# Brand-Driven City Building and the Virtualizing of Space

This book is an investigation of the cultural phenomenon of branding and its transformational effects on the contemporary spatial – and urban – reality. It develops a novel understanding of the rationale behind the construction of large-scale architectural complexes that relate to corporate brands, and of its tremendous cultural effects. The author suggests that what we see today is the creation of "global mass ornaments", of a thorough ornamentalization of the entire globe.

The origins of this are discussed with regard to examples of corporate brand-building from Europe and China (Autostadt Wolfsburg, BMW Welt Munich and Anting New Town). Additional cases are several simulated spaces in Berlin and the space-branding activities of companies like Apple or Prada. Theoretically, the author develops an innovative poststructuralist framework, combining ideas from Gilles Deleuze with the space philosophy of Peter Sloterdijk. He analyzes how the corporate redefinition of space makes the city enter into a mode of virtual urbanity. This idea leads to a notion of a "global urban" and, ultimately, the "global mass ornament".

This concept of a global mass ornament is developed here with reference to Sloterdijk's concept of a world of "spheres". The latter is used to understand the new mode of spatiality of mediatized spaces. The book makes the point that our world is involved in a process of mass ornamentalization that has only just begun. The concept of the global mass ornament is the first to come to grips with a culture in which branding is effectively changing the physiognomy of the earth. The global mass ornament is a banner for a cultural transformation that employs architecture, sign theory and mechanisms borrowed from traditional advertising and from social media, as well as social processes – and that we have yet to properly understand. This book is a significant step forward in this respect.

**Alexander Gutzmer** received his PhD and his MA in Cultural Studies from Goldsmiths College, University of London. He also holds a business degree from Berlin's Freie Universität. He has worked as a cultural and business journalist for the last few years. He reported from London and Berlin for the German national newspaper *Welt am Sonntag*, and worked as Editorial Director for the Burda Creative Group, where he also edited a business magazine for the global consulting firm Roland Berger. He is currently Editor-in-Chief of the architecture magazine *Baumeister*, and Editorial Director of the publishing house Callwey. His academic interests include cultural and architectural theory as well as concepts and processes of communication and branding.

**Routledge Research in Planning and Urban Design**
Series editor:
Peter Ache
*Radbound University Nijmegen, the Netherlands*

Routledge Research in Planning and Urban Design is series of academic monographs for scholars working in these disciplines and the overlaps between them. Building on Routledge's history of academic rigour and cutting-edge research, the series contributes to the rapidly expanding literature in all areas of planning and urban design.

**Brand-Driven City Building and the Virtualizing of Space**
*Alexander Gutzmer*

**The Empty Place**
Democracy and public space
*Teresa Hoskyns*

**Deconstructing Placemaking**
*Mahyar Arefi*

**Public Space and Relational Perspectives**
New challenges for architecture and planning
*Chiara Tornaghi and Sabine Knierbein*

# Brand-Driven City Building and the Virtualizing of Space

Alexander Gutzmer

Taylor & Francis Group
LONDON AND NEW YORK

First published 2014
by Routledge
2 Park Square, Milton Park, Abingdon, Oxon OX14 4RN

Simultaneously published in the USA and Canada
by Routledge
711 Third Avenue, New York, NY 10017

*Routledge is an imprint of the Taylor & Francis Group, an informa business*

© 2014 Alexander Gutzmer

The right of Alexander Gutzmer to be identified as author of this work has been asserted by him in accordance with sections 77 and 78 of the Copyright, Designs and Patents Act 1988.

Every effort has been made to contact and acknowledge copyright owners. If any material has been included without permission, the publishers offer their apologies. The publishers would be pleased to have any errors or omissions brought to their attention so that corrections may be published at a later printing.

All rights reserved. No part of this book may be reprinted or reproduced or utilised in any form or by any electronic, mechanical, or other means, now known or hereafter invented, including photocopying and recording, or in any information storage or retrieval system, without permission in writing from the publishers.

*Trademark notice*: Product or corporate names may be trademarks or registered trademarks, and are used only for identification and explanation without intent to infringe.

*British Library Cataloguing in Publication Data*
A catalogue record for this book is available from the British Library

*Library of Congress Cataloging in Publication Data*
Gutzmer, Alexander.
 Brand-driven city building and the virtualizing of space /
Alexander Gutzmer.
 p. cm.—(Research in planning and urban design)
 Includes bibliographical references and index.
 1. City planning--Social aspects. 2. Urbanization—Social aspects.
3. Urban sociology. 4. Place marketing. 5. Urban economics.
6. Branding (Marketing)—Social aspects. I. Title.
 HT166.G88 2013
 307.1'216—dc23
 2012033775

ISBN: 978-0-415-81534-5 (hbk)
ISBN: 978-0-020-30663-4 (ebk)

Typeset in Sabon
by Swales & Willis Ltd, Exeter, Devon

Printed and bound by CPI Group (UK) Ltd, Croydon, CR0 4YY

For Almut, Emil, and my parents

# Contents

|   |   |   |
|---|---|---|
| | *Acknowledgements* | ix |
| 1 | Introduction | 1 |
| 2 | The cases: Autostadt Wolfsburg, BMW Welt Munich and Anting New Town | 9 |

*Branded force fields: Autostadt Wolfsburg 1*
*Architecture of combustion: BMW Welt Munich 18*
*Hybridizing Shanghai: Anting New Town 22*

| 3 | Branding and the spatialization of capitalism | 27 |
|---|---|---|

*Brands as an extension of marketing 27*
*Cities as an extension of brands 28*
*Virtual spaces, new media cities, mass ornaments and Schäume 32*

| 4 | Actualizing the virtual of capitalism? The functions and functionings of brand space | 41 |
|---|---|---|

*Methodology and knowledge production: researching brand cities, brand cities as research 41*
*Virtual cities and moments of actualization: why and how brands conquer urban space 48*

| 5 | Virtualizing the actual of space: brand city as new media space | 86 |
|---|---|---|

*Researching the abstract, or how brand space changes the focus of the cultural study of the urban 87*
*New layers, new complexities: how brand space is virtualizing the urban 90*

| 6 | The rise of the global mass ornament | 122 |
| 7 | Conclusion | 148 |

*Glossary of German terms*     154
*Notes*     155
*References*     158
*Index*     173

# Acknowledgements

I want to thank Celia Lury and Scott Lash for their amazing support of this project and for their countless helpful comments. I also want to thank Liz Moor and Adam Arvidsson for their valuable input. I am grateful to Maria Schneider (Autostadt), Gunter Henn (Henn Architekten) and Johannes Dell (Albert Speer & Partner) for sharing their insights during our interviews. I want to thank BMW AG and Autostadt GmbH for the image material they provided. Finally, I want to thank Maria Schneider and Autostadt for supporting this work.

# 1 Introduction

> We are not witnessing the flow of information so much as pure spectacle, or information made sacred, ritually unreadable.
> (Don DeLillo, *Cosmopolis*, 2003)

During recent years, capitalism has developed towards an ever more abstract, purely technological and indeed increasingly invisible system. With abstraction at the very core of capitalist process, the only thing that can be said about capitalist reality today is that it has a tendency to escape the world of the physical, of borders, of everything that evokes notions of substance and substantiality. At the same time, however, capitalist institutions have started to engage in more and more active ways with space and its (permanently changing) structural and processual principles. One way is through architecture, and the relationship between capitalism and architecture appears to grow in intensity just as it grows in complexity. Hence, one can at the same time also talk about a "spatialization" of capitalism, or of capitalism's very specific *spatial turn*.

This spatialization should not be interpreted as a sign of failure of capitalism's abstraction; rather it seems as if capitalist spatialization and abstraction were two parallel processes. Capitalist abstraction has often been presented as a way to organize space (cf. Harvey 1985). Put very succinctly, one could even argue that the need for a certain spatial footprint is the logical outcome of the abstraction.

From this perspective, such spatialization would seem to be the result of capitalism's principle of permanently extending its own boundaries. Deleuze (1995, Chapter 5) has developed an approach to capitalism that focuses on its change-related characteristics, and shows how capitalism is driven by a permanent urge to change and to integrate new exteriors into its functioning principles. Therefore, an engagement with space or "the spatial" seems to be a consequent development of contemporary capitalism *especially* if it is at the same time featured in a non-physical, non-actual reality. It is this ambiguous and complex relationship that this book will analyze.

## 2  Introduction

The spatial engagement of capitalism is omnipresent in today's urban landscape. Billboards, logos, corporate headquarters or brand-driven events are three-dimensional representatives of a thoroughly capitalized urban reality that is arguably driven by one concept, increasingly at the heart of capitalist productivity: the brand. Branding is the "subsystem" (to speak with Luhmann, 1984) most visibly and vividly represented in the spatial structures that make up our cities today. Brands are thoroughly spatial urban phenomena. They impact on, and change, the cityscape – and our perception of it. It is this interactive, in the broadest sense, relationship that this work will focus on.[1]

In cultural analyses the brand has replaced the decoding of advertising messages as the prime focus of marketing-oriented critique. This implies a shift from textual analyses of the language of advertising to the development of more complex models which take account of the virtual and abstract characteristics of brands as well as the economic forces that drive their production and circulation (cf. Arvidsson 2005; 2006; 2007; Halstead 2002; Lash 2002; Lash and Urry 1994; Lury 2000; 2004; Moor 2003; 2004; 2007). Although there is no single accepted *theory of the brand* (yet), certain common features are increasingly visible. Primarily, most brand writers agree that the relationship between brand and product is one in which the brand comes first. Brands are increasingly assigned a certain independence; the products merely play the role of actualizers. It seems as if the brand creates the product (Lury 2000: 168).

However, brands are usually treated as an entity with a rather fragile ontological basis; something that is merely the result of corporate efforts towards communication management. They have not so far been attributed any independent or productive spatial reality, which is why in the existing literature on space, architecture or cities, brands do not play a major role. Space theorists, whether geographers, architecture critics or cultural theorists, usually emphasize the messy, ambiguous and not easily interpretable characteristics of space (Thrift 1999: 32). Space is often read as that which escapes meaning. In this context, a systematic analysis of brands as institutions assumedly aimed at the *creation* and *exploitation* of meaning might seem a contradiction.

The assumption underlying this book is that such an analysis is not all that contradictory, for the following three reasons. First, one could argue that brands have always been spatial, in that they are present in the urban landscape through visual representation strategies (product design, billboards, etc.). Second, the growing impact they have on spatial categories such as the city or architecture today increases the necessity of the aforementioned analysis. Finally, most brand analysis is in one way or another engaged with the extent to which the brand can be seen as a "medium". This creates the necessity to approach the topic with categories developed from a critical perspective on space, as media production and media use have been the object of a lot of spatial analysis (see, for instance, McCarthy 2001 or Morley 2006). Anthropological media ethnography in particular has diverted attention away from the mainly historical currents of analysis, as put forward, for instance, by McLuhan (1962).[2] Therefore, the development of media theory actually calls for a more detailed analysis of the relationship between media and the spatialization of branding.

However, this book does not aim at developing yet another anthropological perspective on media space. My question is not primarily "how does branded media space impact upon people?" Rather, I want to offer a cultural interpretation of the interplay between brands on the one hand, and space and the city on the other, in which the position of human agency will be a central, but open question. I will ask how the principles of branding transform space and our thinking of it. I will analyze how the mediatization of a particular brand-oriented architectural activity – constructing entire city-like structures oriented at the assumed characteristics, values or functioning mechanisms of one or several brands – changes the ways in which cities can, and do, function today. Furthermore, I will discuss how space and its own distinct principles affect the ways in which brands are created.

I will let my analysis be guided by poststructuralist understandings of geography and the urban sphere (cf. Murdoch 2006). Actor-network theory (ANT) and Deleuzian poststructuralism both develop an understanding of "the spatial" and "the urban" that transcend the dominance of concepts of linear identity, distinct, isolated places and relative stasis. They contrast territorialization with deterritorialization, outlining a vision of the spatial in which concrete places are influenced by other spaces and are constantly subject to change. In this poststructuralist perspective, the urban is not given, but is *created* by spatio-temporal processes beyond its confines. ANT claims that these processes result in what the theory calls "network relations" (ibid.: 80). And even if this book departs from ANT, arguing that its concepts are at certain points insufficiently flexible or architectural to understand a media-rich urban environment, it can be stated that to the extent such relations exist, they create and recreate different kinds of "multiplicities" (Deleuze and Guattari 1987: 33). These multiplicities are a central concept for understanding the media-rich spatial reality that this work is concerned with.

Deleuze and Guattari see such multiplicities as differing "layers" coexisting at one physical point. These might influence each other, as well as simply coexisting without touching. What is clear, however, is that any division of a layer or any element being added changes the multiplicity in nature (ibid.). It is these change processes that I will follow up on through the workings of brand space. Thence, this work will be Deleuzian, at least to a certain point. In later stages, I will extend the Deleuzian conceptual frame, linking it to the spheres theory of Peter Sloterdijk. While not at all a fundamental reversal of Deleuze's multiplicities, the thinking on spheres will help to develop a more nuanced understanding of processes of spatial change (and the difficulty of it).

The Sloterdijk perspective notwithstanding, I will suggest interpreting a brand – and the processes that constantly create, recreate and change it – as a particular kind of intensification, or "virtualization", added to the externality of space. By entering space, the brand changes a spatial setting or even a city in nature. A *brand city* structure is not a neutral space, but a city loaded with content, hence displaying a certain proximity to discourses on themed urban environments (cf. Gottdiener 2001; Sorkin 1992). It is also, as I will show, mediatized space, or space becoming medium. By referring to the media theory of Friedrich Kittler I will argue that, in a peculiar way, brand city is an instance of the urban becoming an element of new media (as opposed to a generic concept of "medium").

With the employment of a philosopher like Sloterdijk, who is often seen as a core proponent of what is commonly called a *spatial turn* in philosophy, the reader might be tempted to put this work into a camp of writings that propose a relative higher relevance of the concept of *space* to that of *time*. And while it is too early to debate this question now, I want to emphasize that this work takes into account space in its *relation* to specific notions of temporality. Specifically, I will engage with the ways in which a concrete spatial environment deals with its own past; this is why a significant part of this work will be concerned with how certain spatialities employ notions of history and "the historical" in their functionings.

While doing so, I acknowledge that history has always been an element in the construction and self-identification of space(s). It has been the "intensity" that has negotiated much of the efforts by individuals to create a sense of identity by relating to given spatial settings (Williams 2003: 164). In this book, I want to show how different informational structures such as brands can be said to relate to space, and how this is far from ahistorical. It does not leave the "historization" of space untouched, nor does it create or support a harmonious or tension-free version of history. Rather, partly by interacting with ideas of the historical prevalent in the spatial structure in question or in the society in which it is situated, it creates new tensions – tensions in city space, but also for brands as forces that play out in space, and, ultimately, for contemporary society and culture.

This spatialized perspective on history is necessary for any analytical engagement with media as soon as processes of what is often termed "new media" are dealt with. This might seem surprising, as common sense has it that new media are essentially spaceless. However, they are not. Consequently, as Fornäs (2008: 899) points out, historical analyses of new media are often concentrated on the spatial dimensions of new media. Taking this further, one can argue that new media history develops a new spatial dimension for the analysis of media in general. Vice versa, new media history also makes it necessary to approach the analysis of space in general with a new historical focus and so, on a meta level, I will ask if history as such is not a spatial as much as a temporal phenomenon. These are the tensions that the presence of brands in space adds to, and the tensions that I want to analyze in this book.

Specifically, I will argue that brands need space to "actualize" culturally and economically. But I also want to show that neither brands nor capitalism as a whole can simply *appropriate* space. Once they actively engage with architectural and city-building practices, the complexity within and around a brand grows significantly. The combination of the functioning mechanisms of a brand and of space creates a situation in which neither of the two remain unchanged. The brand aims at a new level of actuality; simultaneously, however, the urban sphere is entering a state that I will characterize, once more following Deleuze, as "virtual".

I will not merely *use* this notion of the virtual, however, but extend it by linking it to the concept of "Ornament der Masse" suggested in the 1920s by Siegfried Kracauer, and to Sloterdijk's philosophy of globalization. The virtual–actual interaction in brand space will be argued as adding to a new, post-globalized reality, characterized by what I will call a "globalized mass ornament". This is not to say that brand space *is* globalization. I will agree with Sloterdijk who sees terrestrial globalization as a process essentially finished by 1945. Rather, the argument will be that we are encountering today a *new kind* of globalized space, and that the altered version of the mass ornament is indicative of that.

The rise of this globalized mass ornament through the invasion of urban space by brands will be discussed by focusing mainly on three concrete examples. The first orientation point is a case of corporate brand-building that can be seen as almost "classical" today: the "Autostadt" (car city) in the Northern German Town of Wolfsburg. Autostadt is an architectural ensemble supposedly representing the individual brands of the car company Volkswagen and the values and ideas they stand for. It has been the first project of a brand-building company trying to use entire city-like structures as marketing tools. This is interesting because the engagement between the brand city of Autostadt and the existing city of Wolfsburg highlights particularly clearly how the media spaces created by brand cities engage with spatialized history.

I will draw parallels with, and differences between, Autostadt and other urban developments or concrete cities such as Los Angeles and Berlin. I will also analyze two other concrete, corporate-influenced, urbanist developments. The first one is a rather directly connected development: the brand space that Volkswagen competitor BMW has opened some years after Autostadt at its corporate headquarters in Munich, "BMW Welt" (BMW World). Given that it is set in a very different urban environment, I will discuss the extent to which BMW Welt parallels Autostadt. This will bring up the question whether BMW Welt was influenced by Autostadt, or whether both developments ran parallel simply because certain structures or developments within brand capitalism made it opportune to become involved in large-scale urbanist activity. The answer to this question is not just indicative of the relationship between two companies, but may, I will argue, also be relevant to the way in which the urban landscape as a whole might develop in the future.

6  *Introduction*

The third case I want to use to understand virtualization and becoming-media of city space is an urban development in Shanghai: Anting New Town, an urban development where, apart from middle-class professionals working in central Shanghai, people with jobs in a nearby car industry cluster are supposed to live. Started more than ten years ago, it is still incomplete and has been subject to a lot of architectural criticism in Western media (cf. de Muynck 2012). It is connected to the concept of Autostadt Wolfsburg in a rather indirect way – through certain ideas of what is "German". Anting New Town is a simulated German town. The architects had the task of building an urban complex that bore aesthetical and planning characteristics which local and national political decision-makers perceived as "German" – in direct proximity to an industrial area dominated by Volkswagen. The ways in which the corporation of Volkswagen and the values of its brands influenced and perhaps motivated the creation of Anting New Town will be looked at.

Also, the question will be addressed as to what extent a place like Anting New Town extends certain principles of brand space or of (new) media space, and whether it is perhaps the model for an urban development that might be taking place elsewhere too. This meta-local perspective on the mediatization of the urban sphere will be developed into an argument for an increasingly complex relationship between different spatio-political concepts; the point will be made that in today's capitalism, the idea that "Western" concepts are simply "adapted" elsewhere no longer holds true. Specifically, Shanghai will be argued to have the capacity to not only intensify, but also reformulate the idea of spatialized branding and of the development of the urban landscape globally.

This work is divided into three major parts. After giving a short introduction into the history of the brand spaces I will look at, the historical development of brand-driven spatial concepts, and the theoretical frameworks that I will base my core analysis on (Chapters 2 and 3), I will show in Chapter 4 the way in which brands aim to use space to get rid of their purely virtual character. I will focus on the Deleuzian concept of the virtual here because it offers the most encompassing way to deal with the degree that a capitalist invention such as the brand is charged with features that both constitute it, while also creating an inherent deficiency. I will then change the perspective, looking at how the efforts of brands to create their own actualization impact on cities and alter our notion of the urban (Chapters 5 and 6). I will argue that by trying to develop a certain actuality, brands change cities, adding to and accelerating the process of virtualization currently underway (Chapter 5) and I will demonstrate how this thoroughly transforms any notion of globality, nationality and locality (Chapter 6).

The way in which I understand the particular virtual–actual interaction that brands initiate is closely connected to the idea of a mediatization of space. I will try to show that through the kind of mediatization brand space is performing, the urban is developing features that can be understood as media, or specifically, as *new media*. The processes of spatialized branding, I want to make clear, transforms urban space into a space of new media.

The fact that brands engage openly and strongly with space today, and my understanding that the processes they initiate can be conceptualized as new media processes, results, one could argue, from a certain emptiness that is typical for brands. For a company, it is easy to "invent" a new brand. But that means little. Once a brand has been declared as such, it can only succeed economically and survive culturally if it manages to create real social processes that are in some way "linked" to it. This is harder to achieve than ever, as today brands are no longer perceived as a radically innovative form of management, instead being threatened with becoming a kind of commodity themselves; present everywhere, but not always with significant effect, sometimes struggling in vain to be recognized at all, especially through the transformational effects entailed by social media, which also imply a radically changed notion of "consumer". This is where space comes into play. It is here that, in a way similar to other new media communications, brands are momentarily endowed with a new kind of actuality. What kinds of cultural process are at work in brand space I will show in Chapter 4.

In this context, the aforementioned link between the notions of spatiality and temporality will be a major theme throughout my analysis. History will be one core concept in this, as the increasing use brand builders make of concepts such as "history marketing" shows that brands tend to appropriate temporal dimensions for their own strategies. They do so by offering certain spatial interpretations of past or future. The creation of lasting links between its own set of values and a concrete spatial structure effectively means that a brand has managed to develop a certain brand-specific spatio-temporal reality, thereby diminishing the threat of simply disappearing from the social cosmos of capitalism. This has real urban effects; the brand thereby continuously transforms what it means for a spatial ensemble to *be* a city, as well as for us to perceive, and live in, one. In Chapter 5, I will show the way in which brand city space is fundamentally different from city structures as we know them. The consequential vision of the city does not simply demonize brands as evil capitalist agents in space. Rather, I want to make a contribution to a better understanding of how cities and architecture develop today. The argument is not that something good has been substituted by something bad, but rather something that has always been very dynamic (the city) is in the course of being transformed into something new.

I will analyze this innovation in Chapter 6, with a focus on Sloterdijk's claim that we are living in a "post-globalizing" world (Sloterdijk 2005, Chapter 28). This world, I will argue, thoroughly transforms the relationship between medium and extra-mediated reality. As I will show, the medium comes first today. Media are no longer added to any pre-existing reality (or spatiality), rather they are the basis on which any such extra-mediated actuality is constructed. In fact, I will make the point that the medium has the capacity to become, in a still-Deleuzian sense, the new "actual".

Based on what can be termed an "anti-essentialist" concept of space (cf. Murdoch 2006, Chapter 1), constituted by demonstrating that space is subject to a specific kind of mediatization, I hope to develop a new understanding of the relationship between space and the built urban reality on the one hand, and time on the other. The so-called "spatial turn" has often been interpreted as an indication of an irrelevance of categories of time. And indeed, I will show that temporalities no longer dominate cultural process. However, I will not renounce the relevance of time as an analytical concept for cultural thinking. Rather, I will try to determine the extent to which my notion of new-media space has the capacity to take into account the fact that architectural practice seems so heavily engaged with notions of the temporal or the historical. The question will be addressed as to where, in such a topological perspective that takes as its starting points Sloterdijk's topology-inspired spatial concepts, is there a productive role for a sense of temporality.

At the beginning of this introduction I have already indicated that the reinvention of space through the mediating activities of brands is highly relevant for the functioning of contemporary capitalism. The ways in which brand architecture and brand urbanism change capitalism will be reflected throughout this book – even though this suggestion of a "politics of brand space" does not reduce brand buildings to new ways of social manipulation, spatial control, and corporate power. And yet branding and politics are connected, and perhaps even more so as we approach a brand-driven capitalism that lives off a "political entrepreneurship", as Arvidsson (2006: 89) argues. Consequently, this work does not completely *abandon* the notion of politics. But as capitalism changes through the urbanization of brands, the question is on what grounds political processes can actually unfold. Just as the transformations that the urbanization of brands creates for any notion of capitalist politics, it is these grounds that the next chapters will investigate.

# 2 The cases
## Autostadt Wolfsburg, BMW Welt Munich and Anting New Town

### Branded force fields: Autostadt Wolfsburg

"Autostadt", an architectural ensemble in the Northern German town of Wolfsburg, opened in June 2000 with the intention of displaying and strengthening the brands of the car company Volkswagen. Its political economy is connected to the development of the automobile industry. Twenty or 30 years ago the car industry entered a stage that is referred to by business writers as a "mature industry". In the West, demand for cars did not continue to grow as fast as during the 1950s and 1960s, until in the late 1970s Japanese companies put increasing price pressure on Northern American and European multinationals. Consequently, the competitive battle entered a stage of what business theorist Richard D'Aveni (1994) famously termed "hypercompetition". In this situation, Volkswagen started, like its major competitors, to build a multi-brand car empire, under the assumption that building a broad product range under one brand was not enough. Hence, the company started to take over smaller companies, usually to strengthen its presence in product categories or markets where it was rather weak before.

One economic idea behind this was the "platform strategy" that became popular for all major car producers in the 1980s; one production platform is used for different car models, even from different brands. That is, the different brands are increasingly based less on differences in production, and an *appearance of difference* is produced on the basis of a thorough sameness, as far as physical production is concerned. Hence, any company pursuing a platform strategy will be in need of ways to differentiate its brands, and to communicate its strategy and perception of the relationship of the individual brands both internally and externally. Autostadt will be interpreted in this book as a (partly subconscious) reflection of this political–economic situation.

### *The origins of Autostadt*

The initiative to build Autostadt has been driven by the former Volkswagen chief executive Ferdinand Piëch (CEO from 1993 until 2002). As a financier,

Piëch is, together with his family, a major shareholder of Volkswagen, and considered the "strong man" at Volkswagen even today. He is grandson of Ferdinand Porsche, inventor of the Volkswagen Beetle.

The idea to build an "Autostadt" in Wolfsburg has been seen by many as a sign of Piëch's need for personal self-representation (cf. for instance Reichle 2003). However, it would be too easy to interpret Autostadt as a mere private interest of one CEO, however powerful he might be. Such an interpretation would underestimate the complexity of decision-making processes in publicly listed companies. It would also mean misinterpreting the role of a CEO. Business literature does not conceptualize CEOs as potentates with unlimited power, but rather as the main strategist of a company (cf. for instance Kim and Mauborne 2005). With marketing arguably the critical success factor of companies today, the centrality of the CEO also implies that he is in fact the company's main marketer. What is more, the personality of the CEO is today seen as an asset to be managed, to create what in business discourses is called corporate reputation (Gaines-Ross 2002).

And not only can CEOs be assumed to take marketing strategy into account in their decision-making. It means that, effectively, the CEO as a person with personal interests is an integral part of the positioning of a company, and of its brands. It therefore does not make sense to isolate any decision a CEO makes completely from a company's branding, even if it is in line with personal interests. This is also how architect and Autostadt master planner Gunter Henn interpreted Piëch's decision. In our interview, Henn described Piëch's involvement in the building of Autostadt as significantly marketing-driven.

Located on 25 hectares on the northern bank of the "Mittellandkanal", an artificial water line next to the main Volkswagen factory and north of central Wolfsburg, Autostadt includes a number of pavilions representing the individual corporate brands: VW, Audi, Lamborghini, Bentley, Bugatti, Skoda, Seat, Porsche and VW Nutzfahrzeuge (trucks and vans). Apart from the "Premium Clubhouse" hosting Bentley and Bugatti, each pavilion represents one brand, and each tries to combine a unique exhibition concept for the brand values with an architecture that in some way "suits" the brand. No pavilion looks like the other, and all are more or less equidistant from each other.

Given that any pavilion is to display, reflect or interpret the essence of the brand in question, it does not come as a surprise that the architectural style of Autostadt can be described as eclectic. Each pavilion has been designed by a different architect and has its own architectural and stylistic language. This creates a sense that there is no direct architectural communication between them, even implying a certain "architectural autism". However, with each building and its respective (symbolic or affective) force field positioned in relative proximity with the other pavilions, there is of course a certain, even if involuntary, interplay.

Even if creating brand distinction was one core target of the pavilions' design, Autostadt is not a showcase of a radical branded diversity. The ensemble is centrally managed, and everyone is aware of that. Autostadt is an expression of the central management of different brands from different cultures as much as a sign of the brands' individuality and uniqueness. The singular as Autostadt's principle (put forward by Uhlig 2000: 10) is centrally framed.

*The pavilions*

The "Premium Clubhouse", originally built to represent the British car brand Bentley, is a very gentle building, apparently dissolving into a small artificial hill. Most of it seems to be a cave in the mound. Its main material is green granite, yet does not evoke an atmosphere of extreme "hardness".

The building's curved structure is supposed to evoke associations of the racetrack of Le Mans, where Bentley cars started their fame (Henn 2000: 37). Interestingly, the brand took off with a notion of speed and wildness that are quite the opposite of today's brand values. Perhaps this Bentley past made it logical for Volkswagen to reconceptualize this pavilion as the "Premium Clubhouse" in 2008. Since then, it is also a representative for the luxury sports car brand Bugatti.

The conceptual opposite of the Clubhouse's nonchalance can be seen in the aggressive form of the Lamborghini pavilion (see Figure 2.1). It is a solitary element, a self-centred black cube. Its title: "cubo della violenza" or "violence cube". Its position, in an awkward angle rising from the grass, and the roaring sounds coming from its inside, strengthen the impression of solitariness and aggression. It is positioned in the centre of Autostadt, visible very much from everywhere. Most paths seem to lead to and around the cubo. Combined with the cubo's shape, this peculiar topography evokes associations of the Kaaba in Mecca. Even if unintended by the Autostadt planners, this association might still be interpreted as a sign that the idea or motivation to create a certain "holiness" or "spirituality" has driven the cubo's design.

The Skoda pavilion is rather unimpressive at first sight. It looks like a snail with three wings on the outside. The idea behind the bowl in the centre was to evoke feelings of honesty and security (Henn 2000: 45). Even if difficult for the visitor to see, however, the construction of this pavilion perhaps has the richest conceptual background of all Autostadt pavilions. Its layout has been explained to me by the former head of the Skoda division, Klaus Homann. The pavilion design started off with a model of thought process, considered in line with the intellectual values of the brand. It was conceptualized as a circuit which starts with the notion of "learning", goes on through "use/experience" and ends with "reflection/memory". These three abstract categories were to guide the construction of the pavilion, and are how the pavilion got its snail-style shape. The materials, dark blue glass and white concrete, express a version of modernism that we can read as an expression of the brand's history with its Czech modernist roots – the company was set up in 1925 and was bought by Volkswagen in 1991.

12  *Autostadt, BMW Welt, Anting New Town*

*Figure 2.1* The Lamborghini pavilion (Autostadt GmbH)

In contrast to this, the Seat pavilion, in its white ceramics, is the obvious effort to capture the Mediterranean spirit the Spanish brand wants to represent (Figure 2.2). Henn calls it a "sensually shaped, white sculpture" (Henn 2000: 49). He even explains that it is supposed to be reminiscent of the shapes of the female body, claiming that "from the bridge, the walkway leads directly into the female, erotic form" (ibid, original in German).

*Figure 2.2* The Seat pavilion (Autostadt GmbH)

Less obvious, more abstract and conceptual is the way in which the Audi pavilion wants to give architectural reality to the essence of the brand. The building is made up of two round semi-buildings intertwined with each other. One of them is larger on top, the other at the bottom. Hence, the visitor can divide the building into four distinct ring forms – the four rings of the Audi logo.

Interestingly, the building with the least "interesting" or "original" design is the pavilion of the core brand of the company, Volkswagen: a glass box enclosing a completely round shape – two basic geometric shapes supposedly representing perfection (ibid.: 56). In terms of corporate micro-politics, one is tempted to interpret the less than impressive form as a bow from Volkswagen to the other brands. However, from another perspective, the opposite can be argued to be true – the Volkswagen brand does not have to fight for its position, as it is so closely associated with the company as a whole.

In 2012, Autostadt added a new pavilion, for the newly integrated sports car brand Porsche. It is a sculpture of stainless steel, dominated by a roof that reaches out 25 metres above an artificial pond. This is the first pavilion designed by Autostadt master planner Gunter Henn.

### KonzernForum and structuring buildings

All visitors enter Autostadt through the "KonzernForum", designed as an atmospheric starting point of the Autostadt experience (see Figure 2.3). It

*Figure 2.3* KonzernForum (Autostadt GmbH) © Joerg Modrow

can be accessed through a footbridge leading to Autostadt from the South, the railway station or the city of Wolfsburg. Alternatively, visitors coming to Autostadt with their own cars will be directed to KonzernForum from the parking spaces east of Autostadt.

Six revolving glass doors make up the entrance, each 20 metres high and usually partly open. In fact, they don't appear to be doors at all, rather reminiscent of temple columns. Through these doors visitors enter the forum and are confronted with the first significant design element pointing to the character of Autostadt as a "connected place": "World Processor – Globenfeld", an installation of globes by media artist Ingo Günther. Obviously this is supposed to express what is, in business discourses, called "corporate responsibility", meaning that corporations develop a responsibility for broader, non-economic issues. At the same time, however, the installation can be read as a sign for a sense of spatial connectedness.

Six more glass doors lead inside the main area of Autostadt. There is a recommended walk, but the many paths, bridges or alleyways allow for individual movement. Autostadt here is similar to other theme parks; the concept of limited choice distinguishes theme parks from, say, theatre events (for a critique of this kind of "limited freedom" see Cohen and Taylor 1992).

The closest Autostadt comes to being a "museum" is the "ZeitHaus" (house of time). Here, the engagement of brand space with notions of history becomes obvious for the first time. The ZeitHaus concept makes an explicit claim for Autostadt to offer its own account of what counts as history, hosting exhibitions about the history of driving and the past of the company. However, the idea of linear history writing is broken up by the building's architecture. In fact, the ZeitHaus is a built contradiction, deconstructing any notion of linearity. It is made up of two completely different buildings attached to each other. There is the "rack", a cuboid-formed glass building containing cars like a collector's box (Henn 2000: 32). Left of the rack (seen from the centre of Autostadt) is the "corpus", an organically shaped building with a steel façade. Henn writes that the intention of this double building is to represent the collision of two different ways of information processing: the analogue and the digital. The rack, invoking values of rationality and linearity, represents the digital. The analogue is supposed to be visible in the organically shaped forms of the corpus.

The architectural contrasting of analogue and digital is of course in the first instance a media critique. But the integration of exhibition-based corporate history writing can also be interpreted as a critique of grand historical narratives. It even appears to express a certain consciousness regarding the effects of message-distribution through architecture.

The link joining the two building parts is a staircase apparently wedged inbetween. The bridges and staircases connecting the two building parts are supposed to evoke the impression of the links between the left and right side of the human brain (ibid.). This architectural approach to creating buildings by allusions to the functioning mechanisms of the human body seems to be part of Autostadt's basic idea set. We will see later that this is in fact countered by the much more radical, and newer, approach: the implication of real human bodies into the basic functioning mechanisms of an architectural space.

Although Autostadt is not designed as a place where people live, the site includes a hotel. Formed like a ring open towards the southeast, towards Autostadt and the visitors, the Ritz-Carlton is playing with a basic architectural form. Its rounded structure differentiates the hotel from modern hotel architecture with long hallways. The impression of a supposedly inhuman emptiness is to be avoided (ibid.: 74).

Finally, there are two towers from which buyers pick up their cars, the "AutoTürme" (Figure 2.4). This is where Autostadt comes closest to incorporating a concrete business process; the towers store new cars before they are picked up, each with a capacity of 400 cars. As a car is picked up every 40 seconds, there is constant movement. In that sense, the towers are the counterparts to the production towers two kilometres west. Here, production is replaced by extravagant delivery. The towers are a signature of the new source of productivity in consumer capitalism.

In English, Autostadt means "car city". However, in which sense is Autostadt an urban phenomenon? The answer to this, as will become clearer later, is by no means straightforward. At this point, I want to summarize core features to be taken into account in this context. Autostadt encompasses urban elements, such as squares and streets, narrow points and spacious

16  *Autostadt, BMW Welt, Anting New Town*

*Figure 2.4* AutoTürme (Autostadt GmbH) © Marc-Oliver Schulz

areas, restaurants, bars and a cinema. The language used to name its main elements is that of city planning: "piazza", "forum", "axis". The visitor is not bombarded with a structured programme of activity, as would be the case with non-urban theme parks. However, Autostadt is not a "Stadt" in the sense that anyone is actually living in it. The only people staying overnight are Ritz-Carlton guests. The fact that visitors pay an entrance fee demonstrates that the planners' primary target is not to create a social reality that is as urban as possible. Creative Director Maria Schneider clearly stated in our interview that the makers of Autostadt are aware of the symbolic meaning of taking an entrance fee.

Neither did the Autostadt makers simply want to build as centrally in the city as possible. Autostadt is removed from the centre of Wolfsburg. Presumably, one reason for this is a very practical one – it might have been difficult to find a place within the city centre. But the position opposite the Mittellandkanal also has a symbolic meaning; Autostadt is not simply another part of Wolfsburg, and it needs a certain distance in order to function the way it does. Apparently, planners were conscious enough to reflect that, from an urban thinking perspective, their endeavour can be seen as problematic. This reflexivity is also demonstrated by the complete lack of driven cars (part and parcel of any urban structure).

I want to conclude with a topographical/topological remark. Autostadt is traversed entirely by a diagonal path, the extension of the main pedestrian area in Wolfsburg. The axis is called "Koller axis", named after the initial city planner of Wolfsburg, Peter Koller. At the Northeast end of Autostadt it points to the Renaissance Wolfsburg Castle, the solitary building that gave the city its name. This axis is an expression of a sense of connectedness – spatially as well as temporally. It aims at creating a link between city and castle, thereby expressing the relevance of the notion of the historical in a city usually described as a place without history.

## Autostadt and Wolfsburg: brand space in a city of production

The urban significance of Autostadt is connected to certain specifics of the city it is part of. Hence, I want to give a brief introduction to the development of Wolfsburg, a development that has as much to do with the economic processes surrounding the company Volkswagen as it has with the development of Germany during and after WW2. A development, more fundamentally, whose historical relevance has always been contested. Wolfsburg contradicts many elements of a "good" city. Instead of having developed smoothly over centuries, it was founded – by the Nazis. On 11 June 1938, the Nazi party officially founded the city as a place to build cars. The newly built plant for the "Kraft durch Freude-Auto" ("strength through joy car") needed workers, and those needed housing.

The naming of the city is no Nazi heritage. Wolfsburg got its name after the Second World War from the British Military (Assheuer 2006: 65). Before, it had the absurd name "Stadt des KDF-Wagens bei Fallersleben" ("City of the KDF Car close to Fallersleben").

After 1945, the newly founded company Volkswagen took over the remains of the Kraft durch Freude plants. During the German Wirtschaftswunder time, Wolfsburg grew quickly. So did Volkswagen, at first largely due to the success of the iconic mass-produced car Käfer ("Beetle").

In 1972, Wolfsburg had 131,000 inhabitants (ibid.). The city extension focused on the modernist idea of "autogerechte Stadt" ("a city fit for driving") introduced by city planner Hans Bernhard Reichow (Reichow 1959). Interestingly, Reichow had already been involved in Wolfsburg planning during the Nazi times, which did not make a later career impossible (Acker 2000).

Just as Wolfsburg thrived when the car industry did, economic setbacks for car producers in the 1970s directly affected the city. Not much was built then. Only in 1994 did architectural activity kick in again, with the construction of the major art museum. The architectural passivity in the 70s and

80s is one reason why Wolfsburg architecture appears to be a melancholic showcase of a lost modernist optimism. The general sense of loss felt when looking for a centre or for a place where ideas of tourist "beauty" prevail seems to prove critics right. Also, the lack of any old town with ancient churches or nineteenth-century townhouses increases the impression of a city without a visual identity (Borgelt 2005).

The development of Wolfsburg and its peculiar urban legacy have to be seen as a background for the construction of Autostadt. While Wolfsburg's urban growth always followed macroeconomic developments, now economy and urbanism become one altogether. Consequently, Chapter 4 will discuss Autostadt, and brand space in general, as a productive element of corporate strategy.

The initial thought behind Autostadt was to build a larger service centre and a place for customers to pick up their cars, but the idea quickly extended beyond that. CEO Piëch wanted something architecturally impressive; at the same time, the company was looking for ways to integrate its many recently acquired brands. Also, the world exhibition Expo 2000, to take place in Hanover, increased the political pressure on Northern German companies to contribute to the region's architectural activity (Roost 2007: 287) and was an incentive to build.

## Architecture of combustion: BMW Welt Munich

Seven years after Autostadt had been completed, Bavarian carmaker BMW opened its own brand space – "BMW Welt" – close to the company headquarters in Munich (Figure 2.5). Similar to Autostadt, BMW Welt combines an atmospheric display for the company's products with a delivery centre and a place to offer what is vaguely described in many marketing discourses as "experiences" (cf. Schmitt 1999). BMW Welt was planned by Viennese architectural firm Coop Himmelb(l)au.

BMW Welt consists of only one building: a 75,000-square-metre colossus with a highly dynamic, asymmetric shape. It is an abstract shape that does not evoke very concrete comparisons, the main association being that of dynamism itself. As a building, it tries to make movement visible.

The main architectural element combining all individual parts of the building is the roof; sloped, curved, irregular, carried only by eleven columns, the roof connects the two main bodies, a smaller showroom area (called by the architects the "Double Cone" – Figure 2.6) and the larger, slightly lower, two-story main area. Together, the Double Cone and main area make up a space dominated by manifold nonlinear elements and less-than-square micro spaces.

These micro spaces develop their spatial specifics in relation to the roof as the conceptual core of the building. Coop Himmelb(l)au reverse architectural thinking by developing a top-down philosophy of architectural form creation (Prix 2007: 23). An iconic architectural feature, the roof is

*Figure 2.5* BMW Welt. © BMW AG

*Figure 2.6* Double Cone. © BMW AG

supposed to evoke associations of technological avant-garde, thereby defining urban form and structure while at the same time reflecting a whole new way of building.

Coop Himmelb(l)au got the assignment for BMW Welt in a three-stage architectural competition. BMW decided in 2000 that the building was to combine, similar to Autostadt, car delivery with emotional, aesthetic, experience-based features to define and represent the core of what BMW "stands for". In the competition to follow, 275 submissions were received, 28 of which were short-listed. The two first-prize winners Sauerbruch/Hutton and Coop Himmelb(l)au were asked to review their concepts, and the Viennese group won.

The architecture of BMW Welt is characterized by two basic approaches to architectural form: an engagement with the dynamic characteristics of phenomena of nature; and an engagement with the aesthetics of technology (Feireiss 2007). The principles of both were effectively woven together, indicating an understanding of a "machinic" urbanism as conceived by Amin and Thrift (2002: 78). This suggested a poststructuralist urbanity developing a sense of architectural unity by combining the natural and the technological.

Regarding the forces of nature influencing BMW Welt, it is mainly the phenomena of clouds and of combustion that it seeks to employ architecturally. The architects experimented with these spatial formations of nature to develop new ways of creating architectural form. For them, nature is not so much a creator of environments, or *atmospheres*[1] as a generator of models, or *forms*, in the most basic sense. In this sense, it is not a mere metaphor when Kwinter (2007: 8) claims Coop Himmelb(l)au developed an architecture of "combustion". Combustion (as a natural phenomenon) is an integral part of the architectural process, and the (surprising) resilience of the physical is a mere proof of the almost metaphysical strength of architecture itself: the strength to integrate nature into processes of culture.

This thought is effectively developed further by the second level of external influence on the specific architectural reality of BMW Welt, one that is closely related to Coop Himmelb(l)au's success in the competition: technological innovation. In fact, it seems to have been the centrality of innovation as a motif of their architectural concept (not merely as a tool) that made the jury choose their design. Their submission, rather than simply "using" technological innovation to solve certain architectural problems, is supposed to "express" innovation; and to do so by the way it is built.

This rather direct articulation of a concrete brand value does not make the BMW Welt a solitary complex, nor integrated in an existing urban structure. On the one hand, the area in Northern Munich can't be described as dense urbanity. Large streets create an urban grid, dominated by architectural icons such as the 1972 Olympic Stadium, the Olympic Village and the BMW headquarters. And yet, BMW Welt features a certain openness. The proximity to the Olympic Stadium is articulated through the dominance of open views and visual axes, and the impression of streamlined shapes reminiscent of the stadium's architectural language, extending the apparently unlimited architectural presence of the stadium's shapes and materials which seems to be "fading out", merging with the surrounding landscape, rather than displaying a definitive borderline.[2]

BMW Welt's capacity for architectural interaction is not limited to the stadium. It is to the BMW corporate headquarters by architect Karl Schwanzer that it is particularly open. Although separated by a broad street, BMW Welt pays constant reference to this milestone of early corporate architecture, realized in the 1960s. There are countless visual axes exposing the tower, as if it were part of BMW Welt itself (Figure 2.7). This impression is furthered by the fact that from a visitor's perspective, the boundaries between inside and outside are blurred. There are many spaces that are outside yet roofed. One never quite knows whether one is in- or outside, whether at the building's centre or far away from it – and whether still at BMW Welt or already on the tower premises.

*Figure 2.7* Schwanzer Tower and Double Cone. © BMW AG

The irritation this evokes is not only visual. Being outside yet half inside has a bodily and, in a way, biopolitical reality. Also, the bodily position inside and yet half in the street is countered by the absence of noise, which creates a constant activity of multi-sensory irritations. These are surely not part of the architectural "programme". And yet, they influence the way in which building and visitor interact, which is in itself strategic (and thence biopolitical).

## Hybridizing Shanghai: Anting New Town

My third case, Anting New Town, has a rather indirect connection to brand spaces like Autostadt or BMW Welt, for it is not a space planned by a capitalist actor to represent brands. There are indirect yet strong connections between the Shanghai case and the concept and history of Autostadt in Germany, making Anting New Town another instance of the virtualization and mediatization of urban space. Furthermore, Anting New Town is, in Deleuzian terms, indicative of the rhizomatic character of brand space, with certain elements, images or virtualities of a brand becoming active drivers of urban development. Finally, the case of Anting New Town might be offering a glimpse into the change that concepts of the national and national history (or historicity) will be confronted with in a world in which mechanisms of ubiquitous-mediation-driven image-building play a significant role in the public sphere.

The writing that follows is based on the assumption that the construction of a "German town" in China has to be understood in the context of the current political, cultural and economic situation of China as a whole, and of Shanghai as its most vital business metropolis. China's fast economic progress thoroughly changes the country's consumer culture, which is clearly distinct from Western "advanced economies". Anting New Town is not a mere instance of Shanghai "becoming Westernized", and yet its construction illustrates my claim that certain brand space principles that might have concretized for the first time in Autostadt have the capacity to spread virally or rhizomatically, changing somewhere, then coming back as a different quality. It is then indicative of a multi-centred capitalism, void of a stable structure of "global cities" effectively controlling the global flows of capital (as suggested by the global cities discourse; cf. Brenner and Keil 2006: 3–16).

In Anting, German city planning firm Albert Speer & Partner (AS&P) has been developing – and is supervising – the construction of a completely new city space. Anting New Town, part of the industry cluster Shanghai International Automobile City (SIAC), is an element in the major city development project "One City, Nine Towns" (de Muynck 2012). In this, Shanghai municipal government had planned to erect nine towns at the city's outskirts, each designed in a certain style reminiscent of a place outside Shanghai (Britain, Italy, etc.).

Writers such as Waldmann (2008: 4) see this plan as influenced by older ideas of decentralized city development as exemplified for the first time in the "Greater London Plan". However, there is a distinctly late modern or postmodern element in the Shanghai project. (Although it can also be argued that the building of Anting New Town adapts a certain colonial pattern – bringing the whole world into an assumed centre.[3])

The Anting province of Jiading is 35 kilometres northwest of Shanghai. Volkswagen erected its first production facility there in 1984, the first Western car company to set up a joint venture with a Chinese firm. Today Volkswagen has two Chinese joint ventures (Ruhkamp 2010: 18) and China is seen as the biggest growth market for the global car industry, with all major companies having set up major production facilities in the country (Frauenfeld 2005: 47). China's strategic relevance is expressed by public statements of Volkswagen, pointing out that the Chinese market transcends the notions of "home market" and "export".

While this work will analyze Anting New Town under the label of "brand space", it has to be clear that the case is less obvious than, say, Autostadt. It is not built by Volkswagen, but by the governmental Shanghai Urban Planning Administration Bureau of the Jiading District and the official development body Shanghai International Automobile City Real Estate Co. Ltd. These two government-run or government-influenced agencies decided that Anting New Town was to get a German character.

AS&P got the job for the central planning in 2000 in an international competition. Their expertise in large-scale city planning might have played a role here; but equally relevant, or so it seems, was their German origin. Chief architect Johannes Dell believes this, as he told me in our interview. Interestingly, Dell links this point to his belief that Anting New Town is significantly a marketing project. The argument is that as a marketing instrument, Anting needs to have a German architect/master planner for credibility reasons. In this way, Anting New Town transforms nationality into a marketing tool.

When driving around Anting, the place seems to be rather empty (Gutzmer 2009, de Muynck 2012). During my visit in 2009, there were showrooms promoting the flats on sale, but no customers were to be seen. Most flats were not yet occupied. Johannes Dell estimated that (as of mid-2009), only 500 of the 20,000 existing flats were inhabited. Building activity at the time of my visit seemed to have stalled, while apparently having started again in 2011 (de Muynck 2012: 30).

AS&P were not only planning, but also building in Anting New Town. Five other architectural firms had also obtained assignments to build in the Western part of Anting New Town in 2002 – all of them German. That is, Anting New Town was supposed to be a German-looking town for 50,000 inhabitants, planned and built largely by Germans.

For AS&P, one key question in the early planning phases was: what does "German" or "German-looking" mean? There was significant disagreement about this during the initiation phase. The Chinese idea of "Germanness" did not fit with AS&P's idea of what makes a good, future-oriented city. The Chinese wanted a medieval-looking place full of "Gemütlichkeit", but

*Figure 2.8* Flagging Germanness: café in Anting New Town (author's picture)

Speer and his colleagues were more interested in building something ecologically sound and stylistically driven by Bauhaus ideals (Frauenfeld 2005: 49). The result appears to be a compromise, with a slight upper hand for the architects. AS&P managed to give Anting New Town a modern look. Town planning features of Anting are following German or European city planning traditions. Anting has a round, inside-out form. On a smaller scale, this round form is repeated through the many squares reminiscent of such squares found in smaller European towns. It seems to be oriented at European concepts of public space. Johannes Dell conceded the extent to which Anting was to be "un-Chinese": "The main idea is that of a certain internationality. This fits with the ultra-international history of Shanghai." (Dell 2008). In the nineteenth century, its different quarters were run by different national governments. Up until today, the identity of the city is based on its international character. "This identity was to be expressed and strengthened."

The assumption of a supra-Chinese character of Shanghai is reflected by the way Anting New Town is built. The straight-angled structure typical of Chinese towns is not found here (Waldmann 2008: 43). Neither is the place orienting strictly to the idea of North–South flats. Today, Dell considers this a mistake, because the respect for traditional rules seem to make potential Chinese buyers shy away from acquiring property. This holds true also for every investor interested in a solid investment.

While not featuring any "Chinese" building traditions, neither can Anting be argued to be devoid of reminiscences of pre-modern European building traditions. Cai and Bo (2007: 52ff.) have identified seven Anting design principles supposedly derived from a medieval logic of building, from changing façades to green back yards and a diverse mix of urban functions.[4] Architectural compromises have also been made regarding individual urban elements of German towns. For example, the classical perimeter block development has been transformed into what Waldmann (2008: 45) calls the "Anting Block": a block slightly slimmer than the classical square dominant in many German towns since the 1920s (Heineberg 2001: 219).

While the Anting Block as a new architectural form can arguably be seen as a productive confrontation of two diverse sources, this notion of productivity is difficult to uphold with the architectural elements dominating the central square. The square has a theatre and a church in its centre, its architectural outline implying city structures that are typical of Western middle-sized towns. This concept of the central market square is clearly European, and a key orientation for discourses on (European) public space. Chinese city planning, on the other hand, does not know the concept of the market square (Cay and Bo 2007: 57). It is hard to imagine just what kind of urban life this square will develop once Anting New Town is fully inhabited (if indeed it ever is). Whatever will happen won't be "Chinese", and it won't be "European" either. One might expect a hybrid urban reality, arguably an extension of Penelope Harvey's notion of hybridity (Harvey 1996 – I will come back to Harvey's hybridity concept later).

The tensions of the colliding architectural traditions in Anting New Town are nicely illustrated by a small planning episode. The central market square is dominated by a building slightly higher than the rest, in the style of Bauhaus modernism (see Figure 2.9), intended to be the city hall. However, as Dell explained to me, upon finishing, the government realized that Anting had a city hall already, which made this representational building obsolete. The solution: it was redefined as a hotel.

One of the stranger architectural statements is a pair of statues of Goethe and Schiller, presiding over a smaller square close to the main one. With their original standing in Weimar, they seem to display involuntarily that Weimar functioned as a very concrete role model for the Chinese officials as well as for the German planners. Anting carries elements of a copycat Weimar (Siemons 2006: 41). The intervention of AS&P with regards to what Anting should look like seems to have referred not so much to the basic approach of building one city with clear reference to another. Rather, they intervened *because* they did not feel the medieval role model to be "properly German" – they saw Germany better represented by modernist allusions (Waldmann 2008: 43).

The other main planning issue of AS&P was ecological sustainability (Waldmann 2008: 48) and Anting is more in line with contemporary Western sustainability standards than most other Chinese cities. Interestingly, this implicit criticism of general Chinese urban practice was not much of a problem for the

*Figure 2.9* Anting, Bauhaus-inspired Central Square (author's picture)

Chinese; one can even argue that the very choice of AS&P as the main planning bureau, a firm known for its emphasis on ecologically sensitive building, is a sign of a certain symbolic value that Chinese officials ascribe not only to the process of how Anting is being built, but by whom. Ecological sensitivity is becoming a marketing selling point (Gutzmer 2009: 27).

Despite the obvious connections between Anting New Town and Autostadt Wolfsburg, the relationship between the two seems to be far from one-dimensional. Although Anting is often referred to as "Autostadt Shanghai" (for instance by Rebaschus 2005) or as "Autostadt Anting", thereby indicating that the development in Shanghai was a follower of that in Wolfsburg, how exactly these names came up is unclear. Autostadt Wolfsburg officials told me that they did not intend to "export" the idea of Autostadt in any way, even though Volkswagen is the oldest international incumbent on the Chinese car market and remains one of the main investors in Anting. In a newspaper interview, Speer himself denounced the idea that Anting is to become an "Autostadt" (Erling 2007). What he has in mind when he uses the term "Autostadt", however, is a place exclusively for the physical production of cars, a place more similar to the old Wolfsburg of the 1950s than to the image-driven architectural ensemble at stake in this work. The question of how certain architectural ideas spread between different brand spaces will be dealt with in the following chapters.

# 3 Branding and the spatialization of capitalism

## Brands as an extension of marketing

In order to understand the complex relationship between brands and marketing-driven capitalism we have to look at the emergence of marketing as concept and practice. In the US, marketing was not initially an instrument for promoting the liberal vision of free markets, but a way to secure state regulation and to control markets. Cochoy (1998: 208) argues that marketing in fact emerged from the Roosevelt administration's efforts to "master the economy". The government's aim to control markets in those days needed standardizations and measurements to define to what extent a product or company met the set targets. The company that not only met these targets, but was also able to prove that it did, would gain what business theorists later called a "competitive advantage" (Porter 1995).

The close relation between government intervention and marketing is not really surprising. Marketing practice does not aim at supporting free markets. Marketing is a means of preventing pure market situations, interested in establishing a set of individual or social desires that *force* the consumer to buy certain products. The consumer does not have free choice. Marketers want to create a solid power structure regarding consumer behaviour, and this power structure is also a knowledge structure; they want to *know* that the consumer will choose product A, and why.

In terms of strategic terminology, marketing discourses have established their own wording for the category "consumer": the "customer". Apparently, there are implications of the term "consumer" to do with frantic purchasing and an orientation towards the blunt process of exchanging money for goods, presumably considered too banal, that are to be avoided. As the "customer", the consumer is the fetish of marketing. At the same time, he is also the main problem, stubbornly refusing to be the calculable object marketing wants him to be. Hence the degrading terms used to describe purchasing behaviour patterns in which consumers do not act according to some predefined models, such as the "ambiguous consumer". Or, the other extreme, such customers are called "smart shoppers", a term which seems to express the surprise about the fact that the customer has the capacity to make individual decisions.

When it comes to conceptualizing the role of the consumer in the microeconomic process of consumption, a rift exists between business discourses and cultural analyses. Even though marketing literature by now acknowledges that consumers are not passive entities that can be manipulated at will, the idea that consumption and production increasingly merge is still driven mainly by cultural theorists (cf. Beller 1998: 61, or Arvidsson 2005). It is they who claim that as soon as labour becomes immaterial, the consumer obtains an active, and perhaps even productive, role. They are putting forward the view that the definition of production as that which is done in companies by employed workers seems incomplete.

The introduction of branding into the conceptual frameworks of business literature further decreases the level of potential corporate control. My argument is that the brand cannot easily be used as a control tool. I will put forward the idea that the brand became the key focus of business and business-related discourses through a gradual acceptance that the aim of a complete control of consumer behaviour and therefore markets is an illusion. Even if business theory is not giving up on this idea of control completely, the integration of the concept of branding into its core frameworks is a step towards a more complex future business theory.[1] And there are marketing discourses questioning the corporate aim for control (for instance Brownlie *et al.* 1999).

While traditional marketing approaches would like to uphold their deterministic ways of thinking, it would appear that branding gains increasing dominance in practice and theory *because* it is neither deterministic nor rationalistic. Lury (2004: 25) argues that there is a tendency towards intuition to branding. Following up on this, the brand becomes a holistic concept accounting for the fact that conventional rationalistic marketing concepts have fallen short of defining or framing capitalist reality.

Marketing, one could argue, opens up to complexity theory. If that is the case, then this would mean that it would have to begin to develop a more cultural approach to and a more situated model of the consumer (Lury 2004: 38). This tendency can indeed be seen, and it is connected to a theoretical movement called "postmodern marketing" (see for instance Cova 1999). Lury (2004) argues that "marketers have increasingly become advocates of the view that consumers are active and reflexive". Arvidsson (1999, quoted in Lury, ibid.) adds that this new view of the customer has undermined the usefulness of traditional tools of market segmentation.

## Cities as an extension of brands

Brand spaces are not the first endeavours into establishing a link between a city and a content- or ideas-based capitalist structure. Mainly in the Passagenwerk, Benjamin has shown with regard to early modern metropolises how commoditization was mediated by practices of cultural representation (Bridge and Watson 2001: 354). The whole idea of themed environments is concerned with ways in which capitalism tries to appropriate space by giving it a certain "theme" (Gottdiener 2001). Practically as well as conceptually, the city has often been understood and used as space of representation (cf. Westwood 1997). Particularly the work of Lefebvre almost seems as canonical in this respect (Lefebvre 1991).

However, the capitalist phenomenon of entrepreneurial, profit-driven activities trying to connect to city life is not limited to representational distortions through capitalist agency. Benjamin's and Simmel's analyses of capitalist urban transformation processes are broader than this, pointing to the combined effects of money, media, a culture of "thingification" and the tendency to a permanent acceleration of social life as key drivers of the capitalization of urban space (Amin and Thrift 2002: 32–33). This thinking has been developed further by theorists of consumer culture, resulting in a significant part of the literature on both historical and contemporary regimes of consumption being distinctly urban. Mark Jayne (2006, Chapter 2) shows how the modern city has consumer culture at its very core. "Consumption-driven" and "real" have never been opposites.

Theorists focusing more on the production side of capitalism have also aimed at developing an urbanized notion of the economy. In their critiques of classical equilibrium economics, thinkers like Hirsch or Myrdal aimed at explaining the efficiency bonuses city-focused economic strategies can create. Hirsch (1973: 3) highlighted the particular strength of urbanized corporate modes of action for the generation and distribution of information. Later, theorists developing Weberian or Marxist perspectives on urban space have conceptualized the relationships between urban space and capital formation (cf. Castells 1977; Massey 1984; particularly also Harvey 1985).

Many of these approaches were partly working in a Marxist framework while extending certain claims central to orthodox Marxism. They challenge Marx's claim that capitalism aims to annihilate space over time (Marx 1983: 539). Capitalism always needed space (and it knows as much, as intra-capitalist discourse shows; see von Oettinger 2004). Many Postmarxist writers have accepted the impact that capitalism has on space. Sennett criticized that capitalism creates the fall of public man. David Harvey argues that "the production of fixed and immobile spatial configurations" is what capitalism aims at (Harvey 2001: 327). However, like others, Harvey seems to underestimate the proximity to change that capitalism brings to a city. Capitalism does not need immobile configurations. It is precisely through its high degree of non-fixity that capitalism can be seen to have undermined the identity-creating structures we might once have found in cities. Because, and only because this is the case, the question can be asked whether there is room for any kind of criticism of brand space as furthering the vulnerability of the city. Is it undermining the idea of the city as we used to know it? This criticism would then work along the lines of stating that brand space is not a "real" urban phenomenon, but simulating the "real" city, thereby weakening the essence of "real" real cities. The point I want to make in Chapters 4 and 5, of course, is Deleuzian: that brand space is real, even if virtual.

Parallel to these theoretical engagements with the urbanization of economic strategies, there have been different ways in which companies tried to establish urban links. There have also been earlier efforts to create the kind of reflexivity that can be said to be at work in Autostadt. A much-discussed example of the former is the city-building activity by entertainment giant Disney, another the British workers' city Bourneville, built by the chocolate-bar producer Cadbury. The intellectually challenging and, one could argue, critical design of certain retail areas (see the Prada works of Rem Koolhaas) is another proof of the effort by brand builders to use space to give their brand substance.

Bournville is a small town on the outskirts of Birmingham, home of chocolate company Cadbury (taken over by Kraft Foods in 2010). One of the early Cadbury owners, anthropologist George Cadbury, had erected Bournville as a model village around the turn of the century (Harrison 1999).[2] Its architecture has a certain Arts and Crafts appeal to it, and has been a blueprint for other communities in England and the USA. Just as many later model villages or ideal cities, Bournville has arguably been characterized by a clear overarching idea of a *good life* (Bridge and Watson 2002: 452). In this sense, it was a spatial and a social project at once. In terms of architecture, it "speaks about itself".

Model cities have been a major idea in architecture since the Renaissance (Vidler 1992: 179). These cities are monuments of themselves. Their functioning mechanisms have been designed to *speak of* the city right from the start. First step in the creation of a model city is the definition of which urban processes are supposed to take place. The question is whether this is the case with brand cities, too. There are no predefined urban processes. Rather they have to develop a high degree of openness, due to their inherent emptiness. This is why, when entering the urban landscape, a brand has to maintain an openness as to the ways in which people deal with its spatial offerings. Whatever urban process there is enhances the content of the brand, the set of images, phantasmagoria, or sentiments that essentially *are* the brand.

Nevertheless, one can see model cities as an important step towards brand cities. This is because in order to give a certain interpretation of what cities are, or are supposed to be, they work with daily process; they work processually. They do not take the concrete daily flows in the city as given, but claim to manage them in the interest of some higher definition of what it means to be urban. This basic approach is similar to how brand space works. It sets the stage for the interpretation of the city as a site of a permanent conflict between chaos and order, manageable abstract principle and messy reality. One peculiar effort to deal with this conflict can be seen in the corporate architectural urban project "Celebration", a town built in Florida by the Disney Corporation. Celebration is a highly planned space, but one that put a lot of effort in minimizing the above-described confrontation between principle and chaos. It can be described as an abstract space – in which a rigid ideological content wants to *break* with the domination of the city by abstract categories such as money or exchange value, thereby involuntarily creating its own abstractions. It has been broadly criticized for that, for instance by Ross (2000) or by Zukin (1995).

Not so much an abstract city, or a "non-city", but rather a case of display capitalism that has certain similarities to brand space, are world exhibitions ("Expos"). In the early world exhibitions, major companies, their products and ideas of the future world of consumption played a significant role. They developed an image of a *better* capitalist world, free from the nastier sides of early industrialism (Gottdiener 2001: 31), a world of clean, "pure" consumption. Furthermore, they added an element of abstraction and multi-levelled intellectual demand to consumption itself. People *saw* products at expos, they were expected to *think about* them, but they could not *buy* them. Being a consumer, this seemed to communicate, is not an easy, straightforward task (Frisby 1985: 254). An anthropological analysis of the system "world exhibition" has been offered by Harvey (1996). She interprets the world exhibition in Seville as a "hybrid": a hybrid between modernity and postmodernity, and, connected with this, between *experience/dwelling* and *picture/reading*.

There seems to be a strong connection between Harvey's "hybrid" concept and some of Rem Koolhaas' endeavours in retail architecture. Several of his retail spaces seem to *think through* the notion of a capitalist hybridity in architecture, while in fact *being* such hybrids themselves. Also, Koolhaas makes us understand better the aforementioned relationship between dwelling/being and reading. His Prada stores in New York, Tokyo and Los Angeles reflect on the role of the "selling place" and of the brand in society. They have often been seen as a reflection of how technology is shaping our lives. But they are more. Toy models sunk into the floor of the LA store entrance can be seen as a critical reflection and a critique of the contemporary consumer. And Koolhaas makes his criticism explicit; on the upper floor walls in the Beverly Hills store, the visitor is confronted with wallpaper writings and drawings by Koolhaas' think tank AMO. This breaks up the linearity of the concept "selling point", creating an awareness of the role of the shop, and in fact of any shop, in a whole range of cultural, architectural and urban processes. Koolhaas forces the shopper to read, thereby creating a situation of involuntary criticism. This has the capacity to create, in Harvey's sense, a "hybrid experience".

Another example of a hybrid consumption space configuration is the global network of flagship Apple stores. While not interested in promoting any sort of "critical customer", the minimalist and spacious design of the stores draws attention to the environment. Being here means reading. The customer is reading the very Apple brand itself – exactly by means of reflecting upon his own bodily integration into the store and its physical appearance. This is enhanced by the wide-open window front many of the stores showcase. Before going in, we are aware that we will be entering a consumerist stage. Once inside, the experience of this stage is read by all of us.

## Virtual spaces, new media cities, mass ornaments and Schäume

In recent years, poststructuralism has begun to focus on the development of the city and its relationship with architecture, thereby changing our perception of space and of the urban itself (cf. Murdoch 2006; Whatmore 2002). Sloterdijk can be argued to build on this, developing concepts that philosophically integrate a notion of a culturally productive role of space and a thoroughly poststructuralist reading of key concepts of cultural theory, such as subjectivity, flow, or media-induced cultural change (van Tuinen 2007: 28). Similarly, media theory and the thinking of the mediatization of contemporary reality have overcome the assumption of a strict distinction between what is urban and what is a medium.

Within a poststructuralist understanding of culture, space is seen as relational (Murdoch 2006: 1–4). Relationality can be defined through giving process the lead over structure (Harvey 1996). Place formation then "becomes a process of carving out permanences" from the various flows that define any possible spatiality (ibid.: 261). "Space" is the area where places are related to one another, and "place" is that which can be related.

*Networked space*

The concept of relational space has been formulated by actor-network theory (Law 1999). Law points out a need for a theory that sees spatial formations as constituted by a heterogeneous set of relations. This is what actor-network theory is aiming at. Space is no longer an empty container, but contained, or rather, produced. So is the relevance of the individual elements within space. In a network, "elements retain their spatial integrity by virtue of their position in a set of links or relations" (ibid.: 6).

It is obvious that this understanding complicates any possible reading of spatial structure. What belongs to the relevant network? What is an "actor"? What is an "element"? But despite this ambiguity, the concept of relationality is vital for the idea of a spatialized brand; the brand is relational, and even when spatializing, it can be understood to exist through relations. Furthermore, I will argue that the brand actually *creates* a new kind of relational space.

However, the network concept might not be sufficient to fully grasp the complexity of the brand spaces discussed here. This is because we might need a theory that allows also for processes below the level of objectivity. In a network, elements are argued to have a certain objectivity. Either something or someone is an objective part of a network, or it isn't. This is where the concept of fluid space, also developed by Law, comes in. In fluid space, "it's not possible to determine identities nice and neatly, once and for all" (Mol and Law 1994: 660). Fluid space is softer, more open. We need not decide yet whether Autostadt, BMW Welt or Anting New Town *are* this fluid space. It is sufficient to have in mind this theoretical concept in order to understand phenomena that network-oriented thinking cannot grasp.

*Virtual space*

The degree of change this implies for space leaves the latter weak. What, after all, "is" space in that respect? If these multiplicities interact with spatial elements, being physical in one moment, then escaping the boundaries of spatiality, then space is no longer a *container* of process, but process itself. This is why Doel claims to no longer even see space as a noun.[3] "To space – that's all. Spacing is an action, an event, a way of being" (Doel 2000: 125). In that sense, from a poststructuralist perspective, this extreme openness is a central feature of any space-related process. This is why we can argue that space has the capacity to become "virtual". It is not only that which can be seen or perceived at one particular moment, but also the potential processes it might trigger through the application or combination of certain multiplicities.

The concepts of the virtual and the actual seem to be suitable for understanding the complexity of brand urbanism as architectural, commercial as well as cultural space and practice. They seem to allow for the development of an analytical framework to describe the process of architecture becoming medium at one point while resisting mediatization at another.

Deleuze distinguishes the "virtual" as discussed here from the "possible". The virtual has the capacity to be actualized, the possible to be realized. Without realization, the possible cannot properly be argued to "be". The virtual on the other hand can very well be argued to be, even without its actualization. This actualization might occur at some point, at a given moment. But even if it does not, the virtual is not nothing. It has the capacity to be different at any given moment; "the sheer contingency of an unactualized event, a program that may successfully run" (Doyle 2003, quoted in Shields 2005: 281). There is a high degree of *complexity* and *contradiction* involved in virtual processes (Castells 1996: 372). Permanent change is a central feature of the virtual. For what "is" something that has the capacity to be different at any given moment?[4]

This does not mean that the idea of identity loses all relevance. In virtualization, identity still matters, albeit not as an actual or given, but as a partly virtual construct. It is in this way that it relates to my interpretation of media urbanism. Virtual cities are not cities without identity. This can be seen with regard to the global cities discourse (cf. Brenner and Keil 2006), and in particular to Sassen's notion of global cities (Sassen 2002). Sassen does not think of them as places without identity. Rather, they get their identity from the interaction with other cities; globalization is a new source of identity. For Sassen, cities are a site for *new types* of cultural and subjective operations (ibid.: 112; see also Watson and Bridges 1999).

As a concept, the virtual is central to explaining another key feature of Deleuzian thinking that this work will engage with and use as an undercurrent of the understanding of the formation of brand space: his philosophy of time. For Deleuze, following Bergson, time is not the ordered sequence of actual events. Or rather, it is that, but also the opposite: linear time's interruption and permanent threat of being interrupted by nonlinear, one could say, virtual temporalities. In particular, for Deleuze, "impersonal memory" (Colebrook 2002: 33) is continuously cutting through the layers of Cartesian time.

This leads to a new relationship between past and present. For Deleuze, the past is not only an element in the construction of the present; rather, it grows into a role as the present's other side. It is the present, reconceived as a virtuality (Eisenman 2001: XIII). It will be with this idea in mind that I approach the many, almost obsessive ways in which brand space engages with the history of the spaces it inhabits. The putting-together of products, architectural styles and human subjectivities within brand space creates a new relativity with regard to any notion of history. It introduces different histories, different perspectives on the relationship between past, present and future, and, therefore, different perspectives on time itself. Time becomes a variable. Similarly, Anting New Town refers architecturally to a history that is not its own.

### The lens of new media theory

The outlined concepts of time–space interaction have a strong media-theoretical background. Deleuze connect this background to the advent of modern cinema (Deleuze 1989). In our context, this connection between the philosophy of time and a *medium* (cinema) is central. It makes sense to approach brand cities with categories of media theory. Specifically, in brand space, architecture has the capacity (or is threatened) to become a medium. And as medium, I will show, its effects pertain to our sense of time, and to the ways we deal with time in our daily life.

In terms of theory, I want to suggest that it might make sense to employ the thinking of Friedrich Kittler when explaining the ways in which urban(ized) space works as a medium. The general idea of "the city as medium" is thereby broadened. Specifically, Kittler allows for a view on mediatization in the urban sphere that abandons a reduction of media productivity to the creation of symbolic, consequential, and linear modes of communication. For Kittler, media processes today are in the last instance *matter*, and *material*. This is the essential link between his thinking and the – material, physical, architectural – reality of the urban sphere.

In Kittler's writing, the new focus on the physicality of mediatization processes is connected to the dominance of the internet – a central element in the creation of the cultural regime of "new media". Hence, for the Kittler perspective on the city to develop its full potential, I suggest extending the notion of urbanized mediatization processes, claiming that the city is not just *any* medium, but specifically an example of a *new media process* (cf. Massumi 2002: 192). When we look at the writing of new media theorists such as Manovich (primarily 2001 and 2003), there seem to be three main arguments to support the claim that the developments I am looking at can indeed be described as a new media process.

First, new media are inherently connected to mechanisms of interactivity (Manovich 2003). Wherever a consumer of media input is put in the position of actively engaging with this input, co-creating it to a certain extent, this can be seen as an instance of transforming classical media into new media. The actual–virtual interactions taking place in brand space offer this kind of transformation. They have the potential to be generated interactively, for the consumer/visitor has to become actively (even if perhaps involuntarily) involved.

Second, connected to the point above, brand space works along a notion of "doing", rather than exclusively of "communicating". The expectation of interactivity pulls visitors into the position of "immersing" fully into a process of "doing" something with the brand, rather than simply picking up or even sending out bits of communication. Similarly, it can be argued to be constitutive of new media processes to be defined by the principle of doing in the sense of economic productivity, with people becoming active in processes of production, rather than by the triggering of communication processes as an end in itself (Lash 2002: 67).

Finally, these interactions and "doings" that a brand triggers by becoming spatial are not limited to the concrete brand space, or brand city alone. They are taking place on a potentially global scale. The fact that, for instance, Autostadt provides a new kind of centre for the brand does not mean that it loses its global character, but is actually increasing the global presence of a brand. The particular media space is connected to other spaces engaged in similar mediatization processes. Different media spaces interact, and engage in intensive modes of exchange (of information, images, products or money) significantly *through* the images created by branding. Hence, the brand is furthering the globalization of the urban as medium. Once more, this is an analogy with the mechanisms of new media, seen by Manovich and others as drivers of the globalization of culture. Flew (2002) even goes so far to argue that the cultural and economic process of globalization has been made possible by new media in the first place.

If we can indeed argue that brand architecture offers functional mechanisms of new media, then it is the endpoint in the becoming-medium of architecture, creating what can be called "intensities" of new media spaces (Lash and Lury 2007: 15). It is through the notion of intensity that we can understand what the specific productivity of architecture in new media space is made up of. Intensity is that which results from the spatialization of information. It is also that which remains once this spatialization has deprived information of much of its symbolic coherence.

The application of Kittler's thinking then allows for a more substantial understanding of how these processes of new media work in brand space. There are two rationales for using Kittler in this context. On the one hand, Kittler (1996) himself has conceptualized the city as medium. With reference to Lewis Mumford, he first states that the city is a place of the recording and transmission of information (ibid.: 721). He then argues that Mumford left out a third element of urbanity: the fact that in an urban context, information is also *processed*. His argument is that because in urban space, information is dealt with on all three scales simultaneously, the city can be seen as a medium (Kloock and Spahr 1997: 167).

This transforming element in urban structures can be argued to be a strong motivation for companies to engage in city building. Brand space, one could say, applies information bits of all kinds – historical, architectural, aesthetical – to brands, thereby processing it and generating (in the broadest sense, information-based) new levels of spatial reality.

However, in the context of Kittler's thinking, the notion of information itself has to be treated with care. Regarding brand space, the question is in which way information bits indeed have "informing" effects. Are people really and primarily seeking information in the sense of knowledge in brand space? My point is that they are not, which effectively means that the notion of information has to be differentiated from ideas of knowledge creation and furthering, be it on a social or an individual level (Kittler 1986: 5).

This brings us to the second argument linking Kittler to the concept of brand city as an instance of new media. Kittler's historical approach to the development of media is based on the assumption that the level of text-based media analysis has to be abandoned in the age of digital media (Kittler 1990). In this sense, Kittler's thinking relates to the concept of "ubiquitous media" (Featherstone 2009). Kittler takes the idea of ubiquitous media to a new dimension. For him, new media get rid of the monopoly of text and content in favour of more purely technical levels of mediated reality.

These levels, I want to claim, can also be conceptualized as spatial. Space is where text and content are deprived of their essentialist character. Architecture plays a central role in this context. When architecture is becoming the carrier of information, this transforms not only the notion of building but that of information itself (architecture is, in Kittler's sense, "processing" information). Information is then the foundation of matter, rather than matter being reduced to information. Matter "grows" out of engaging with, and containing, information. It is in this way that one can talk regarding informational space about ubiquitous media (cf. Lash 2002: 128).

This in fact means that the old and well-learned discourse analysis has to make way for a different kind of analytical practice, what Krämer (2006: 97) calls a "technological media analysis". This necessity to rethink cultural analysis holds also true for the spatialization of branding through architectural brand assemblages. Just like digital media for Kittler, brand space is a move away from the sign-based logic of advertising to the functioning of the architectural, which of course can also connect to signage, but for which the sign is essentially an externality. We are still dealing with images, but no longer with images *of* something external and identifiable, but rather with the *pure image*. This image is beyond the restriction to the visual, because it is lived (Lash 2002: 184). We perceive it by being in it. Architecture as pure form is the creator of this kind of image, because it is an externality to the notion of sign; it is, to speak with Lacan, the real rather than the symbolic. Similarly, for Kittler, digital media turn away from the symbolic and towards the real (Kittler 2002: 38). In this sense, brand space is the "real" of capitalism.

But what is this "capitalist real"? The argument above creates a certain uneasiness with which this work is positioned alongside other ways to capture capitalist reality. Specifically, it seems to indicate a connection with, but also a partial deviation from, the Marxist assumption of a capitalism characterized by a permanence of abstraction, by a culture that makes abstraction the only reality. This work is strongly engaged with the notion of the abstract. What I analyze here is an abstraction of architecture and public space, but at the expense of the partial breakdown of a symbolic order. It is what Toscano (2008: 71) deems as necessary to understand capitalist reality: an "investigation into the effective, productive, material – in brief, real – character of abstraction". However, by looking for these productive effects, I want to maintain a more open analytical position, allowing a search for the productive effects of abstraction beyond the Marxist categories of exchange value and commodity fetishism. Through the confrontation with the urban, abstraction itself changes (Massumi 2002: 165–166). With this in mind, I argue that it makes sense to look for the potential cultural productivities inherent in the abstract, and for the ways in which abstraction creates elements that are the foundation, the "new concrete", in a capitalist culture: lived images, abstract affects (ibid.: 219).

## Capitalism and the mass ornament

However, there is one element central to Kittler's thinking where I adopt a different position. Kittler's writing is concerned with the argument that in the age of new media, the human being, which means human subjectivity as much as it pertains to the human body, loses out in conceptual relevance (Kittler 1989: 115). This exclusion of the human would not do my analysis much good. For this book, it seems reasonable to assume that there is still something like a human subjectivity, however embattled. This notion of subjectivity at least seems to have the capacity to play an active, perhaps even a creative role in the process of spatializing brands. The question is: how? We need a theory that allows for a flexible understanding of the human, questioning the role of the subject, but still making it possible to conceptualize processes in which parts of human beings become a productive element in a greater machine, or in a collective and productive spatial process.

What I want to develop is an approach that acknowledges all the limitations put upon human agency by media and mediatization, but which does not exclude any relevance of the human altogether. This approach brings this work in line with what Thrift (2008: 13) calls "minimal humanism".

In order to understand this minimal notion of the human, I would like to suggest that, alongside recent ideas of the cyborg (Haraway 1990; Hayles 2000; Shields 2006), the concept of the "Ornament der Masse" by Siegfried Kracauer could be of use. The mass ornament is a capitalist event in which human beings enter into an abstract form-creating process. It gives a form to the formless creature that is capitalism; indeed it might be the form of capitalism itself.

Kracauer's key example is the early twentieth-century show combo the Tiller Girls, whose individual members all gave up their self-definition as an individual to become part of the self-referencing capitalist form, the ornament. Human subjects give up their individuality in order to become part of a new whole they don't know in advance (Kracauer 1963: 52). The mass ornament is form, but it is also blind; it is the creation of form without intention and a creator. The human is entering this form – as physical data.

This idea can be adopted by the analysis of urban space. It then yields an understanding of this space as a self-referential post-urban system. This kind of system is what is created by brand space. Physical bodies continue to play a role here. This is a particular instance of McLuhan's idea of media as prosthetics (cf. McLuhan 1964); the city as medium becomes a prosthesis for the humans, just as the humans are necessary to make it whole. In fact, it is they who transform the urban into a medium. They are not receivers of media messages so much as part of the creation of mediated urbanity. The inhabitants of Anting New Town are part of a larger whole, part of a mass ornament. Each human subject changes the ornament through her presence. By "participating", human bodies give the architectural elements in the mass ornament a new (mediatized) level of being.

### *"Schäume" and the creative capacity of fragile space*

In Chapter 6 I will develop this idea further, combining Kracauer with the conceptualization of an existentialized space proposed by Peter Sloterdijk. Sloterdijk develops a philosophical reading of space that aims at establishing space in the centre of the philosophical discourse with the same intensity as Heidegger (1986) did with the idea of an existentialized time. Sloterdijk derives his concept from a reflection on the notion of the global. He puts forward a view on globalization that emphasizes its functioning through the creation of a globalized internal space. Sloterdijk calls this the "Weltinnenraum des Kapitals". It is through this notion of a global inside that we can understand globalized branding and the creation of brand spaces simultaneously as a step towards a globally integrated and globally mediatized capitalism.

With this notion of a globally mediatized space, I approach Sloterdijk's concept of the current globalization phase as one characterized by a logic of "Schäume" ("Foams"; Sloterdijk 2004). Sloterdijk suggests that Schaum is not merely a metaphor, but the structural basis for capitalist spatial practice and contemporary globalized culture. The world (of global mediatization) is becoming increasingly Schaum-like.

The notion of Schaum allows us to understand the functioning of mediatized space as one that simultaneously totalizes and de-totalizes. Schaum is potentially global, but also creates multiple niches that allow for the generation of local vernacular forms. It demonstrates how the most diverse microspheres are linked together in the globalized urban sphere, and also creates a sense of unity in a world characterized by permanent ruptures and symbolic heterogeneities.

In a Schaum structure, different microspheres interact. This creation of different "strata" (Schichten, ibid.: 59) is not dissimilar to the understanding of society put forward by Deleuze and Guattari in the sense that the existence of an absolute outside is substituted by a dominance of the in-between (van Tuinen 2007: 144). The basic idea: if we can think the outside, we are always already partly inside.

Sloterdijk, however, extends Deleuzian concepts by introducing a more thoroughly spatial, more explicitly three-dimensional philosophical perspective. In this concept, space is an anthropological as well as sociological core category. Spatial reality determines what it means to be human. Therein lies the relevance of Sloterdijk's understanding of culture as Schaum: that it puts forward an anthropological sense of spatiality.

The multifocal structure of Schäume is creating a spatial regime radically different from that of distinct territories, limited cities and media as mere tools to communicate precreated messages. In Schaum, media create space, and space enables the perception of media messages. Sloterdijk understands Schaum space as fragile, changeable; principally unlimited, but also multiple. Schaum is Sloterdijk's conceptual reaction to the failure of models to develop an understanding of human culture from a perspective of the one uniting globe. Globalization is a fact, but the idea of the globe as an organizing meta-principle is obsolete (Sloterdijk 1999: 582). It is substituted by the multiple (and poststructuralist) logic of Schäume.

This thinking carries urbanistic relevance. Cities for Sloterdijk are "schaumige Agglomerationen" (foamy agglomerations, Sloterdijk 2004: 47). Vice versa, Schaum can create urbanities. Hence, he sees contemporary cultural process as yielding to the creation of "foam cities" (ibid.). Like Kracauer, he is intrigued by the architectural form of the stadium. The stadium is an important concept for foamy urbanity because it is responding to a desire for an outburst of human and architectural mass intensity.

For Sloterdijk, urbanity is not simply "occupied" by the workings of Schaum; rather, the urban is where a foam structure grows. This is what I will develop further under the heading of a globalized mass ornament.

Sloterdijk and his understanding of Schaum as central feature of the current phase of globalization will be the link between Kracauer's mass ornament and the globalized phenomenon of brand space. Moreover, it will help us understand the extent to which the mediatization of the urban through brand space indeed has the capacity to transform contemporary capitalism.

The notion of Schaum allows for a reformulation of the relationship between surface and substance. Schaum is both, substance and surface. It is essentially made up of surfaces, but creates a feeling of three-dimensional density, forming a substance one cannot see through. It is productive, undermining any orientation on substantiality or stability as a measure for cultural or philosophical relevance (ibid.: 39).

This de-substantialization of thought, simultaneously implying a de-substantialization of space, also allows for a very concrete understanding of basic mechanisms of capitalism. Specifically, Schaum allows for an understanding of the developments of capitalist corporations in relation to each other. Globally operating companies are like Schaum structures in that they are connected with each other, and in that the activities of one company affect the procedures within the realm of the other. Also, they have the tendency to swallow each other, or become part of one another, like two bubbles[5] within one foamy structure. The activities of companies in relation to each other have real spatial effects (production lines and corporate headquarters being transferred, workers being laid off, etc.). This spatialized reality of capitalist activity can be understood by a very concrete application of Sloterdijk's concept of Schaum.

In this context, I also want to apply another central Sloterdijk idea, that of our (in a narrow sense post-globalized) world being at the same time post-historical. Sloterdijk (2005, Chapter 32) effectively connects the end of the nautical globalization process with the death of the grand narrative of history. In looking at three concrete building endeavours obviously engaged with their own idea of a history, or many histories, we will see that the end of the grand narrative of history, while certainly a suitable concept for understanding the project of terrestrial globalization, is not sufficient to account for the built reality of the urban. Specifically, the construction of highly mediatized places such as the brand spaces in Wolfsburg and Munich allows for an application of notions of history after the end of its grand narrative. Furthermore, I will propose that it is consequently China that employs not only its own historical narrative, but also what is left of the grand narratives of other countries, to create its own version of a transnational, and translocal, form of post-historical, but historizing city space.

# 4 Actualizing the virtual of capitalism?

## The functions and functionings of brand space

### Methodology and knowledge production: researching brand cities, brand cities as research

*The readability of the city*

The conceptualization of brand space as a place for research from a corporate viewpoint has to be understood in relation to a certain crisis of the research of cities (Amin and Thrift 2002). Conventional urbanism is seen as a thing of the past, but more concrete, multisensual approaches, such as the idea of reading a city by wandering through it, did not offer an easy solution. The city is becoming an increasingly abstract place (ibid.: 37). It is subject to economic, cultural and political processes which are not visible and do not all take place in the streets.

This argument is the background for what Volkswagen aims at in Autostadt, or BMW in BMW Welt. In times of knowledge capitalism, creating organizational knowledge is seen as a source of competitive advantage. At the same time, however, companies mistrust the given tools of knowledge creation and storage. This holds true particularly for the world of marketing, which is seen as especially opaque. Even marketing theorists acknowledge that there is an "extreme disorder in consumption" leading to what is perceived by marketing theorists as a venerable consumer crisis (Cova 1999: 64). In this context, when a company engages with the city, this should not be interpreted simply as a way to create certain clearly predictable reactions on the part of consumers. Rather, it can be interpreted as a way to understand urban space and the brand in this space (perspective one mentioned above) as well as the consumer as a thoroughly urban being; the subject(ive) is read through the object(ive) (perspective two; cf. Appadurai 1986). Autostadt master planner Gunter Henn quotes management theorist Tom Peters who claims that management of space is today becoming an essential way to enhance learning by globally operating companies (Henn 2000: 2–3). Through Autostadt, Henn and Volkswagen want to foster such learning processes.

They thereby employ a mechanism developed by utopian modernist architecture. Architectural modernity always had an element of epistemology in it

(Sloterdijk 2004: 657). It was an effort to understand. It aimed at creating understanding through new modes of cultural synthesis in what Sloterdijk calls "Verdichtungsräume" ("spaces of densification"). Brand space is creating those Verdichtungsräume. It is typical for Verdichtungsräume to create complex modes of a spatial multi-dimensionality. Brand space is essentially doing the same. In particular, the design of multi-levelled three-dimensionalities is indicative of this kind of experimental-analytical architecture. Concretely, Autostadt Wolfsburg is characterized by several problematizations of the dimensions of traditional urbanity, particularly with the AutoTürme and the Audi pavilion. The latter not only transforms the Audi logo into a building, but also deconstructs the iconic rings the logo is made up of, putting two of them on top of each other. This can be read as a parallel research of the social effectiveness of the capitalist modality of the logo, as well as of the degree to which the idea of media space and mediatized urbanity can be appropriated by branding.

The AutoTürme deprive the car as an iconic product of its inherent link to the street, lifting them 50 metres above ground. Cars are thereby essentially becoming properly three-dimensional for the first time; or maybe the sky for them is dimension four. In both cases, Autostadt creates what Sloterdijk calls "emporgehobene Meta-Städte", super-cities fit to replicate at any imaginable height the basic three-dimensional structures from ground level, and which thereby use dimensionality to create uncommon and even disturbing urban experiences.

Hence, Autostadt can be argued to be testing car- and brand-driven urbanity by engaging with those peculiar features of the urban real that Sloterdijk is so fascinated by. It is thereby becoming an urban or hyper-urban *laboratory*. In this laboratory, what is tested in particular is the non-linguistic essence of a brand, its "doing" in urban space. How can a brand be brought to the urban sphere? How is it "done" in an urban context? Through brand space as semi-controlled corporate environment, this processual essence of spatialized branding is brought at least partially into the realm of the company. This creates embedded knowledge. The company "knows", at least to a larger extent, what is happening within the realm of the brand when it relates to urban space, when it "plays out" in urban reality. In this way, brand space can be seen as a response to the crisis of traditional market research. If new ways to investigate brand-related urban reality are sought for, then brand city can be seen as such a research innovation. It is the object of a new research methodology (of what von Borries calls, with regard to the inner-urban activities of the shoe giant Nike, "Nike urbanism"; von Borries 2004: 19). This holds true for the company Volkswagen as well as for me as cultural researcher.

The urban involvement of brand initiators in order to create knowledge can be seen as a reaction to a growing corporate awareness for an increasingly active consumer. The many brand-specific strategies that today want to engage with active and sovereign consumers are often urban ones (cf.

Bieber 2000: 149 ff.). One example: in a complex game of action and reaction, of image making, image transformation and even image subversion and destruction, inner-city youth cultures "make" certain brands, rather than simply consuming them. From this perspective, the efforts of the brand Nike to engage in an active and creative way with the urban sphere in its Niketown campaign seem to be a way to get closer to the consumers – and to *understand* them better. Through Niketown, the company developed procedures to read youth cultures – by interacting with them. Niketown was urban research through urban intervention.

It is interventions like these that this work wants to trace. It is, therefore, a work of cultural and architectural analysis as much as it focuses on the daily social reality. In Chapter 4, I am trying to define the capitalist rationale behind constructing brand spaces, and to demonstrate how it plays out spatially and architecturally. Given that this implies a strong emphasis on architectural practice, an engagement with previous writing on these concrete spatial arrangements and their history is central. This background is added to by observational practices, based on several visits I have made to each of the three places researched. During these visits, the individual buildings have been studied regarding the way they define space, their relation to each other, and also the way in which they shape bodily movement and set the frame for affective experience.

Given that it is significantly a capitalist rationality I want to trace in Chapter 4, a critical engagement with marketing theory is required. However, my writing will always acknowledge that neither marketing theory nor concrete brand-oriented decision making can be assumed to be based on an awareness of the cultural complexity of capitalist space. This will become even more evident in Chapter 5, where the focus on the development of capitalist modes of space management will be left for a broader perspective on mediatized space.

In the course of my research, I have also spoken to individual visitors to the brand spaces in Munich and Wolfsburg. These conversations will become part of my argument, without, however, being the basis for my overall work. This is because much of what I am writing will be based on the assumption of what Murdoch (2006: 10) calls a "decentred", fragmented subjectivity. Tracing these new forms of subjectivity means tracing how the self-awareness of "the subject" (understood as an individual capable of reporting its own emotions or, especially, affects) is undermined. This will become most obvious in Chapter 6, where the programme of what I will call the global mass ornament is very much *defined* by a transformation of possible modes of subjectivity.

And yet, the focus on the architectural and urban effects of current modes of capitalist activity does not mean that the consumer is merely subject to encompassing systems of capitalist manipulation. Rather, the very notion of new media urbanism that this work puts forward is based on conceptualizing a new notion of consumer activeness and an embodied corporate knowledge as the starting point for a very specific consumer culture. In this culture, what Holt calls "postmodern brand management" offers brands as cultural resources for consumers, rather than trying to prescribe certain consumer practices (Holt 2002: 94). The customer interacts with the brand, thereby establishing a lasting relationship with it. The way he does that, especially in its pre-cognitive, pre-rational and immersive ways, is more insightful for a company than any abstract brand value a customer might attach to the brand and which could be investigated through traditional market research methods. The definition of own settings in which the production/consumption processes around a brand take place seems to be the only way for a company to grasp these levels of space-mediated capitalist productivity. Similarly, for me as a researcher, it is a way of understanding how knowledge capitalism works – that is, a capitalism in which the creation of knowledge is a directly productive process.

Indicative of the strong link between productivity and research is the fact that Autostadt commissioned AMO, the research arm of Rem Koolhaas' architectural practice, to study for Volkswagen the "Phenomenon Automobility". An unpublished research paper was the result, which I had the chance to read, but not to keep. Obviously, the way in which Autostadt wants to foster the productivity around the brands in question is conceptually related to doing cultural and space-related research. The research eventually turned out essentially as an analysis of the *phenomenon brand*. The question AMO addressed was how Volkswagen can again become the brand it once was, a brand for the "Volk", for all the people.

## Koolhaas: criticism as corporate strategy

AMO's research methods often have a degree of eclecticism to them. They draw from urbanist data, research material, cultural thinking and personal analyses and observational techniques. However, other research institutions could have used these methods, too. It might therefore appear surprising that Koolhaas, an architect known for his spatial critiques of capitalism, was chosen to do research for Autostadt. I want to suggest that exactly this critical experience attracted Autostadt. What made him suitable for creating brand knowledge is the fact that Koolhaas is in fact a practice-based cultural researcher of spatializing capitalism. His research idea is to build, and to deal with building contractors, thereby getting to know how capitalism works. Volkswagen uses this intellectual production to get to know itself as a capitalist actor. Architecture (Autostadt) and architectural criticism and theorization (Koolhaas) both become ways of corporate self-understanding. Or, as Koolhaas (2003: 118) himself writes, a building is no longer merely an issue of architecture, "but of strategy".

For Koolhaas, this combination of architecture and corporate strategy also implies a necessity to architecturally "think" through the notion of the brand as it pertains to a business strategy. A key example for this is his unrealized plan for the Universal headquarters in Los Angeles (Koolhaas

2004). Here, his team not only tried to accommodate all potential capitalist processes into a complex architectural structure characterized by an extreme openness, but also engraved the brand history of the company in the physical shape of the building. Specifically, the different high-rise structures they suggested alluded to liquor bottles, the core product of the old Seagram company that was to be merged with the movie and music business of MCA, which also included Universal Studios Hollywood.

This thinking-through of a core capitalist process (the takeover of one company by the other) in a Hollywood context is of double relevance. On the one hand, Universal here is a major multinational company, and its architectural presence is an instance of what can be called, with reference to Kracauer (1963), capitalist form-making. On the other hand, an encompassing analysis of Koolhaas' project would face the difficult task of following through the virtual creation of a new corporate world in an area (Hollywood) that has specialized in the creation of virtual worlds all along, and that, bluntly speaking, transforms the whole world into an increasingly virtual entity. In a way, this kind of world building by Hollywood set certain standards of what brand builders do. With Koolhaas' design for the Universal headquarters, branding strikes back, developing a frame for the framing process that Hollywood is very much defined by.

In his work for Autostadt, Koolhaas mainly concentrates on the ways in which brands are produced socio-culturally. One of his suggestions is to have brand fanatics produce their own specialized version of their car in Autostadt with the help of engineers. This suggestion builds on the notion of consumers as co-producers of brands, because they define what the individual brand means or represents for them. The AMO suggestion would mean nothing less than mass customization proper. In terms of knowledge, the realization of individual car visions by members of the brand community would mean that Autostadt allows the company to understand more about the dreams and desires of the customers. They not only show what they associate the brand with, but also what production process or production material they perceive as suitable for it.

*Reintegrating productivity*

The centrality of consumer activity to the understanding of capitalist productivity is connected to the changing role of images in brand space. Arvidsson (2006, Chapter 4) shows how consumer branding is effectively commoditizing consumer activity in concrete social environments. This effect of such a commoditization process can be seen in consumers, creating through mental/imaginary or social processes the reasons that make them buy certain products or brands. This productive process is connected to new ways of the processing of images. This is what makes Beller (1998: 61) argue that "looking is posited by capital as labour". Seeing things, recognizing them as images, and transporting them as such, is what gives brands value.

Hence, corporate efforts to build city-like structures are not so much a step towards an increased domination of the social sphere by a company, but rather a reaction to the fact that consumers take up significant parts of the production process. From this perspective, brand space is a way to reintegrate contemporary production into the corporate processes, thereby broadening the borders of the organization. For cultural research, this means that attention has to be paid to the differences between spatial and architectural processes inside and outside brand space, in order to trace capitalist lines of urban transformation. Simultaneously, we have to be aware of the possibility for brand space to develop features of rhizomatic space, thereby delimiting its scope.

## Public space redefined

The spatial argument above leads to an extension of post-Marxist thought around exploitation. Arvidsson (2005) argues that if consumers devote more and more time to the extension of brand images (thereby creating brand value), then the time they sacrifice is what they are exploited for. Following my arguments above, this thinking can be extended; not only is physical production now intertwined with knowledge production. What is more, this new level of knowledge creation thoroughly transforms notions of public space. With city space becoming a source of capitalist production, and with production no longer confined to a factory or even a modern office, Marxist thinkers could argue that public space is not only privatized to a larger degree than ever, as argued most distinctly by Richard Sennett (1974; 1994) or Jane Jacobs (1961), but even places that are still public are now deprived of their potentially anti-capitalist essence. Public space is *becoming* production space. This has methodological implications. One now has to trace capitalist transformations *within* the public sphere. The separation between public and private largely disappears – not because everything is private, but because a decentred capitalist knowledge production process develops the capacity to conquer all levels of public space and public discourse. The brand has the potential to become the new centre of this discourse. It is not the outside of public discourse, not merely the object. It is changing it from within. Cultural research has to trace how it does that.

## The challenge of a methodological openness

With the research perspective I develop here, I hope to avoid a simplifying notion of global homogeneity often used to criticize capitalism. This notion, I want to point out, fails to grasp capitalism's capacity to produce difference. What is required is a perspective of global, temporal as well as spatial heterogeneity. It is impossible to predict beforehand the flows a brand will initiate, and the ways in which brands are affected, strengthened or weakened by certain flows. This also pertains to the relevance of technology in this particular capitalist structure (Sandiwell 2003: 118 ff.). The question is in which way certain technologies and flows are becoming part of the multiplicity of a concrete brand, how they develop spatiality and, methodologically, how to study these flows. One can argue that the thinking above brings the approach of this work close to Whitehead's understanding of empiricism: to develop the methods and the degree of interdisciplinarity with which one approaches an object with reference to the specific object (Wightman 1961). Every object has a specific set of faculties and references with which it is best studied (an idea put forward by the critical ethnography discourse; Hepp 2004: 258).

What makes this openness vital is the inherent cross-disciplinarity of the brand. The brand is so effective as a tool for capitalism exactly because it works cross-disciplinarily. A research that follows the brand will have to be flexible enough to continuously follow the disciplines the brand itself uses, because these change over time (which is itself part of the strategies of branding). This also justifies my combination of cultural studies-influenced, architectural, marketing-oriented, philosophical, sociological and ethnographic approaches.

An interesting additional way in which the spatialization of branding is researched is the brand's implication in contemporary works of art. Specifically, certain contemporary photographers like Andreas Gursky engage strongly with brands and logos. Gursky's 1999 work *Toys "R" Us* (Dexter and Weski 2003: 231), for example, is displaying an almost hyperreal setting of white storage spaces with the brands Toys "R" Us and Toyota attached to them. Gursky is investigating the destructive power of the brand here. In order to understand what his work means for the essence of branding, methods derived from arts theory would be necessary. At the same time, the brand-related effects of a contemporary artist investigating brand-influenced culture will not necessarily be limited to discourses of arts history, which means that any cultural analysis of those effects will have to maintain a critical distance from these discourses.

Concretely, the Gursky picture is interesting in two respects. Firstly, it is an example of arts driving and furthering the meaning of brands. In his art, Gursky is essentially taking the role of a researcher of the capitalist real, and the brand is an icon for his effort to understand what is left today of any possible collective memory. Gursky aims at writing and researching a *history of the present* (Honour and Fleming 2005: 901). For his project, Gursky applies the brand, using it to highlight the abstraction and the aggressive ordinariness of our capitalist reality (Searle 2003). Building on the work of pop artists or of Los Angeles painters such as Ed Ruscha, he points out the ambivalence of the logo, between signifying something and destroying the significance of space (Schwartz 2010: 100), or rather, of architecture in space. In the Gursky work, architecture is not filling and structuring space. Rather, it is subtly reflecting on the almost dreadful blankness the logo needs to develop its full effectiveness. Through the influence of the logo, then, architecture in this piece seems to turn against space, researching the limits of spatiality.

Secondly, the Gursky piece is interesting in terms of cultural research because the artist *uses* an architectural setting to understand branded reality. To him, the strength of the brand seems to be to create hyperreal, somewhat abstract spaces (and the abstraction in the picture is obvious). It is this abstraction that his work seems to investigate. One could even go so far as to discuss whether the whiteness in the picture implies a certain artistic reality to a brand (with connotations of the white cube as the ultimate arts space).

Hence, from this arts-focused perspective, the brand is not only a driver of today's image-based social and cultural complexity. It is also a vehicle for arts to try and analyze this reality. Tracing these processes of analysis, while being a complex and difficult task, will be necessary for understanding the relationship between the capitalist creation of knowledge and the way in which capitalism aims at organizing space.

## Virtual cities and moments of actualization: why and how brands conquer urban space

How do we conceptualize the brand in space? How do we analyze the brand as an architectural presence that is always partly absent, that unfolds and changes constantly, thereby permanently redefining its centre and boundaries? How do we analyze something, furthermore, that exists through the processes it initiates and the transformations it undergoes? Something, finally, that is undeniably spatial, but at the same time transcending spatial boundaries and traditional categories of spatiality and ways of spatial ordering? In order to properly understand spatialized brands, we need a concept that allows for a description and a definition of a being that has permanent change and the co-presence of different places as well as different times at its very core. This work claims that an appropriate theoretical framework is the poststructuralist, often implicitly or explicitly space-related writing of Deleuze. Specifically, it argues that the Deleuzian, Bergson-informed conceptualization of "the virtual" offers all the features mentioned above. I will show that the going-spatial of brands can be interpreted by means of the virtual in the Deleuzian sense. I will link the virtual of the brand to the branded spatialities that this work is concerned with. In this way, I will be able to show that exactly this virtuality is what ultimately makes the brand strive to become architectural, and that this contains a business-strategic rationale.

In the next paragraphs, I will lay the ground for this argument by demonstrating the brand's thorough virtuality and how this impacts upon its spatiality, focusing on the following features of brands:

a) the omnipresence of change;
b) the independence of the image from any notion of an image-less "real";

c) the co-presence of past, present and future;
d) a transcendence of the binary opposition of actual, therefore real, and not actual, and therefore not real;
e) the simultaneity of spatial and temporal groundlessness.

## a) The omnipresence of change

The Deleuzian distinction between the virtual (that has the capacity to be actualized) and the possible (to be realized) involves a high degree of contradiction and change (Castells 1996: 372). This holds true for brands. There never *is* a moment in which a brand remains unchanged. The lack of change would mean that no one engages with the brand, which would also imply its death. This change is spatial; it is the result of the rhizomatic character of the brand in space. Every action involved anywhere in the world will change what the brand "is", for it might add or subtract a certain level of intensity.

## b) The independence of the image

Our Deleuzian understanding of the brand is strongly connected to his concept of the image. For Deleuze, the image is creating what functions as reality. It is not "reflecting" or "extending" any "real world"; Deleuze substitutes this dualism with the concept of a multi-levelled, yet strangely frictionless world. Similarly, the brand is virtual because it is neither the image *of* something, nor some actual essence that we could understand *through images of it*. The brand is an image of itself as essence; it is its own image.

This liberation of the image is the driving force for a specific, image-based spatiality, and for a new intensity of image-production in space. If a company builds a new office space connected to certain assumed features of a specific brand (take as an example the landmark Bacardi office buildings in Downtown Miami), then this is an effective becoming-image *of* the building. This image-production influences and changes what the brand *is*, not just what it *means*. If the fantasy of a consumer is directed towards a certain brand, if he or she is, in Deleuzian terms, *affected* by it (Massumi 2002: 43), then this changes the brand itself. There is no *inner core* of the brand that is not affected by such developments; they cannot be judged as some disturbing processes *at the edge*. The spatiality of the brand does not presuppose any centre-periphery duality.

In terms of the production of images, the permanent change described above is enabled and strengthened by the fact that human beings as generators and/or receptors of images cease to obtain centre stage in Deleuzian concepts. Deleuzian image-production and the interaction of images take place without a necessary human reference point to allude to. Spatial images can run through human beings, but also have the capacity to be creative and productive on their own: "Images are constantly acting and reacting on each other, producing and consuming. There's no difference at all between images, things, and motion" (Deleuze 1995: 42).

The spatiality of brand-driven image production transcends the confines of business-strategic activity. While certain images of brands in space are more or less consciously produced by companies, each of these images creates new images; as soon as corporate advertising is exposed in an urban context, for instance hanging down a well-known inner city church (as has been common for a while at Berlin's Gedächtniskirche), this is a different image. This newly composed image might itself set off a new production circle of images. For a company, this "production of production circles" is no longer containable. But it is also, and this brings it so close to the Deleuzian understanding of the virtual, enabling and productive.

### c) The co-presence of past, present and future

As explained above, the virtual is complicating the relationship between these three. The past is not simply that which has ceased to exist and the future is in some ways always present. In Bergson's thinking, the virtual is the force of the past still present with us now (Rajchmann 1997). This co-presence of the past is a central feature of brands. Brand value is created by past user processes and brand intensification developments. For instance, it would be impossible to distinguish the brand *Coca Cola* from the fact that the company had been the first to gain brand presence in the newly capitalized Eastern Europe. This capacity to actualize or "presentify" the past is part of a brand's virtual quality.

### d) The broadening of the real

The brand is transcending the binary conceptual opposition of actual (therefore real) and not actual (therefore not real). The brand is real without being actual at a concrete point in time and space. This means that this work is no capitalist critique along the lines suggested by Baudrillard, trying to find a hyperreality that disconnects us from the material essence of reality. Branded spatiality allows, or makes "room", for an interaction of virtual and actual. Virtualization of reality needs a mediatization of space, thereby creating interactions of virtual and actual. It is these interactions that the brand aims at through spatialization.

The underlying understanding of the virtual then is one in which the virtual has the capacity to become other, and to create differences in space. It creates spaces of difference. This is why the spatial understanding of brands as virtual is different from understanding them as "hyperreal" or simulacrum. Simulacra and the hyperreal don't initiate real, substantive change; spatialized brands do (Lash and Lury 2007: 6).

### e) Spatio-temporal groundlessness

Brands' engagement with space seems to result from a feeling of a certain lack of solidity. A brand has no temporal or spatial starting point. It is, as both Deleuze and Sloterdijk have it, always "in the middle". Brands are everywhere and nowhere at once. If a marketing executive in Wolfsburg or London defines what his brand is, then he might be proven wrong at that very moment in time by a different process involving his brand anywhere in the world. Deleuze and Guattari (1987, Chapter 1) call this *rhizomatic*.

This spatio-temporal simultaneity is a precondition for the particular virtual–actual interaction that brands provoke; a car crashing, a logo destroyed or a billboard transformed through graffiti are clearly actual processes. But at the same time, the implications of such micro-events for future brand development are open. This openness, or groundlessness, is driven by the peculiarity of the interaction of space and the image outlined before. A logo, for instance, is clearly also an image; or better, it is different images to different recipients. Let us take the example of a car crash. In fact, the logo as image is then multiplied and transformed thoroughly. It is suddenly a very different image for the driver; the driver of the other car involved in a crash; for spectators; for the media; for the production facility engaged with repairing the car – including the logo – later.

What is more, this multiplicity of images is also characterized by multiple interactions between images. In space, images impact upon each other. The brand values of car A imply certain physical features of the car, which then affect another car via a crash. This means that the image of car A affects the image of car B after a crash.[1]

These processes are sudden outbursts of actuality around a brand. But, just as quickly, the actuality vanishes again. What is more, it is entirely open when and where such actualization takes place. The actual here is intimately connected with a notion of chance, and even of catastrophe in the sense suggested by Koolhaas (2001). The interaction of two different brands during and after a car crash might or might not "actually" happen; be it through the drivers, visitors, TV cameras or corporate analyses of cars' performances during accidents.

## Brand semiotics

This complex position between virtuality and actuality is a reason for branding's complicated relationship with concepts of the "symbolic" as opposed to the "real". In which way does a brand, or a logo, apply the logic of the symbolic? What, then, is its relationship to semiotics? We understand this when thinking through the notion of the logo, as one core element in the cultural structuring of brands, and applying it to semiotic thinking. Lury (2003: 74–85) develops an understanding of the logo in terms of Peircian semiotics. On the one hand, she states that a logo is a symbol. On the other, this symbol (Peirce's realm of "thirdness") has to mediate the other Peircian levels on which signs function ("firstness" and "secondness"). It is therefore also index, and icon. Brand management "involves the management of the ability ... to mediate aspects of secondness and firstness" (ibid.: 78). These mediations involve the producer as well as the consumer. Who participates in these concrete mediations, and how, remains completely open.

The incomplete virtuality of the brand brings together symbol, index and icon all on one plane. Hence, the reality of the brand undermines its own symbolic clarity. Purely virtual, the symbolic communication of a brand would be all there is. The brand would then simply tell something about a product. However, it would not register. The brand is not *about* a product, but *in* the product just as much as elsewhere. Hence, the confrontation with the actual is necessary for a brand to thrive (including the essential process of capitalist success, the selling of product, as a way to simultaneously distribute and change the brand). Paradoxically, the brand needs and thrives on its own meta-symbolic undermining. A merely symbolic brand would lose dynamism and participation. The brand needs Peircian secondness and firstness. At the same time, secondness and firstness threaten to undermine its symbolic functionality.

I will get back to the affects of the logo on spatial reality in Chapter 5, dealing with the application of the logo in architectural structures, such as the Audi pavilion in Autostadt. Now, I want to concretize the meta-symbolic reality of brands with other references to built reality, demonstrating how the above-mentioned combination of advertising poster and real building is relevant in this context because it indicates how a (two-dimensional) image can become real. In Peircian terms, this will show how brand space undermines the distinction between symbol, index and icon.

The first example I want to give is that of the Brandenburg Gate in Berlin. In 2008, the gate was completely covered with a poster of Telecom sub-brand T-Mobile for several months. What the poster conveyed was: the Brandenburg Gate. The structure of the building was hidden underneath a brand-driven version of itself. The symbol took over the icon, thereby becoming iconic itself.

Now, were that poster and the ideas and images it communicated "unreal"? No. For the duration of the renovation they were more real than the building underneath. The reality of the poster lay in its productive capacity; it was a "producing" image in that it actually allowed for new imaginary processes in the visitors to Pariser Platz, the tourist-crowded square in front of the building. It did so through exploiting the fantasy of the consumer, taking up the visitors' visual attention for a branding campaign. This transformed the gate into something that could be consumed, together with T-Mobile product or service offers.

And not only was the poster gate presented in a new, clean state; as it turned out, it was also cleaner than the gate after being unveiled. This points to the capacity brands have to develop a new context for urban life and reality. The poster positioned the Brandenburg Gate within a context of success and dynamism, telling the story of a city engaged in its own relentless progress. It integrated the image of a cleaner and, in a way, "purer" future Brandenburg Gate into the often gritty and economically rather poor reality

*Actualizing the virtual of capitalism?* 53

of Berlin. It was an urban phantasmagoria, a version of what city marketers imagine Berlin to be.

This brand-driven development of alternative urban micro-realities can be illustrated with two other examples of architecture-cum-advertising from Berlin's historical centre. One is the virtual re-erection of the famous "Bauakademie", originally built by Karl-Friedrich Schinkel and opened in 1836. The academy had been severely damaged during WW2; the GDR government then gradually abandoned it. Today, there are plans to rebuild it, following the general idea of Berlin city-planning to reconstruct pre-war Berlin (or an idealized version of it).

This context of rebuilding/simulating the past was the background for a distinct advertising strategy; the virtual presence of the building was made visible for branding purposes. A plastic version of the original Bauakademie building was positioned at the original site, with four poster-style walls, no roof, and only one corner which is actually built in stone (Figure 4.1). This architectural simulation has been made possible through sponsoring money from a Swedish energy company (which rather bluntly explained this on a big poster covering much of the entrance side of the virtual Bauakademie).

What is interesting is that visually the simulation worked to a certain extent. It really gave an impression of the space with a real, physical Bauakademie. Therewith, the plastic façade as a medium expressed the idea of another Berlin. In terms of branding, the construction of such an

*Figure 4.1* The two-dimensional Bauakademie, and branding (author's picture)

54  *Actualizing the virtual of capitalism?*

alternative city image can be seen as strategic in that it articulates the brand promise that in the virtuality of cities like Berlin (or Shanghai, Dubai or Kuala Lumpur; Sloterdijk 2005: 248) branding can play a productive role.[2] This points to the power of capital-driven city building. The implication is that in a brand-driven world the scars of the historical past hurt a little less, and perhaps can even be erased. Branding here suggests that it can help urban space to develop a new, more flexible social and historical imaginary. The virtuality of branding here is not an obstacle to be overcome, but a potential for alliances with other virtualities.

That such an approach apparently has a significant attractiveness for brands and for cities is shown by yet another example, also from the centre of historical Berlin. In 2009, on the walls of the historical "Alte Bibliothek", BMW displayed poster promotions for its Model "X5 Gran Turismo" (Figure 4.2). The megaposter was facing Bebelplatz, the square where the Nazis burned the books of left-wing writers.

Thereby, the square became subject to brand-driven operations of symbolic urban historical disintegration. The first one was the link the BMW campaign was drawing between poster and façade, visible at the right side of the poster; the poster advertising *quoted* the façade, but suggested an image of a brighter, less ageing Alte Bibliothek. This façade simulation was

*Figure 4.2* Virtual newness on historical architecture: BMW advertising in Berlin (author's picture)

the background for the actual BMW advertising, hanging above the façade simulation poster. It was the (apparently necessary) link between urban structure and advertising image.

On top of this simulation, the urban sphere was not simply confronted with *any* BMW poster. Rather, the poster on top exposed yet another building, apparently a hyper-technological fantasy structure. This integrated a notion of virtual newness to the image-based conquering of historical form. The historical building (Alte Bibliothek) was first deprived of its essentialist bricks-and-mortar quality in order to be confronted with its architectural opposite. In addition, the use of colour in the simulated poster-façade pointed to a potential transformation of the original building into something more closely resembling this fantasy architecture itself.

Clearly, this advertising activity played on and made explicit the contrast and contradiction between the new and the historical. However, this contradiction was not resolved. With the historical façade of the Alte Bibliothek mirrored with a brighter version of itself, the question is: what is historical here? The Alte Bibliothek was forcefully pulled into the present, and into the virtuality of branding.

While all these marketing measures use the city as background, they succeed because of the crisis of the urban, here exemplified by Berlin's obvious desire for a clearer, less ambiguous identity. It is this desire that creates Berlin's willingness to become part of such image interactions. The city appears to be desperate not only for advertising money, but also for symbolic elevation. If we assume that mediatized identities are principally possible, then the architectural branding initiatives outlined above might even help Berlin in the creation of this kind of identity, or "self". And although this new self is again subject to new change processes, the city seems to function culturally not *despite* of, but *because* of this problematic nature, and because of the permanent, unfulfilled fantasies people produce around it. Berlin's constant quest for identity seems to be what keeps it going (this is also why Berlin is sometimes termed "virtual global city"; Ward 2004). Hence applying architecture to advertising campaigns might not create identity that is based on a significant symbolic stability. What it does do, however, is to extend the mediatization processes that seem to drive a lot of urban activity today, thereby creating a new sense of identity based on the possibility of transforming architecture into image.

## Brand space and industry crisis

The last paragraphs have largely presented the brand as external to architectural reality; using it, transforming it, but not essentially building. I now want to look more closely at how brands become a spatial internality, striving for actuality and actualization through building. This will lead to a deeper understanding of brand *space* as an integral element in branding's drive for a calculated and managed actualization, as opposed to the chaotic and catastrophic actualization that potentially happens everywhere and at any time.

Such a strategic going-spatial has to be interpreted with reference to a sense of crisis that has become a defining feature for capitalist activity particularly in the car industry, the industry most actively employing brand-space strategies (cf. Stoffer 2008: 8). What is more, the car industry as a whole as well as its major companies are confronted with the problem of keeping up a sense of being different amid the tendency of multi-brand empires and platform strategies to exploit the advantages of sameness (cf. Bernhart and Dressler 2008). What is more, also the fact that top designers switch from one company to the other (VW chief designer Walter da Silva, for instance, used to work for Alfa Romeo) generate not difference, but sameness.

The problem of sameness is aggravated by the argument put forward by sociologists that there are tendencies within society to generate new ways for substantial differentiation. The internet, far from levelling out all difference, has contributed to it. But even more beyond the net, some thinkers identify a tendency of today's society towards new forms of community, towards what Maffesoli (1996) famously called the tribe. The problem for branding is not any potential "tribalization" as such, a tendency with raised significant awareness in marketing theory (Cova and Cova 2002), but that car brands apparently find it difficult to develop ways of substantial differentiation necessary for becoming part of any "tribe".

Partly, their failure so far to create or engage with such tribes is the result of a crisis of sociality as such. Knorr Cetina (1999 and 2001) indicates that notions of relationships, and of socialities as a whole, have become problematic and need to be disassociated from their fixation on human groups. This is not to say that the need for social belonging has vanished. But it is difficult to create lasting social formations that could be seen as a community, with shared values, clear entry and exit codes, and a mutual understanding of the world and the community's position in it. This holds true far beyond the functionings of branding. But for brands, it is a particularly poignant problem. One is not "born" into a brand community, and traditional educational systems put no value into membership in such communities. At the same time, the claim that such communities exist and might be worth joining can be seen as an effort of "hidden persuasion", to speak with Vance Packard.

What is most important, especially in our context, is that there is no place to *join* a brand community per se. There is no clubroom, no site that represents the holy place of the brand. There is, of course, the internet, a sphere often argued to allow for a new kind of community building beyond spatiality. But net-based communities are fragile. The net is a parallel world that can easily be escaped. On the one hand, double-digit growth rates in online advertising are fostering hopes of compensating for recent losses in traditional advertising forms. On the other hand, companies find it difficult to influence web-based opinion processes. Efforts of brand builders to influence blog-based opinion-forming are often unveiled, thereby backfiring and creating significant brand damage (Roland Berger Strategy Consultants 2009). These are explanations why, even in times of the net, and maybe particularly in times of frantic online activities of brand builders, companies might feel the need to actualize their brand in the physical world, creating physical places that might become the centre of a community.

The connection with the spatial can therefore be seen as a result of the frantic search of car brands for actualization as a source of uniqueness. BMW Welt at first created uniqueness for the company's core brand; in 2012 it also integrated the acquired brands Mini and Rolls Royce. Similarly, Volkswagen aims at spatializing its corporate brand as well as the product brands. The new actuality of the brand is created architecturally and enforced culturally – by the visitors to BMW Welt or Autostadt. These visitors sense that the virtuality of the brand is connected to this specific place, while at the same time becoming part of it. There is a bodily presence to the brand, and this presence is connected to the bodily presence of the visitor as an "actuality" in the Deleuzian sense (Massumi 2002: 43).

The engagement with the actual does not occur randomly. Rather, it is particular spatial settings that are chosen. Brand space seems to have a tendency to engage with the ultimate concreteness of capitalism, the factory spaces where real production takes or took place. Autostadt and BMW Welt both try and generate architectural links with the old, industrial production plants nearby. They connect them with the world of globalized, image-driven, Post-Fordist capitalism. The virtual production of brands is engaging with the actuality of car production.

In business-strategic terms, the effort to create a connection between a brand and an actual place can be seen as a strategic marketing action to gain competitive advantage (Porter 1995). If a company manages to include the placedness of a brand into the set of images considered valuable by the customers, the reasoning is that this cannot be imitated. If we take this seriously, then competition between brands as capitalist constructs would also be one between places and their image capacities. Actuality is then a competitive advantage, allowing for new interactions with the virtual.

However, what complicates this idea is that urban spaces do not only compete, they also form various relations with each other. Therefore, if brands compete regarding certain places (like the site of their historical origin) they also compete regarding the connections of this place to other places. This links brand space to Sassen's thinking about competition between global cities based on mutual access. Then, a competition of urban networks is at stake, undermining the notion of the network as an almost rhizomatic structure evolving two-dimensionally on one plane, like the smooth space envisioned by Deleuze. The competition of networks implies a collision-based network reality. Networks aren't all working on one plane, supportive of one another. Rather, there is an almost three-dimensional mutual entanglement of the differing networks.

The capacity of individual networks to limit each others' development is reflected by Sloterdijk in his concept of "Dichte" ("density"). The denser a structure, the less freely its individual elements can develop (Sloterdijk 2005: 280). This density is created partly by what is commonly referred to as "communication". Communication in this context is not the enabler of a universal understanding, but rather the opposite; it blocks any notion of free flow. What used to be the connecting capacity of "communication flows" is now creating walls. Similarly, all communications activities of a brand limit the possible communication activities of other brands.

This does not imply the end of communication. Rather, the reaction to this new kind of communication will be more communication. Hence, the network is densifying virally. Of course, this logic is impressively used, and greatly enhanced, by the internet. There, the only way to prevent unwanted information to appear on top of Google searches is to block the view – by means of other information. That is, the "information society" is a society that creates information and communication to prevent people from actually being informed (Lash 2002, Chapter 11).

This understanding of communication as that which creates walls apparently collides with the sense in the business world that communication maintains a key role in capitalism, especially in brand space. But this contradiction is not as far-reaching as it seems. Communication through architecture is the creation of intensity, rather than the spreading of information. This intensity can function as a membrane in Sloterdijk's sense. These membranes are aimed at creating communication – not as the spreading of some sort of information; but as the pure and blind production of intensity.

The available material for this production (space) is limited. The earth can only be conquered once. Furthermore, as I have already shown, it is not "any" kind of space that is at stake, but space that is in some way connectable to a brand. Hence, the drive of branding to conquer space can indeed be seen as a quest. This is very much a Sloterdijkian process, as this conquering is an attack on space that has already been conquered. A brand entering a spatial arena and occupying space for its positioning represses other possible cultural processes, or, in Sloterdijk's terminology, the development of other Blasen. From this perspective, spatialization of brands, just as any more conventional communication activity, means primarily a "Spielraumbeschränkung", a limitation of the playing field (ibid.).

## Productive history

The brand-strategic effectiveness of spatial actualization is connected to its capacity for historical references. For instance, the modernist architecture of the pavilion for the core brand VW in Autostadt deliberately evokes notions of Bauhaus and early modernism. Thereby, it links the brand to an earlier epoch of German culture. Koolhaas conceptualizes processes like these in his claim that today, history is treated as a service to the present (Hajer 1999:

142). In a similar manner, Zukin (1995: 17) claims that in posthistorical times history is a scarce resource of capitalism. Marketing tries to exploit this resource, for example by developing strategic competence through training its practitioners in "history marketing".

The ways in which brand space actively engages with history through architecture points to a general change in the relation between architecture and history. Architecture is increasingly involved in cycles of intensification and extensification, with intensity used in the Deleuzian sense as that which is at the limits of perception (Deleuze 1994: 144). History, too, is at these perceptional limits. If it is to develop a capacity to intensify space, then it has to do so through architecture. In a way, the criticism of postmodern historicized buildings has essentially been a criticism of a failure to *produce* such an intensity.

In this respect, brand space historicism is different from postmodern architecture. This is vividly expressed in Autostadt through the "ZeitHaus"; the building designed to engage with ways in which people try to make sense of the past. The exhibitions inside tell the history of cars rather conventionally by exposing historic products. What is new is the way in which architecture comments on the storytelling within. The building does not simply repeat the historical statements inside, but is engaging critically with them.

## *Rethinking copycat capitalism*

The establishment of a place (of origin) for a brand has to be seen in the context of the economic and legal situation of branding. Primarily through developing modes of protectability of the logo, brands are configured as entities permanently threatened by copying and to which therefore intellectual property law applies. The law thereby establishes the brand as a cultural form, defining its specific objectives (Lury 2004: 98). Spatialization can be seen as an extension of this. Giving a brand an architectural frame and protecting it through legal practices are both cases of establishing a notion of the "original" as opposed to the "fake".

Nevertheless, the virtual–actual interactions of brand activities in space are fundamentally different from those employed by the law. Here, notions of the original and the "authentic" cannot simply be argued to "be" there; rather they have to, and can, be *created*. Architecture in this respect is generating a new layer of what *makes* a brand or a branded product "real"; the brand is interpreted as real *because* it is given an architectural reality. From this perspective, the brand can make certain (legal or other) claims regarding its own boundaries *because* it is engaged in architectural practice. In particular the notions of history employed for the creation of brand places add to this constructed originality. The fact that a brand can architecturally employ certain historicities (although this is, as I have shown, largely a rewriting of history) creates a situation in which the brand evokes ideas of originality within the customer and the business community (as much as within the legal profession that is constantly engaged with finding solid ground for what can be protected by property law); originality is created through the combination of product or image production with architectural reality.

From this perspective, the combination of space and notions of originality in branding seems to be vital to the functioning of a brand. However, the relationship between the notion of an architectural "original" and the process of protecting this original is reversed; brand space develops architectural originality only *by defending this originality*. How this works can be seen in Anting New Town. The whole area is strongly guarded. When leaving the M30 motorway at the Anting exit, passports are checked; when entering the actual premises of Anting New Town proper, a security guard once again approached us (even though I was in the car with the master planner of the area).

When I took pictures within Anting New Town, another private security guard intervened; even architect Johannes Dell did not manage to make him cooperate. I asked Dell whether this was connected to a fear of Anting architecture being copied. "Yes", he replied. "It has already occurred that parts of Anting New Town have been copied elsewhere. People are very cautious regarding copying these days." What they can do against being copied? "To be frank – not much." And yet, the control mechanisms in Anting are highly relevant for the functioning of the area as an "original" because they create this originality *performatively* by protecting it. Being copied implies that there is something worth copying, something with an independent architectural presence.[3]

However, the imminence of architectural copying in Anting is real. And it is connected to the fact that Anting New Town itself is copying a non-Chinese architectural style. Dell is aware of that. "It is not as if we designed this place from scratch, so it would be difficult to fight for any kind of copyright. If anything, copyright would belong to the Bauhaus people."

## *Space brands and mobility regimes*

So far, we have seen how getting involved in urban construction seems to be a way of creating a sense of originality and uniqueness for a brand. But there is another rationale for going spatial, one that has to do with the car as a particular culturally charged product. It should not be seen as a coincidence that it is mainly producers of cars who engage with space and architecture today. There is a specific affective intensity connecting car, driver and the urban setting they are positioned in (Featherstone 2004). Cars and the process of driving have always been spatial. Hence, the spatiality of brands makes particular sense in this industry; in an abstract way, the product of car companies is not cars, but urban space.

From their beginnings, cars have impacted on the development of, and life in, built environments. In their early days, they were perceived mainly as a disturbing external force, interrupting the daily flow of city life. Peter Hall (2002, Chapter 9) describes how by the 1920s mass motorization had

*Actualizing the virtual of capitalism?* 61

thoroughly undermined American cities. This initiated a debate about banning cars from inner cities.

This critical public reception of cars and mobility has not continued. Although cars have remained a social problem, intellectual (and architectural) discourses started to engage with them in a progressive way, searching for new forms of spatial (and simultaneously social) mobility. Hall (ibid.) argues that this spirit was the basis for the construction of highways in American cities, first in New York, later in the paradigmatic highway city Los Angeles. In Europe, Le Corbusier developed an analytical approach to future urban life that engaged with the idea of an ever-increasing proximity of cars and architecture, and of driving and living. For him, architecture had to provide the means of a life to be lived under the condition of permanent mobility.

In his writing on Schäume, Sloterdijk takes this one significant step further. He points out that this modernist idea of a life under the condition of hypermobility bred a new architectural form, which Sloterdijk calls the "Wohnmaschine" (Sloterdijk 2004: 550). These large-scale combinations of one-floor flats abandoned all prior connections between living and the more culturally charged concept of dwelling. The Wohnmaschine articulates the disintegration between individuals and a larger, stable, cultural-spatial setting, which in German is expressed through the suggestive term "Heimat". With modernity, the idea becomes dominant that people live merely to be on the move. "Parking" and "living" are essentially the same process.

The extreme point of this would be a concept in which building and car essentially form a coherent unit. Interestingly, Sloterdijk thinks it worthwhile to find a name for this unit. The term he suggests is "Soziomobil" ("social mobile"). This *social mobile* he defines at once as "Gruppenbehälter" ("group container") – and as "Volkswagen" (ibid.). The idea of a "Volkswagen" is apparently closely related to the new, mobile architecture.

Therefore, not only is it no coincidence that car companies were the first brand builders to give their brand ideas physical shape. It also makes perfect sense that the company "Volkswagen" (the founding myth of which was to build mass cars for the people, the "Volk") was the one linking brands with space. The cars that Volkswagen has developed throughout its history were the ones most distinctly involved in redefining the relationship between architectural building and car building. Through building peoples' cars, Volkswagen (and to a lesser extent Toyota) had been involved in the creation of the street-related background to Sloterdijk's equation of driving/parking and living. Now, they take the visual and symbolic icon of this society of mobility, the brand, to the architectural sphere.[4]

Sloterdijk goes on to develop his idea of a "Soziomobil" into a new understanding of construction; one that has less to do with building than with assembling. The new home is not built, but assembled, just like a car. If we follow Sloterdijk here, then entire cities are built like cars. For Sloterdijk, this yields a new relationship between nature and human activity. From this viewpoint, building is no longer an intermediate between human being and nature. With reference to Buckminster Fuller, Sloterdijk (2004: 553) points to a new independence of this kind of building from its natural or cultural context. Wohnmaschinen have no roots and no links to their environment. Consequently, their individual elements are all constructed with one floor only. Several floors in one flat would effectively create lower floors that function as something similar to *architectural roots*, thereby referring back to the logic of rooting that this architecture wants to get over with.

Regarding brand space, I want to suggest that its relationship with Sloterdijk's Wohnmaschinen is ambiguous. On the one hand, the spaces discussed here clearly have a proximity to the notion of mobility, and some of them may even be constructed in a car-like way. And yet they partly transcend Sloterdijk's notion of contextlessness. With reference to BMW Welt, Kwinter (2007) develops a concept of a new embeddedness of this particular brand space. He aims at developing the building principles of Coop Himmelb(l)au into an understanding of a reconceptualized connection between architecture and nature. For Kwinter, the functional mechanisms of clouds and combustions to which BMW Welt refers, both adapted from nature, point to a new connection between architecture and nature, enabled through a delocalized concept of nature itself. As soon as nature is no longer seen as a pure place phenomenon, synonymous with "the local", any architecture that aims at ridding itself of the confines of place is potentially reengaging with nature as principle. This is, according to Kwinter, what BMW Welt does. It aims at learning from natural conditions or elements, such as weather, or the sea. Kwinter writes that weather

> is in fact nothing more than pneumatic *sea*, and architecture is for the first time an inseparable part of it, realising a three-decade-long preparation by the Coop Himmelb(l)au project to make architecture present itself to experience at once as cloud, panther, and flame.
> 
> (Kwinter 2007: 8, italics in the original)

## Coop Himmelb(l)au architecture: beyond the architecture–nature dualism

In his reading of the philosophical principles of Coop Himmelb(l)au architecture, Kwinter links their way of building to the Kantian concept of a "Dynamisch-Erhabenes" ("dynamic sublime"). From the perspective of this work, in particular its media-theoretical aspects, it would certainly go too far to interpret brand space per se as an example of Kant's dynamic sublime, which describes nature as a force antagonist and superior to culture. I want to challenge, however, the notion of a world in which any mediatization process necessarily implies a development away from an untouched and unambiguously positive concept of nature. The dualism between nature and architecture is not substantialized by brand space, but complexified by architecture adapting to natural processes. Thence, the dynamic sublime is transformed into an "Artifiziell-Erhabenes" (Sloterdijk 2004: 530), the omnipresence of which makes it possible to experience man-created, cultural reality "als eine sublime Umgebung" (ibid.). That is, architecture aims at developing features formerly reserved for nature alone.

In line with this, Kwinter (2007: 10) points out the productivity of the ways in which Coop Himmelb(l)au make form-creating use of their experiments with natural phenomena. From this perspective, it makes perfect sense that they see "architecture as a volatile substance not only capable of burning, but of *realising itself* in the process of combustion" (italics in the original). Kwinter's quote makes clear that the dropping of the term "dynamic" does not mean that Sloterdijk's artificial sublime is in any way non-dynamic. It is permanently change-driven. But these are not the powerful dynamisms of nature for which culture is simply an object. Rather, the dynamism that ensues here stems from an interaction between man, culture and nature that is, in a way, bottomless. It is driven by pure intensity, rather than by a nearly metaphysical ground, as in Kant's model.

## *The affects of driving*

If we accept that the relationship between architecture and (natural or cultural) context is characterized by this kind of artificial sublime, then the question is what links the individual sources of impact in this process. Where does the intensity mentioned above come from? Regarding the current context of the interdependency between architecture and car, the question is what mediates the exchange between the two levels. When looking at the relationship between architecture and urban (or cross-urban) mobility, and when trying to understand the relationship between dwelling and driving, this analysis profits from a closer look at the impact on the personality of the driver. Helpful for this analysis is the concept of affect (Massumi 2002, Chapter 1). It provides us with a possibility of conceptualizing a richer notion of the relationship between driver and product than would be possible by focusing only on, say, rationalistic, target-driven features (getting from point A to B). The concept of affect allows for insights into the intensive process of engagement between driver, car and environment, for it is transpersonal (ibid.).

As a concept, affect transcends that of mere "emotion" or "emotionality". It is clear that there seems to be a particular emotional relation between driver and product (Sheller 2004) that does not actualize in a spaceless way, but that is created in space. However, the process of driving frees affections from their intra-personal boundaries, creating affects that are in the Deleuzian sense transpersonal. As an affect, emotion here *runs through* car and driver all the way to the outside, to the urban fabric. Sheller (ibid.: 221) speaks about a "deep context of affective and embodied relations between people, machines and spaces of mobility and dwelling". The new thing that cars bring to the urban landscape is precisely this transpersonal relevance of affects, affects that transcend the individual. In this sense, a car-dominated urban landscape must no longer be understood simply as "soulless" or neutral. The affects at play are what ensures a certain intensity and cohesiveness, which is far from neutral; it is, however, more difficult to trace.

The technological development of the car as a product is highly relevant in this context. The increasingly complex IT-based technology that makes a car receptive to affects from the outside plays a major role here (cf. Thrift 2004: 48–52); it also creates new lines of flight for the affects in question. Actually, technology can be argued to create significant capacities of the car not only to be affected by the driver and to affect the outside, but also to be affected by the outside and to affect the driver. Together, these affects form a kind of glue between driver, car and urban landscape. A mobile system is created (Urry 2004), based on affective intensities. Thereby, the individual affection actually becomes less isolated and more localized. Contrary to any assumed spaceless and completely mobile character of the car, it is a way to *link* individuals to concrete spaces or even places.

This brings a new actuality to Corbusier and Sloterdijk's idea of a mobile architecture. It also, however, strengthens Roland Barthes' claim that through becoming-image, the car develops new analogies to architecture, becoming, in his terminology, the equivalent of gothic cathedrals (Barthes 1972: 88). Once more, the image becomes a relevant concept here. Images are affect-creating forces. It is *by* becoming-image that the car *at the same time* becomes thoroughly architectural.

The stability of the urban fabric is thereby taken over by the prevalence of images. Vice versa, becoming a city-builder proves that a company is able to deal with the image-driven, flow-based city as conceptualized by Amin and Thrift (2002) and de Landa (1997). Engaging in the image-based construction of urban space is part of the core competence of the Postfordist company.

The flow of cars as images fits with the concept of the urban suggested by Deleuze and Guattari. They developed their understanding of the city from the latter's origination in movement. "The town is the correlate of the road. The town exists only as a function of circulation and of circuits; it is a singular point on the circuits which create it and which it creates" (Deleuze and Guattari 1987: 432). If the town/city is created by flows, then even its static elements and those moments not characterized by physical flow still derive from the principle of movement.

In the same way, affects are the outcome of the principle of movement. This is where the brand comes into play again. For the image activities of companies are always inherently connected to the brand as the main source of, and frame for the creation of, images. Hence, BMW Welt and Autostadt are part of the creation of competitive advantage by their builders *because* both spaces offer new, and perhaps more complex ways of creating brand-driven images; images that are three-dimensional, physical and actual.

In this context, we also come to understand better why it is not a contradiction to the meaning of the car that in all three places analyzed here – Autostadt, BMW Welt and Anting New Town – the actual process of driving and traffic plays a very different role than in the average city. The car is transformed into an image to such an extent that even filling brand space with car flows would be somehow too "ordinary". Rather, by not being present on a massive scale in brand space, the car as product seems to reflect upon its own image-ness. It is the image in purity, without its social entanglement in ordinary, noisy urban space.

The car in brand space is a highly cultural, cultured and staged phenomenon. The visit to the Audi pavilion in Autostadt in 2007, for instance, culminated in an encounter with one car. The visitor approached the product by walking down a dimly lit walkway. At the bottom, the car was presented as a magical, out-of-this-world entity. Highly lit, it was, one could say, the pure image. This becoming-image was made possible by the theatrical architectural setting.

At the same time, the way the product was presented through architecture had transformational effects on the subjectivity of the visitor. She had to step forward into the brightly lit area to actually see and touch the car. As image, the physical car and architecture together created a spatial setting that pulls the visitor out of the position as a spectator into that of an actor. The design of the pavilion created a theatre-like situation in which the brand transforms the visitor, her identity and her social disposition in Autostadt. Watching and acting here became one.

On a larger scale, such a transformation of an entire urban setting into a playground for watching-actors, and the important roles of cars in this, is a central feature of Anting New Town. Here, the transformation is connected to the idea to make a complete urban area a marketing tool for the place promotion. "One has to see Anting New Town as a marketing measure", Johannes Dell claims. Positioned with maximum visibility from the motorway, Anting has been planned to promote itself. At the same time, it has a display function for an idea of the future Shanghai, emphasizing not only the attractiveness of Anting itself, but the idea of a certain lifestyle out of the metropolis. A tool for social modelling and flow management, it succeeds if people indeed adopt the lifestyle envisioned and suggested by Anting New Town.

As a marketing tool, Dell thinks that Anting New Town "is very up-to-date. Chinese consumers want to be stimulated to an ever-higher degree. This is what we are trying to do here." In the city itself, it was easy to feel how the urban stimulation creates watching-actors. The (few) people one saw in Anting New Town apparently had no problem with being looked at. They smiled back, and they didn't even mind having their pictures taken. They were not only watching-actors, but watching-and-living-actors. Thereby, they strengthen the character of Anting New Town as city-as-brand. And this is what it was right from the start, says Dell: "The *Nine Towns* project as a whole had already been a brand, and Anting was planned as one, too."

However, he was sceptical as to whether as a brand, Anting New Town worked well yet. His scepticism was based on "the terrible management mistakes that have been made" (Dell 2008). In terms of the theatre metaphor above, however, such bad planning should be seen as an indication of a play badly played, rather than as a counterargument to the claim that Anting New Town has significant theatrical elements.

If Anting New Town as brand space is playing a role in a theatrical process, of which the whole of Shanghai is the audience, then a possible title could be "The Impossible Quietness of the Urban". Siemons (2006: 41) emphasizes this surprising quietness. Parking is underground, an idea uncommon for city planning in downtown Shanghai. A single car cruising the empty streets of Anting New Town is an individualized, symbolic entity, not part of a mass of cars. This function is emphasized by the fact that unlike in most of Shanghai, one can actually hear the single car, its sounds not absorbed by the urban sound mass of the metropolis.

The almost metaphysical functionality of cars in brand space also provides clues regarding the complexity of the relationship between driving and walking. Thrift (2004) argues that De Certeau's preference for walking as a way of engaging with urban space misses the ways in which driving also engages with, and speaks to, the urban sphere. For Thrift, driving and walking as two modes of movement are strongly related (ibid.: 44), one being implied in the other. A walker, one could argue, walks to see others drive, while the driver wants to see walkers pass by. Similarly, walking in brand space is a reflection on the cultural practice of driving, and on the cultural phenomenon of the car.

In Anting New Town, the individual, non-traffic-jam-threatened car becomes its own image, and develops a different kind of hyper-presence. This hyper-presence is brand-related in a peculiar way. A strong presence of German car brands is seen as an actualization of the position of the whole area as a virtualized Germany. Hence, an actual German car here develops a double sense of virtuality. It is supporting its own brand. But as a supporter of that brand, it is also adding to the self-positioning of Anting as a virtual German city.

*Bodies, knowledge and effects*

As pointed out before, this new urban setting is one of trans-individual effects. In the process of creating effects, the human body plays a central role. It does so in permanent connection to the car, the latter often interpreted as a kind of prosthesis. Car culture creates a sense of embodiment that goes beyond the idea of merely "extended bodies". The car is not just what Morse (1990: 204) called a "second, more powerful skin". It is not merely giving the body a higher degree of "power over" something else, its environment for instance, or other bodies. Body, car and spatial setting enter into a process of what Thrift (2004: 49) calls "fluid transubstantiation". Car and body merge, but at the same time enter into a closer relationship with elements from the immediate surrounding. The process is more complex that that of the creation of a, in itself relatively stable, man-machine hybrid (cf. Featherstone 2004: 11). Rather, they form a complex and highly fluid system of knowledge.

Knowledge is an important element for Thrift's transubstantiation concept, in particular through the increasing technological and informational intensity of current (and, even more so, future) car design. He writes that "knowledges about technological and human embodied practices circle around and interact with each other, producing new knowledges which are then applied and become the subject of even newer knowledges in a never-ending reflexive loop" (Thrift 2004: 49). This creates a new, knowledge-based person–car–environment subject. In this virtual subject, "intelligence and intentionality are distributed between human and non-human" (ibid.).

In terms of the actual driving process, Beckmann (2004) adds to this by arguing that agency is, and will be even more as technology advances, shifting away from the driver and towards the automated mechanisms of the external system. The IT-enhanced traffic environment learns about car and driver, and interacts with them. Also, twenty-first-century cars increasingly develop ways of reacting flexibly to the body. Knowledge is generated by the interaction of car, driver and landscape, and is distributed between them. These loops inform both car and driver, make both smarter regarding the other but, as I want to argue, also regarding themselves. Humans learn about themselves by engaging with cars, because they realize how the car reacts to them.

This implies that driving a high-tech car means opening up your own body to analytical processes. Hence, the human–machine complex that is the car creates a novel kind of knowing, and known, human body. One could even say that the place in knowledge capitalism where we experience and know our body to the full is, increasingly, the car. In terms of embodiment, this knowledge actually creates a situation in which all bodily functions are becoming more effective than in an extra-car environment.

Regarding the larger setting, say, a motorway, this means that it is an own system in which very different knowledge complexes are at work simultaneously; the individual cars, drivers and, lest we forget, the brand systems are also interacting on the motorway, with other brands, but also with the other systems mentioned – through the image form of the cars. The motorway thereby becomes a highly intensive, permanently changing and culturally active setting. Augé's idea of the "nonplace" has to be reread in this respect. For even as a nonplace, the motorway is far from empty. Rather, it has an own past of meaning-creation, as Merriman (2004) has demonstrated regarding the first UK motorway. It also continuously creates new histories, knowledges and image interactions. Furthermore, and significantly, the motorway is not anti-architectural. Rather, the connection with cars as an example of a system of effects that also involves certain (brand) spaces means that the motorway is a prime element in a new, and highly fluid, architectural setting – the architecture of cars.

## (C)architecture

This intimate connection between cars and architecture can be understood better by a counter-intuitive reading of Norman Klein's treatment of the transformation of Los Angeles (Klein 2008). Klein points to the destruction of existing and functioning neighbourhoods by certain misleading ideas of modernity and modernization. However, his writing also shows how powerful an architectural and urbanist force cars and freeways are. In fact, what he outlines is how the idea of a new freeway system has been used as a way not only to improve traffic, but also to transform the social body of Los Angeles (ibid.: 38–50). This transformation might not seem overly appealing today, but it cannot be ignored that particularly in Los Angeles the car has been seen as a legitimate way to transform an existing urban structure. The flow of traffic as an almost ideological presence has been deemed more suitable for what was seen as a functioning city than the urban density featuring the earlier downtown of Los Angeles. This downtown structure was deliberately confronted with its ultimate outside: the freeway. The latter's cars were seen as a productive urban element.

## Car culture and the mediation of the public

The notion of car as architecture transforms the conditions for a distinction between inside and outside, public and private. In this context, the car is becoming the playground for a semi-public exchange. What is public and private, as well as the way in which the public and private are experienced, is mediated by the car (Morse 1990). Bull (2004) outlines that this mediation process is connected to notions of security and fear. The car, he argues, creates a sense of security in an environment experienced as threatening. It is specifically through the experience of sound that car drivers develop a sense of being safe, being inside, and away from the threat that might lurk outside the windscreen. My point here goes one step further. The car is creating the notion of inside and outside as something that is fluid, and changeable by the individual. It offers ways for subjects to be simultaneously inside and outside; to be inside and experience the outside at the same time. In this sense, the car functions as a medium. What is public is mediated by the car, as well as how the outside is perceived. The car mediates sound, vision and the human engagement with the world outside, and how it does so depends on the choice of car.

This can be seen most distinctly by looking at extreme developments within the car companies' product ranges. Let's take as an example the Hummer 2 (H2), produced by General Motors until 2010 (Luedicke 2006).

*Actualizing the virtual of capitalism?* 69

The Hummer was arguably the most "architectural" of all contemporary cars, its shape reminiscent of a highly technological, factory-style building, rather than of an object designed to move at high speed. It suppressed sound from the outside, transforming it into a mere mumble (a process that should be seen as one of conscious sound creation, rather than an involuntary sound transformation). Together with the equally limited vision it allowed, and with the tendency to make the outside appear darker, the H2 created a sense of permanent threat. This was enhanced through its past as military equipment. Not only did the H2 create what Morse (1990: 197) calls a "dreamlike displacement or separation from its surroundings". In addition, it defined a particular way of making sense of the outside. The car read the outside for the driver (also, of course, through technology). And seeing the world through a Hummer's eyes means seeing mainly enemies and threats. It means seeing the world as an action movie. Hence, the meaning of Baudrillard's (1996: 67) claim that cars are projectiles as well as dwelling places depends significantly on the concrete car, its design and its advertising-created image. The important point is that they have the capacity to become projectiles, and that car drivers are aware of this. And as potential projectiles, cars are becoming media, offering mediated perspectives on the world.

It is particularly this car-becoming-medium that makes the subject building by car-related brand space so strong, but also highly fluid. There is always an element of choice in the construction of identities through the creation of particular car-driver microsystems. Recent theoretical engagements with the relationship between car and culture emphasize this fluidity. Sheller (2004: 222) points to the "lived experience of dwelling with cars in all its complexity, ambiguity and contradiction". One such contradiction is the trans-personality of affects. In our context, the car and the car brand are mediators for these affects. Human subjectivities affect each other (and the creation of subjectivities of others) through cars. The interaction of subjects on roads is one of permanent mutual affection.

As well as originating from the individual, these affects are potentially generated by the entirety of sensory human experiences (Gilroy 2001: 89). However, the ways in which our senses are triggered affectively in traffic do not yield to a harmonious and "full" image of urban life. Instead, individual senses suddenly impact on us with a shocking intensity, creating a sense of a permanent state of emergency.

This holds true for the concrete road interaction, but, on a more abstract level, also for the display systems of brand space. In Autostadt, this was exemplified by the pavilion concept of the car brand Bentley, as I experienced in 2009. In this pavilion, certain sensory experiences, such as the touching and smelling of fine leather, were offered in isolation, that is, without any connection to a harmonious whole, or to the concrete car for that matter. The pavilion thereby implied that the brand Bentley has the capacity to "define" the experience of smelling and touching. From now on, so is the implicit claim, all experience of leather-ness had to be judged against this experience of ultimate leather-ness. The entire human sensory system was reorganized with reference to the brand.

## Affect as production

The entire argument above, I want to claim, is the basis for a new understanding of the capitalist production process and of production as the capitalist core. Despite all abstraction, brand spaces are not transcending the centrality of production. Rather, the notion of production itself is broadened. A new mode of social production increasingly undermines the mechanisms of the capitalist economy. In brand space, the very notion of affect enters into a new production logic. Brand space creates affect *as* production. The production processes in brand space, however, have little to do with physically building a product. It is production as excess – an excess of images, and of the transpersonal intensities implied by the notion of affect (cf. Massumi 2002: 219). Irrational excess here creates surplus value. Physical production does still happen, but does not lead to the purchasing of a car. Even the non-physical, corporation-based processes of research, development and design (Latour 2009) are not sufficient to explain eventual purchase processes. There is a non-rational process of intensity and affect that creates uniqueness for the individual brand.

This is where brand space becomes productive. It does not just *display* brands. Autostadt and BMW Welt provide the corporate brands with a physical epicentre, thereby becoming the core of the brands and the affects surrounding them. I described this process as one of simultaneously actualizing and creating new levels of virtual–actual interactions. When applying the terms of virtualization and actualization to production, the partial physicalization of brand production does not make production in general more actual in the Deleuzian sense, but rather more virtual. Here, brand production becomes physical. But this also means that classical production (of physical cars) enters brand production – as a virtuality. What we understand as production (the creation of value in capitalism) becomes meta-physical, multi-temporal and virtualized.

## The functionality of vagueness

The specifics of brand production outlined above are connected to a regime of almost violent inclusion created by capitalism (Negri and Hardt 2002); we are all part of it, but in which way, we are not told. This not-telling is central to the functioning of brand production; it creates a bad conscience, which presumably develops into a driving force. Architecture in Autostadt or Anting New Town is characterized by a solemn quietness, by building styles and spatial contexts explicitly not driven by information, concrete (brand) messages, logos or symbols. Generally speaking, an architecture of vagueness generates a new concreteness outside itself.

The symbolic vagueness of brand space architecture is in line with current thinking on brand strategy. From the perspective of the individual company, the production process of brands has to be vague. It is not something that the company controls entirely. Many parties are involved, each of them with its own agenda. Klingmann (2007: 62) conceptualizes this as a process in which a top-down logic is partly substituted by one that works bottom-up. This search for bottom-up creativity is currently driving many marketing discourses (cf. Cova and Cova 2002).

However, even this combination of bottom-up and top-down categories seems to me as inadequate. Rather, today, we are looking at many different social, hierarchical and spatial movements, most of them neither bottom-up nor top-down, but sideways. For instance, at times in social media, customers do not mainly communicate "with the company", but with *each other* about a company and its products.

Therefore, brand space has to allow for a high degree of openness. This openness also explains why architecture in brand space is dealing with functions and functionalist processes, but should not be interpreted as implementation of a linear functionalism. Functionalist architecture would know exactly what the functions taking place within its walls are. Brand space does not. It is an investigation into the impossibility of functionalist architecture in a world of global capitalist flows. In his praise of Richard Rogers' Lloyds building, Sorkin writes that "functionalism [...] has offered a number of clear visions of social relations in space" (Sorkin 1991: 321). In brand space, this clarity of social relations has gone. Branded capitalism transforms consumers into producers (Appadurai 1996). But how and what exactly they produce (in our context, what kind of brand or brand image) remains unclear in advance.

## History becoming productive

The arguments above might seem to indicate that brand space, topographically and topologically independent, can be anywhere. This is not so. Brands need a place where the outlined co-presence of the past is not only there, but can become productive. This co-presence is inherently connected to a brand's spatiality. Through spatial arrangements, brands can provide the past with a kind of permanence in the present. This is why the history of a place is of relevance and why Autostadt and BMW Welt have been built in direct vicinity to areas considered relevant for the brand's history. Both are referents to the companies' industrial past.

Autostadt is surrounded by architectural "presentifyers" of its own past. By creating visual references to those buildings, such as the outlined "Koller axis", it provides these buildings with a new brand-related historical actuality. Another way in which Autostadt re-presences the past is through its many explicit architectural references to history.

The engagement with the past in brand-space architecture is driven by the capacity for architecture to become medium. We understand this better by looking at BMW Welt's engagement with history. New architecture here integrates images of the old (the Schwanzer tower) into its visual concept. History writing is closely linked to images of the company's past, and to the function of architecture (as medium) to make this past visible and readable. This making-visible of the past is indicative of the becoming-medium that brand space works through. BMW Welt is the building as medium in the most thorough sense, its design creating architectural screens from which its visitors can perceive the past in the tower.

There are elements in its interior design that even seem to emphasize this screen-like situation. During my visits, I encountered tables in the middle of a staircase that have no function apart from demonstrating that visitors could theoretically stand here, looking out of the huge windows. Interior design is thereby becoming a tool of corporate attention management.

Functioning as screens, the architectural frames constructed in brand space emphasize the collision of different times. Just like a history film, or better even, a historical film, they are screens through which to see the past in the present, to "presentify" or actualize, the past. And what we see through these screens is primarily other buildings. In this way, built space is becoming both the screen and the content to see on this screen. Architecture thereby loses its present character; in the screen of the other buildings, architectural monoliths like the BMW tower obtain features of pure pastness.

### The threat of the past in brand space

And yet the establishment of a certain productivity in architecture in the outlined, mediatized way does not happen without resistance within architecture. Even if mediatized, the presence of history in architecture is not easily "manageable". Rather, it haunts the present, making it difficult to create history versions at will. This can be understood with reference to Walter Benjamin. Benjamin develops a sense of the city as medium that at the same time points to its unmanageability. In the Benjaminian city, the flâneur is subject to formations of pastness in the city that he can merely record, but not manage, be it visually, intellectually, or in terms of business strategy (Gilloch 1996: 67–68). The Benjaminian city is a medium, but a medium as a labyrinth (Chikamori 2009: 151) – the labyrinth of the past in the present.

Through the constant recreation of this historical labyrinth, the notion of a voluntary historicity or "history marketing" is countered by a more involuntary element of actualizing the past. This involuntary presence of the past is architectural, too. This is made apparent through a very different development, present in all urban settings, but obtaining a problematic urgency in brand space: the fact that architecture ages, and that brand architecture ages with particular speed. Architecture with such an immediate connection to capitalist display mechanisms is threatened with decay, to speak with Koolhaas, catastrophically, simply by no longer being new. Brands can be argued to have an almost tragic entanglement with notions of newness. Hence, aging architecture confronts the brand with something outside its functional mechanisms. The no-longer-new of buildings creates a kind of vulnerability. In terms of the relation between the presence and the past, this means that the past can become a threat to the present.

The past for capitalism must always also be seen as a ghost (Derrida 1994). Capitalism has a significant ambiguity when dealing with notions of the past. In terms of economic theory, the idea of path dependence is a more systematic way to deal with history as concept. For instance, Penrose (1959) developed an entire economic theory that points to the past of a firm as determining its present condition. Even his theory, however, is too focused on the immediate surroundings of a corporation's activity to grasp the complexity with which history haunts the corporate presence. The past remains, in business-strategic terms, simultaneously asset and liability. It is the "other" putting pressure on the company.[5]

In this sense, despite all its capitalist-productive capacities, brand space is threatened by decay and death in a very peculiar way, thereby exemplifying what Vidler conceptualized as "dark space" (Vidler 1992). Vidler describes space as a category inherently characterized by a certain other, by objects of fear. Interestingly, dark space is in itself not necessarily dysfunctional; Vidler uses dark space as a metaphor to describe one particular functioning mechanism of city space (ibid.: 172). Dark space also has its own "content". But this content is fundamentally opposed to being "informational" (ibid.: 175). Dark space is the threat to transform what used to be informational, "positive" content into its opposite.

The threat this concept of dark space poses for brand urbanism is obvious. If brand space were to lose all its informational content, for instance because a brand itself is taken from the market, then it seems hard to imagine the buildings simply being taken over by some other urban process. Without the brands they support, the buildings themselves are at risk of "dying", because what used to imply a certain "meaning" is then the skeleton of former meaningfulness. In this sense, there is a ruinous potentiality specific to spatialized brand capitalism.

The ways in which architecture in brand space is dependent on and inherently threatened by external economic developments can be grasped with Koolhaas' concept of junkspace (Koolhaas 2001). Junkspace is deserted yet cultural space. The concept allows for an extension of the argument above, effectively showing that urban space is not only threatened when the brands that influenced its creation die; rather, Koolhaas points to the destructive capacities within brands themselves. Junkspace refers to a brand culture that no longer creates meaning, but dissolves the possibility of the generation of any meaningful communication. This destructive potential is, for Koolhaas, the downside of branded capitalism. "Brands in Junkspace perform the same role as black holes in the universe: essences through which meaning disappears" (Koolhaas 2001: 410).

Still, my point is not that brands always create junkspace. But when space is "weak" anyway, either because of a strict opposition to another, more "vital" spatial area, or through destructive, antiurban processes within, then branded information carriers such as logos or old advertising messages have the destructive capacity to perform an emptying-out process that renders the space in question vulnerable. If one assumes that socially shared meaning gives space if not structure, then at least content, then the absence of this meaning and the social connections through which it is upheld render space vulnerable to emptiness. This emptiness might occur rather rapidly, as Koolhaas remarks (ibid.); there is a threat that "an entire Junkspace – a department store, a nightclub, a bachelor pad – turns into a slum overnight without warning".

In this context, history itself unveils a similar double face. It is the creator of spatial intensity, but can also be the de-symbolized ghost that appears when all intensity has disappeared. Vidler (1992: 13) points out that capitalism hands it over to architecture to fill the voids created by modernism. The engagement of brand space with historical allusions is an instance of just that. But the voids are never filled permanently, but only on a fluid, unstable basis.

In that sense, brand space is subject to Vidlerian feelings of the uncanny, which is an extension of Freud's "Unbehagen" (Freud 1930). This Unbehagen lies in the threat of being emptied out and thereby neutralized, with the remainder of historical allusions becoming dead matter, the effect of an architectural death drive inherent in capitalism (cf. Lash 2002: 213). It is also part of brand space's Unbehagen to potentially lose any sense of time. Given the way brand space is dealing with notions of history, it is certainly not "de-temporalized" space per se, but is characterized by a fragile temporal regime. In brand space, the notion of a slow, evolutionary ageing is confronted with another, abrupt, potentially catastrophic temporality. The virtual time of the brand is colliding with the actual, concrete time of the building. The latter is deprived of its temporal development, forced to enter a system of permanent newness. The decay of matter becomes catastrophic; the brand's virtuality and the links to the past it carries are confronted with a movement of time which is not its own. Space is the playground for this conflict between different time systems.

This results in an irritation of the brand system. The confrontational character of these different time regimes is currently felt strongly in Autostadt, as well as in Anting New Town. Both places are relatively new, but yet they have, at certain spots, an atmosphere of antiquity in them. In Anting *New* Town, cracks in façades, streets and murals undermine the sense of the new. Nevertheless, the management in both places is forced to concentrate on keeping it forever new. In our interviews, the planners of both Autostadt and Anting New Town admitted that brand space coming-of-age might pose a problem to the urbanities they masterminded.

## Newness and the politics of brand space

The fact that the notion of an eternal newness is undermined in brand space is not only a sign of a malfunctioning. It is also an element in an involuntary capitalist reflexivity. It is because the cracks in façades and other impressions of age entering the ageless space come as a surprise that the visitor is bound to reflect on the temporality of brands. In Autostadt, I saw visitors photographically documenting even the slightest deviation from the impression of slick newness. It was as if they were driven towards the cracks. Visitors to spaces aiming at an eternal newness are sensitive towards the old, adopting the role of cultural critics. Hence, brand architecture is creating its own criticism by creating its own critics.

This new degree of space politics is a development away from the "nonplace" politics writers like Augé or Castells had suggested. Augé (1995) claims that in nonplaces, the flows of people become political; nonplaces force individuals to flow frantically, thereby losing any kind of control or self-confidence. Castells (1996) even claims that certain spaces that seem to be non-political in their intention in fact have been created to serve a political function. International elites, he argues, have developed an architectural culture that serves as a tool of power (ibid.: 415–418). This culture is defined by an architectural system to which only these elites have access.

This kind of exclusion politics cannot be argued to be at play in brand cities. My argument throughout this work is that these are not places of exclusion so much as of power through inclusion. Brand places invite us to participate. In this context, the sense of insecurity outlined earlier might be interpreted by many visitors as a reason to participate. Even the abstract notions of sensory experience I described will only obtain actuality if somebody "actually" experiences them. Similarly, the ubiquitous mediatization at play in brand spaces will always need receivers in order to be real. Thrift (2000) has shown that the strength of any effort to use architecture as medium depends on whether it is actually perceived as such. Hence, brand cities need people to become effective. This generates consumer power, and even more so if the existing symbolic constraints on a complete integration into urban reality – entrance fee, etc. – will at some point be abandoned.

## Architecture of new media?

One result of these arguments is that, especially through the threats it encounters, the concept of architecture itself is changing thoroughly. Architecture is no longer the outside of culture or economy, an unchangeable, pure shape. It is becoming a tool for economic and cultural change, a platform for image-based transformation processes, not all of which are planned by the architect. Without affecting social or economic process, an architectural structure today would be seen as failure. Or, as Henn (2000: 3) puts it, architecture has to "work". The question is, however, what "work" means in this context. Clearly, Henn is not promoting a narrowly functionalist understanding of architecture in which function would merely mean "use". Brand space has to be more open than that, for its capitalist "function" is not the necessary outcome of innovations in production, as would have been the case with nineteenth-century plants or even with 1950s modernist office buildings (such as the Volkswagen headquarters). Functioning in brand space means functioning as a medium.

In this context, I want to make the point that functioning as a medium means that architecture functions beyond registers of the symbolic. It is in this sense that architecture is becoming not only a medium, but a "new" medium that in Kittler's sense reaches beyond meaningful communication. In fact, one can argue that the whole architectural ensembles of BMW Welt and Autostadt function as new media. They are media for the brand to initiate actualization processes, but also potentially for counter-forces to deliver their counter-images or new virtualities, which might then also become part of the brand. This means a) that they are subject to processes of interactivity and b) that this interactivity transcends the level of mutual understanding – two of the conditions of new media suggested by Manovich (outlined in Chapter 3). And the effects of this are global, which means that Manovich's three criteria of new media are met.

*Flow and the virtual–actual*

I have described above that the mediatization of space is significantly the mediatization of different kinds of flows, which can, with reference to Walter Benjamin, be interpreted as resulting from, but also creating, different levels of "porosity". Even the apparent boundaries brand space puts up to flows into its realm are made up of flows (ticket-purchasing – money; canal between Autostadt and Wolfsburg – water; broad streets between Schwabing and BMW Welt – cars). From this perspective, space in general and the city in particular are subject to, are perhaps even made up of, flows. Regarding Autostadt, creative director Maria Schneider outlined in our interview how in particular the footbridge from the train station and the Northern end of central Wolfsburg to Autostadt is supposed to create a sense of permanent flow and movement. She explained: "The footbridge is part of the great energy axis of the city, the Koller axis. An extension of the Porsche Street in central Wolfsburg, it crosses Autostadt and continues north towards Wolfsburg castle. We want to use the energy from this axis. People move here, they bring about their specific energy. Everything dissolves into movement." In her statement, Schneider seems to conceptualize flow similarly to Amin and Thrift (2002, Chapter 4) in their concept of the "machinic city". This city is made up of flows – and flow here is a productive force, productive of what they call the "city of passions" (ibid.: 83). Flow creates passion, which is very similar to the transpersonal idea of affect suggested as central to the contemporary urban sphere in this work.

However, there is a tension between different regimes of flow (Doel and Hubbard 2002: 358). The global movement of brand images might become interrupted, for example, by the counter-movement of fake branded products. Imitations of Nike shirts and their movement around the globe counteract the distribution of Nike brand images. They are the brand movements of poorer countries, which were supposed to become smoothly integrated into the global network of brand-image movements initiated by the Nike headquarters.

Similarly, Autostadt Wolfsburg is not seamlessly linked to the pre-existing actual flows of Wolfsburg. The fact that there is an entrance fee naturally prevents certain flows into Autostadt. In order to get even close to Autostadt, one has to traverse the Mittellandkanal. The Koller axis is virtually there, but in terms of actual city life, the Ferdinand Porsche Straße ends some way ahead of the bridge. One does not easily "flow into Autostadt".

The same can be said of Anting New Town. When leaving the motorway for Anting, there is a toll station demonstrating that a border is being crossed. Before entering the town proper, one has to pass a security guard (even though he did not actually approach us). Perhaps even more significant in terms of the collision of different regimes of flow was an incident that took place after we left Anting New Town; the entrance to the motorway was closed and we had to look for another one. The problem: Johannes Dell's driver did not find one. So we drove through endless suburbs, one looking like another, the driver gradually realizing that he was lost. It took us two hours more just to get back into Shanghai. The flows into Anting New Town seemed totally disconnected from the flows of the local street system of Shanghai suburbia.

*Towards a post-symbolic linguistics*

If brand space creates *new interactions between virtual and actual,* then this incomplete actuality translates into a new relationship between the symbolic and the non-symbolic, between the linguistic and the non-linguistic. Just as the brand is not becoming completely non-virtual, it also is not becoming entirely non-linguistic. True, through buildings, a brand seems to substitute its formerly exclusively linguistic character for something new. As long as it was only language, the brand was purely virtual. Now, it is *also* bricks and mortar. But buildings have long been engaged with linguistics too. Ever since the idea of an abstract modernism inherent in any "good" building came into question, it has been accepted that to deal with architecture means to deal with semiology and linguistics. Barthes, Eco and Chomsky have all analyzed architectural strategies of coding (Tschumi 2000: 156).

However, if spatialized branding makes brands less dependent on language and language-based constructs such as advertising slogans, then this complicates the creation and functioning of brands. Language is, and is supposed to be, a strict frame. The architectural approach brings a multiplicity of concepts into the equation – cultural, economic, physical. The brand becomes a hybrid (Delanty and Jones 2002: 456). In that sense, architecture has the capacity to derive brands of the linear nature they have as long as they are *purely* language-based. Architecture frames language, but it also complicates it. It adds its own modes of expression and functionality to the meaning carried by language. So it is not so much architecture that is transformed or subverted by language, but the dominance of language is undermined by the functioning modes of architecture.

In fact, one can say that there is a power play between architecture and signage, or the symbolic. In *Learning from Las Vegas* Robert Venturi and Denise Scott Brown made the point that signage and codes drive architecture. The fact that Las Vegas by today has become a "real" city shows that it is impossible to understand either architectural progress or urban development without simultaneously taking signs and communicated meaning seriously. In an interview with Rem Koolhaas and Hans Ulrich Obrist, Venturi argued decades after *Learning from Las Vegas* that in the information age, "architecture should reject abstract form and promote electronic iconography" (Koolhaas *et al.* 2002: 151). However, this electronic iconography is new media-related rather than symbolic. In and through brand space, the brand transcends the symbolic. It is not only, as explained above, becoming-new-medium. It is also sucking other media in, hence becoming a metamedium, a mediated space that derives its intensity from the *confrontation* of all sorts of media.

This critical engagement with the symbolic can be clearly seen in BMW Welt's use of screens. There are screens everywhere. However, during my visits, to a surprising and irritating degree, these screens were blank. They were not displaying information, but *themselves as screens*. This emphasizes that BMW Welt is actualizing the brand not through information displayed via screens and monitors, but rather through architecture itself. The building in a way *is* the screen in brand space, and the concrete screen becomes a piece of architecture. With this point, this work makes a step beyond Venturi's idea of architecture as iconographic representation. The fact that there is "content" does not matter much any longer. What counts here is the permanent presence of the screen, even and especially when it is turned off. The screen represents the permanent possibility of meaning and content to take over and extend architecture. At the same time, however, it is also proof of the crisis and increasing irrelevance of meaning.

This irrelevance is apparently developed further by another element in BMW Welt's architectural strategy: the use of lighting. When analysing the architecture in- and outside of BMW Welt, one observes a noticeable presence of theatrical lighting devices (Figure 4.3). Sometimes, they highlight certain particularly impressive architectural elements. In other situations, they seem to be just there, not highlighting anything particular. This can be interpreted as an architecture that is playing on the possibility and the limits of meaning. It seems to articulate a specific insecurity as to what really are

*Actualizing the virtual of capitalism?* 79

symbolic and meaningful architectural elements. In this way, these lighting devices can even be seen as the extension of the many blank screens.

It fits with this line of thought that brand space is, in often surprising ways, creating dissonances between notions of solidity/thickness/landscape-connection on the one hand, and hollowness/thinness on the other. The Skoda pavilion in Autostadt, for instance, is designed as a solid, stable, massive building, which is, however, confronted with an architectural opposite; once inside, the visitor is surprised by the floor being broken up repeatedly, unveiling or pointing towards a stream of water below the floor. One is effectively walking on bridges, a situation that creates a sense of spatial irritation. Similarly, in BMW Welt, the dominant architectural statement of the bridge connecting all functional areas within the building as well as the building with the outside, is built in such a fluid shape and is crossing the building at such an irritating height that it creates a sense of dynamism, but also of architectural porosity and fragility (Feireiss 2007: 167).

*Strategic immersion*

The uneasy arrangement of the architectural settings in brand space is part of a larger process that can be described as one of strategic architectural immersion. Brand-space architecture "immerses" the visitor, integrating his or her body into a larger whole; this irritates, because it implies a loss of bodily coherence and independence. This notion of immersion is another instance of brand space furthering and employing certain architectural principles that can be argued to have begun in Las Vegas. There, architecture

*Figure 4.3* The omnipresence of lighting in BMW Welt (author's picture)

was also developed to "immerse" the visitor, by integrating him or her into certain three-dimensional stories (Klingman 2007: 202). Effectively, all Las Vegas casinos tell such immersive stories (and stories of immersion). In front of the Treasure Island casino, for instance, is the story of the "water world", which the visitor effectively joins, thereby "shrinking into a movie" (Klein 2003: 340).

However, despite the apparent, Hollywood-style linearity of many of the stories told by Las Vegas casinos, Las Vegas architecture in a way already seems to integrate the possibility of the end of linear storytelling. Klingman (2007: 203) points out that the staging of stories in casino architecture always contains elements of irritation. Interestingly, water plays a central role here, as it does in Autostadt. This can be seen most impressively in the Venetian Hotel and Casino, built by Las Vegas-based WATG architects and opened in 1999. The complex is organized in a labyrinthine manner. Water does not "structure" the compound, but poses a permanent challenge (a similarity to the "real" Venice). The canal is not only an ornament outdoors, but is repeated on the second floor, thereby once more upsetting every sense of spatial coherence and order. On the third floor, then, there is an outdoor pool, not only posing the question of whether one can or should swim in a canal, but also repeating the outdoor water scenario with another outdoor scenario that is nevertheless also a part of the interior design of the hotel. Klingman (ibid.: 204) writes: "Detached from any conventional architectural logic, such choreographed motifs subvert predictably understood notions of the exterior and also any expected notion of the ground plane."

Klingman and Klein both argue that such a level of irritation is constructive in creating immersion that swallows any visitor into the planned effects of a totalizing architectural experience. Compared to this, brand space seems to follow a different strategy. It does not offer a totalizing experience; the coherence of a complete "story" is no longer offered to the visitor. Instead of being drawn into a story, the visitors are often deliberately left alone with an irritating architectural hollowness. No solution or "easy way out" is offered. Brand spaces are not the "perfect simulation". Immersion in brand space does not mean that the visitor is sucked into a movie, as Klein had it, which would mean that he or she effectively becomes "media content". Rather, just as architecture itself, he or she is part of the mediatization process, and perhaps his or her own medium.

From this perspective, the question is not only whether there is a solution to the feeling of hollowness in brand architecture. The question is whether there is supposed to be one. Mostly, the effects of hollowness and the architectural hints towards elements of pastiche and architectural staging in brand space seem to be offered voluntarily. Brand space apparently wants to irritate. And even if it does so involuntarily, this does not seem to be a major problem. In 2008, I saw several plastic bags covering certain repair works in the pond in Autostadt. These bags were not only ugly; they were the three-dimensional proof that all waters apparently natural are clearly

*Actualizing the virtual of capitalism?* 81

managed, and have to be supported by pumps and artificial barriers. Brand space apparently has a tendency (or even a subconscious desire) to lay open its own character as a highly managed space.

Similarly, in Anting New Town, the low building quality, irritating as it may be, also emphasizes the fact that the whole town carries elements of an architectural imitation. I saw several cracks in the (new) bridges there (see Figure 4.4). This pointed out that this bridge is not of European building origin. Architecture here develops expressive capacities beyond its assumed narrow functionality.

From the perspective of an architect like Johannes Dell, this capacity of architecture to counter its own (display and other) functions is of course perceived as a problem to be overcome. The question is whether it necessarily has to. If architecture is becoming medium, and if, as I will outline in Chapter 6, the mediatization of space is only complete through the

*Figure 4.4* Cracks in the New Town (author's picture)

engagement of human bodies, one could argue that a certain notion of fragility and changeability is an integral part of the entire process. Not only would poor building quality then not be a major problem, but perhaps even a productive feature. Its imperfection emphasizes that it needs the engagement of human bodies to create the perfect global mass ornament.

### The transformation of the national into the "national"

The creation of media space is often seen as an effort to generate a new sense of "identity". However, one has to be careful with the application of identity-related concepts. Just as brands do not simply stop being "virtual" when provided with an architectural centre, it would also be simplistic to claim that through creating an architectural centre for a brand, the brand would then "have" an identity it lacked before. The fact that architecture is not an easy way to create a new sense of national identity has been demonstrated by Delanty and Jones (2002).

This problematic character of any notion of the national is negotiated also in Autostadt (in a way similar to other exhibition concepts, such as World Exhibitions). However, Autostadt does not make concepts of nationality in any way coherent or understandable; it does not create any national "identity". The bigger identity to be constructed in Autostadt is not "Germany", "Spain" or "Europe" but the brand. The notion of the national in the Autostadt brand pavilions offers a constitutive role for branding, helping to create and reflect a distinct "cultural backbone" for each individual brand. The individual pavilions do so, as I have shown, by engaging simultaneously with notions of national history and by the latter's transcendence through the category of the global. Ideas of the "national" and the "European" become thinned-out elements in this reflection (offering physical forms apparently embodying elements of Spanish-ness or Czech-ness, without being explicit regarding what this Spanish-ness might actually mean). The national becomes a quote: the "national".

One can even argue that the actualization of the brand in space is more seamlessly possible if national identity can be reduced to implicitly understandable physical/architectural/iconic elements. The architectural assemblage of national-cultural references in Autostadt is just enough to allow consumers to link the brands in question to pre-cognitive images of the national (Spanish, Czech, German, etc.) without any critical questioning of the meaning of such images in a globalized world. Global capitalism is developing an understanding of the national as strategic resource here; an understanding in which each country has "something to add" to the global functioning of branding, and of the creation of global multi-brand corporations.

Regarding the ways in which the pavilions in Autostadt represent nationality, the focus is limited to qualities (such as the Spanish ceramics that made the walls of the Seat pavilion). The buildings are essentially surfaces on which these qualities play out. Through this "qualitization" the national is

*Actualizing the virtual of capitalism?* 83

becoming material. Capitalism presents itself in Autostadt as the force that promotes (and understands) this "nationalized materiality". It is adopting the role of a mirror, aiming at showing each country what (material or quality) the country "is best at". This effect is then reciprocally strengthening the competitive position of a brand. Hence, nationality in spatialized brand capitalism is essentially a *nationality of surfaces*.

This kind of thinned-out nationality is also a key element in Wang's argument for a need to go beyond the dichotomy of the global versus the local when understanding branding processes today (Wang 2008: 39). Interestingly, and consequently, when analysing the cultural role of contemporary branding, Wang focuses particularly on China. For her, branding in China is not "catching up" with certain branding processes that have been constituted in the West, but is creating a whole new capitalism that she expects to have worldwide effects. In this perspective, Chinese branding is a showcase of the fact that both the global and the local can, and has to be, *produced* in a process involving many different actors, both local and global, East and West. Similarly, in Watson (1997), it is argued that McDonald's has effectively stopped being an American, or even a Western brand. Instead, it is appropriated in different countries in different ways.

In this sense, when we look at Anting New Town, we might encounter something that is not only taking developments in Wolfsburg or Munich further, but is creating its own capitalist reality. The idea of a thinned-out nationality is not only "employed" (rather bluntly) by Anting New Town, but is simply taken as a given. Anting does not even pretend to be based on this traditional national logic; and the notion of the "German" is not an add-on or a mirror to an existing national mindset, but rather the sign of a very different Chinese self-understanding. Anting New Town is using the idea of "Germanness" to foster the development of Shanghai as an inherently *transnational* city. The national is not reduced to qualities as in Autostadt, but rather embraced, including all its most symbolic elements (such as the statue of Goethe and Schiller), thereby documenting that even such symbols are not constituent of any clear-cut national identity any more. Anting New Town is the result of the assumption that Germany (or any other nationality) can "be in Shanghai" just as much as in the place actually called Germany. The dissolution of the national is not a threat to the creation of identity here, but a key driver.

The relationship between space branding and the issue of national identity is complex – particularly in situations of rapid change, as is the case in China and in particular Shanghai. Anting New Town seems to indicate that the city is engaging in a rather uncritical way with the influences a company had on the urban economy in the past, taking up certain assumed characteristics of the brand's homeland, developing from that an idea of an urban space – and implementing it architecturally. One could approach this topic with the analytical arsenal of postcolonial theory, seeing it as a Chinese step towards a subtle countering of its own colonial past and of the colonial European powers.⁶ From that perspective, it would be the counter-creation of what Liu (2004, Chapter 2) calls "super-sign". Unlike in Liu's linguistic analyses of how the British dealt with Chinese characters during their occupation however, here it is China that actively engages with signs and representations from Europe. It thereby creates its own "super-signs", transforming their meaning and potentially providing them with new associations.

From this perspective, Anting New Town can be argued to be an urban investment in a globalization-driven, post-national mode of identity. Economic process and cultural longing here form an alliance. There is an economic layer to the cultural process of identity-creation in and through Anting. The success of Shanghai International Automobile City depends on investments from Volkswagen and its suppliers (Waldmann 2008: 6). Hence, the architectural gesture of building a German town can be seen as an element in a strategy dedicated to creating favourable conditions for the negotiations to follow. The appearance of building "German" (or "English" or "Italian" as in other satellite cities around Shanghai) might be interpretable as an act of politeness towards potential or current investors (Kammhuber 2005: 287).

And yet, there is another argument to explain the ease with which Chinese officials construct an artificial place with explicitly extra-Chinese (German) attributes. Kang Liu (2003: 38) identifies the opening of the country for a postmodern consumer culture as a move towards an economically motivated "universalization" of Chinese culture. This includes mass-cultural products, but also academic and intellectual concepts and ideas. From this perspective, Anting New Town can be conceptualized as an element in this universalization – of both products and discourse. It might be the result of an aesthetic openness that is evoked by certain post-nationalist (Western) discourses and by the (consumer-cultural) possibility of creating national attributes elsewhere. From this perspective, Anting New Town can be interpreted as a training ground for the universalization of the Chinese society. The fact that the Chinese economy and culture is apparently able to put characteristics and images of other countries to use in its own process of adapting to the globalized competition of regions would, in this reading, become a unique strength. Shanghai, this interpretation would go, is able to work with different national characteristics, and does not depend on ideas of national purity.

From a Western viewpoint, this extreme flexibility might be seen as dangerous, evoking fear of the fast-growing Chinese economic power, as well as a certain anxiety regarding the changing face of capitalism in general. In this sense, Anting New Town is becoming the focus point of a "capitalist uncanny". In fact, one can argue that Vidler's concept of the architectural uncanny (Vidler 1992) was always connected to capitalism. In Europe, the idea of the classical European city is commonly employed to find a pre-capitalist self. From this perspective, the trans-local employment of features of a traditional city like Weimar for an extension of Chinese hyper-capitalism will be seen as capitalist uncanny going wild.

Nevertheless, this "working with" national attributes is another link between Anting New Town and the branding culture established by European brand spaces; for it is brands that are core drivers of this kind of capitalist universalization. Anting New Town can be argued to make use of attributes of Germanness distributed significantly through the presence of the brand Volkswagen in China. It can be seen as an element in an involuntary, or rather, strategically unintended, spatialization and actualization of the brand Volkswagen *through its Germanness*. The brand is part of what is mediated through Anting New Town, even if Volkswagen did not intend this (as both Maria Schneider and Johannes Dell made clear in our interviews). The thinned-out version of nationality that Anting New Town is based upon finds it easy to include brand values. The outcome of this is yet another "brand": the universalist brand Shanghai and/or China.

# 5 Virtualizing the actual of space

## Brand city as new media space

Having outlined the extent to which brand space changes the virtual character inherent in brands I now want to switch the perspective; no longer tracing capitalist rationality, but developing an argument around the development of mediatized urban reality. I want to argue for a necessary change in our understanding of contemporary cities *through* the spatialization of brands. The key question from this perspective is whether the city-building activities on display in brand space and in the urban reality I conceptualized as a process of new media add a new dimension of virtuality to (our understanding of) the city. As part of an argument for which concrete brand spaces are only a symptom, I want to discuss whether these cultural-industrial efforts of companies in search for competitive advantage increase the complexity, non-actuality and abstraction that is characteristic of the capitalist city.

This argument will try to determine the extent to which, and the way in which, brand space makes cities and the urban in general "more" virtual. Does, for instance, Autostadt make Wolfsburg more virtual? I will argue that Autostadt initiates a new interplay of images, architecture and flow that has a thorough impact on what and how Wolfsburg builds, and on how city visitors perceive the built environment of Wolfsburg. And not just of Wolfsburg, for my argument will be that brand space has an impact on the concept of the urban as a whole. When brands become spatial, I will point out, they change the character of architecture and indeed of the city itself. By becoming media, they create a new kind of architecture and urbanity.

In this respect, I see the search of brands for moments of actualization as a consequent precondition for the alteration of city space I will outline. From a brand perspective, the eventual conquest of the urban was unavoidable. The change the city thereby undergoes is not just the involuntary effect of the branding process. It is a structural urban development that facilitates the redirection and alteration of the individual and social fantasy creation that is the driver of a brand's productivity. Brands do not simply need any kind of city. They need the openness and specific productivity of what can be termed the "virtual city". I will show the ways in which cities can be argued to become virtual, and why this is not just a development of loss and destruction, but also of urban development and change which has the capacity to foster new generative, perhaps even creative processes.

To start, however, I will once again think through some methodological implications of this book's perspective of the urban for city-oriented analysis.

## Researching the abstract, or how brand space changes the focus of the cultural study of the urban

In which way does brand space change the urban? Or rather, what do I have to focus on to understand the effects of these particular architectural ensembles in the context of contemporary cultural and urban thinking? This question should be answered before delving into any deeper urban analysis. Specifically, it has to be explained why there might be a new kind of urban process involved in brand space, and what this new process entails.

Significantly, this means thinking about what to look at when analysing the cultural characteristics and larger urban effects of a concrete brand space. This is what I want to discuss now. Specifically, I will employ the notion of the "event" in this context, because it allows for a thorough investigation of the relationship between structure and process in space, and this relationship is the key to any spatial analysis influenced by poststructuralist thinking. My employment of the event concept will distinguish the two very different meanings the term has (common-sense "fun event" vs. poststructuralist "thought event"), but also look at the relationship between the two. Massumi (2002: 80–88) demonstrates that both terms are in fact connected and that this leads to a broadened concept of event as a central category for a Deleuzian spatial analysis. I want to follow him in this respect.

One core question any spatial analysis has to discuss regarding "fun events" is their relationship with architecture. My argument at this point is that a) space has to be understood with reference to the specific temporalities it is creating and deconstructing through spatializing brands and b) in order to look for these creations and deconstructions it is vital to determine what has to be taken into account when looking for such events. The assumption here is not simply that brand spaces are part of a capitalist tendency to turn the world into a space of permanent event activity, at the expense of certain "deeper" or more "cultural" processes. This would mean that my analysis would have to focus exclusively on what is "happening" inside brand space and look for the craziest, loudest, most eye-catching activity, with architecture merely being an empty shell, background to whatever event PR consultants come up with. However, the straightforward argument "brand space equals fun event space" or "brand space is an example for Debord's society of the spectacle" is complicated by a surprising empirical observation; in Anting New Town, there is hardly any event activity to speak of. And the character of Autostadt or BMW Welt as a fun event is rather weak. Autostadt is not characterized by an atmosphere of permanent event activity, but by a solemn calm. Maria Schneider emphasized in our interview that in the design process, everything reminiscent of an average fun park, such as a Coca Cola sponsoring, has voluntarily been left out.

Also, the experience of the individual pavilion is not what one would expect in a fun arena. Many pavilions offer sensory experiences, but either in an isolated way or as momentary experiential explosion. In the end, this experience will leave the visitor alienated and irritated, rather than satisfied with the fun he or she had. This is also what visitors leaving the Lamborghini pavilion told me. "Impressive" it was, also "interesting", but not primarily "fun".

To be sure, the lack of linear, simple events in Autostadt is not always planned. Partly, one has to assume that the lack of imagination displayed by those responsible for the individual pavilions gives Autostadt its limited fun appeal. More generally, I perceive Autostadt as only partly corporation-driven. With Autostadt, as with urban intervention in general, companies abandon the aim of complete control. The analysis of who is in which situation and to which degree "in charge" is part of what we have to look at when understanding how brand space transforms the urban sphere and the ways in which the latter rearranges relationships between the public and the private.

However, the lack of a "fun" atmosphere, even if not always intended, is not a contradiction to, but rather an indication of the intellectual ambitions expressed by the makers of Autostadt. Had there been a more easy-going, unambiguously positive attitude towards any kind of consumerist "happening", then it might have been easier for the decision makers to initiate them in the first place. The Autostadt strategy is to develop a certain "life" in a subtle, architecture-based way. While the marketing world starts exploiting urban events to create branded experiences, Maria Schneider seems to have intended Autostadt to surprise the visitors by lacking any feature of the crazy event-based capitalism. In our interviews, she showed she was aware of cultural-critical concepts surrounding global capitalism. In this sense, the decision against a fun park can be read as an integration of cultural critique into capitalism's functioning. In terms of methodology, this implies that it makes sense for any analysis of the cultural effects of capitalist space to start with determining the degree to which individual actors or driving forces within this spatial setting are capable of integrating such a critique.[1]

Even if brand space doesn't offer fun events, on a more abstract and critical level, the concept of "event" is still present. In my conversations with Autostadt visitors just entering the premises, those informed by former visits to other spatial capitalist arrangements like Disney World indeed claimed to expect some "event". Meeting the same persons again afterwards, they did not express disappointment. The reason for this, I want to argue, is that the social position of the visitors here is characterized by insecurity and an openness towards the spatial setting they enter. They are expecting experiences, and perhaps "fun", but leave the interpretation of fun and experience to the institution offering them. In terms of methodology, this points to an obvious complication particularly of the use of interview techniques when researching capitalist mediatized spaces.

This leads to the broader notion of "event" put forward in this work. From this perspective, more abstract and more distinctly poststructuralist, "event" is closely connected to the momentary actualization of the virtual outlined above. This is where affects of any kind are generated. To be sure, this does not always happen in a planned way. The notion of crisis and threat has gained permanence in the mediatized spaces that make up what Sloterdijk (2005: 309) calls the "Große Installation". Just as any installation, Sloterdijk's "Weltinnenraum des Kapitals" is characterized by a kind of over-eventization, creating spaces that (effectively) transform the presence of groups of human bodies into events (collectors and connectors). This notion of spatiality in the end serves to make people simultaneously numb and hyper-sensitive towards the event. This numb hyper-sensitivity is arguably even productive in making the event possible in the first place, creating what Milev (2009: 421) refers to as "zones of emergency". These emergency zones are intimately linked to capitalist accumulation and productivity. Brand spaces can be argued to be such zones of emergency.

If "event" in this sense refers to the creation of affect, then it would be too narrowing to limit the occurrence of an event (and its research) to the perception of the visitor. Events are, from a poststructuralist perspective, trans-human (Deleuze 1993: 77–80; see also Badiou 2007). Drawing on Whitehead, Deleuze describes four core features of the event:

1   a spatio-temporal extension;
2   the presence of intensities;
3   the individual and certain "prehensions" the individuals are involved with;
4   the involvement of objects.

Particularly features 3 and 4 are relevant at this point; individuals and individual bodies are part of the taking-place of an event. They are, however, not directing it, and its taking-place does not depend on their perception.

What is more, point 4 highlights that events are always partly, and significantly, object-ive. Objects (in Whitehead's terms divided into sense objects, perceptual objects and science objects) and their effects are just as relevant in the realization of an event as are humans. In terms of research, this means that we should not focus exclusively on the conscious involvement of brand-space visitors in spectacular events. Instead, we have to trace whatever might have the spatio-temporal effects mentioned above. Architecture might be an "event", just as an architectural void, or a misplaced object or human being in a branded environment.

This thought helps bridge the gap between the philosophical idea of the event and the way the term is used in everyday language. It brings the event in the concrete sense closer to the concept fostered by Foucault: event as thought. For Foucault, an event is not a logical sequence of words or actions. In fact, a logical and target-oriented development of processes as in the idea of museum events makes something a non-event. Rather, an event is connected to notions of collapse, questioning, or problematization of assumptions of any kind of functionality (Tschumi 1994).

In brand space, we find many such deviations of elements from their presumed function. Autostadt, for instance, is a car city, but no one drives in it; cars are expressively put out of context as in the Lamborghini pavilion. In BMW Welt, the only driven cars are the ones leaving the place, and visitors can only see them from a distance. Its architecture and interior design are full of breaks in its own apparent functionality (as demonstrated in my analysis of the irritating use of light installations – see pp. 78–9).

If we deal with the concept "event" in this abstract way, where does this leave the common-sense notion of events as something spectacular "going on" in the streets? The space event as a marketing category is seen as an effort to actively involve people in spatial processes, aimed at getting their attention by involving them in the process of "doing" something in space, or even with space (Metzinger 2003). Following Crary (1996), one can argue that if human attention can be changed by capitalism, then the spatialization of brands is not only an effort to get people's attention in situations in which they are principally willing to pay attention (because they act in or move through space). It is also a way of connecting process and perception, perceiving (seeing, feeling, etc.) and doing. This is why the concept of affect is so helpful in understanding how brand space, as space of new media, works (cf. Colebrook 2004); it makes it possible to understand media space as no longer restricted to the perceptive. And this is where the event as "something going on in the street" still has its place. Perception and attention are now connected to doing something. Place-based perception processes are substituted by urbanized event patterns.

Interestingly, it is the capitalist institution of the company that is constructing city events as ways for consumers to get involved with the city and thereby to perceive it. Apparently, the old criticism of capitalism as being interested in *hiding* what is taking place *underneath* the shiny surface does not capture what is happening any more. Now, a *strategically enabling* capitalism becomes prevalent; a capitalism that is enabling us to perceive it by being part of it, by being affected by it. It is these affections that a critical analysis of capitalism will have to trace.

## New layers, new complexities: how brand space is virtualizing the urban

Based on the analysis of capitalism as a force that produces new relations between virtuality and actuality in space, I will now elaborate on this by analysing the effects and changes brand space has on the urban. The perspective from the previous chapter will be reversed, with mediatized urban space now analyzed not as an indication of a capitalist transformation process, but as a contemporary spatial condition that has real cultural effects. I will start by outlining the ways in which this spatial condition still has the capacity to engage with notions of the historical, thereby arriving at a concept of virtual urbanity which transforms the urban setting as it engages with the built past. This argument will lead to an understanding of new ways in which brand space reconceptualizes architecture as spatial practice and how it transforms traditional notions of urbanity. This will be followed by an inquiry into the concept of the subject: how does brand architecture impact on human subjectivities? Finally, I will show that brand space has the capacity to function as a mirror, thereby influencing the city not only from within, but simultaneously from outside. I will trace the connections between brand space and the larger urban setting it is part of. Throughout these arguments, I will show that brand space is fundamentally urban, while at the same time offering certain features that non-brand city space does not have.

## *Brand city: the posthistorical combat for history*

As explained before, Wolfsburg contradicts much of what is seen as urban common sense. The city has always been characterized by a dominance of planning. This is one peculiarity of its history: that it is a history of planning, not of gradual development. In this, Wolfsburg differs even from "classical" industrial cities like Manchester or Detroit; its foundation is the result of excessive industry planning by a totalitarian government.

Wolfsburg and its Nazi predecessor are economic phenomena without initially having been capitalist. This is why Borgelt (2005: 4) can claim that Wolfsburg is an example of "planned urban development under the maxim of economic forces" *without* at the same time calling Wolfsburg a prototypical capitalist development. Wolfsburg had been planned as a place for production, thereby reflecting certain Nazi ideas of social and urban space as a machine that can be managed and directed towards certain goals.

However, with the Nazis, the rational and a thorough and deadly irrationality always went together. Hence, it would be a misinterpretation to argue that Wolfsburg has a history of economic efficiency maximization. For the Nazis, the place and the auto plant were not just a rational way to produce cars and house the people who build them. The whole ensemble was also a way to represent a society working together on a *grand idea* (Schildt 2007: 212). It was not *just* a social machine. It was this machine; but this machine simultaneously became a stage on which the production process and the living conditions of people function as a representation of the idea of such a machine. It is production for the sake of the creation of an iconic reality (cf. Schneider 1979: 40).

One is tempted to call this representational process "symbolic". The Wolfsburg predecessor would then be a "symbol" of certain meaningful categories seen as valuable by the Nazis. And what is certainly true is that the ways the Nazis often built had a kind of theatricality to them (Taylor 1974: 11). And yet, this theatricality remains rather vague in its representational capacities. In fact, it does not refer to something else, but to itself; the machine represents itself as a machine. In the Nazi-staged production theatre, the logic of technical machines – to produce cars – has a tendency to self-exaggeration, becoming the model for a broader, general social mechanism. Through self-representation, architecture here extends the logic of the symbolic. As cultural practice, it has been so central for the Nazis precisely *because* it defies and transcends the mechanisms of rational, symbolic meaning-creation.

## Modernism without the modern

The Nazi legacy then plants a certain ambiguity regarding the modernization of urbanity concepts into the heart of Wolfsburg's development. The National Socialists' relationship with the modernist movement and with modernist (and industrial, production-oriented) architecture is ambivalent (Krier 1989: 219). Hence, the Nazi predecessor of Wolfsburg can be argued to have used the architectural language of modernism without being modern.

There is, however, a connection between Nazi city building and the uncanny side of modernity (Vidler 1992: 12). In many instances, Nazi aesthetics arguably were indicative of this uncanny, and even seem to be attracted by its presence (Reichle 2006). From this viewpoint, their tendency towards an iconic modernism as it plays out in the architectural staging of grand-scale economic production has to be analyzed regarding its origin in this sympathy for the uncanny side of modernity. On a more conscious level, the idea behind Wolfsburg was arguably to fabricate an architectural ensemble capable of demonstrating the idea of a machinic life in Nazi reality, thereby emphasizing the assumed social and technological superiority of national-socialist Germany (Schildt 2007: 212). This resulted in a significant visual grandness: 1.5 kilometres of impressive red brick production lines, set dramatically alongside the Mittellandkanal and the rail track. Hitler himself opened the plant in a grand ceremony in 1938 in front of a 70,000-strong audience. The architectural semi-language of the original production plant culminates in the four chimneys at the east end of the production facilities.

Directly beyond this culmination point, opposite a small water pond, Autostadt starts. The plant chimneys face Autostadt, the latter's architecture integrating their image into its own design. Autostadt is, if we want to take the concept of affect that far, "architecturally affected" by those hyper-expressive buildings (Amin and Thrift 2002: 87). This architectural affection, however, does not translate as *imitation*. Autostadt is not also building high, which is what one might have expected as a counter to the chimneys. Instead, the high buildings of Autostadt, the AutoTürme, are at its Eastern border. Like a wave, Autostadt counters the brute force at its

Western border with the gentle presence of the former Bentley building and the self-focused roundness of the hotel (a mechanism similar to the concept of movement in architecture outlined by Kwinter 2007).

## Abstraction through production

But why was it so relatively easy for Wolfsburg to take over the architectural remains of a theatricalized production once the Nazis had left? How did Wolfsburg manage to become a capitalist city rather suddenly, having been a showcase production place for the totalitarian Nazi government before? Or why, more precisely asked, did capitalism manage to make use of the remains of the Nazi production place right from the start? One answer I want to suggest is: abstraction through production. Especially in its showcase elements, "productivity" has been part of any idea the place has had of itself. Wolfsburg was always a productive place in the most encompassing sense. This production focus has a kind of neutrality to it, and, from an urban perspective, a high degree of abstraction. As a production city, Wolfsburg was also an abstract city; and the display character of its modernist architecture strengthens this point.

Although not limited to capitalist societies, the abstraction inherent in the focus on production puts Wolfsburg at the heart of capitalist urbanity.[2] Capitalism substitutes targets by processes, ends by means: production for production's sake, movement and change as autopoietic system. These are the elements that Deleuze and Guattari (1980) refer to when writing about the deterritorialization tendencies of capitalist regimes. It seems reasonable to argue that this kind of deterritorialization is what Wolfsburg has always been about. And it is a logic that intrigued the Nazis just as it must have been appealing to the early post-war Germany. At that time, the country mobilized an impressive economic energy, the so-called Wirtschaftswunder. Arguably German society embraced the blindness and neutrality of pure economic production in order to ease the pains of moral self-questioning (cf. Giesen 1998: 149).[3]

## Wolfsburg and Los Angeles

This emphasis on abstraction, emptiness and groundlessness links Wolfsburg to another city, providing us with an unlikely urban couple: Los Angeles. Similar to Los Angeles, Wolfsburg is in a way *groundless,* with both cities being perceived by visitors as *irritating* (Mitchell 2005: 153). They are abstract to the extent of finding it hard to offer their citizens any naturally "grown", readable structure, which makes them aim at developing architectural hints as to what they might "be".

The ways in which Los Angeles is trying to develop such hints were dealt with for the first time by Kevin Lynch (1960). He demonstrates how popular images of a given city are used to define what a city is, in particular when lacking any easily readable structure, like Los Angeles. Lynch demonstrates that the city indeed manages to develop certain images of itself, and points out that this creates a synthetic form of readability.

Central to this development is the Los Angeles freeway system. This complex three-dimensional network, which had been envisioned since the 1930s but was not actually finished until the 1960s, provides human agency with an opportunity to develop a process-based (driving-based) understanding of what Los Angeles "is". One has to drive on the freeway to realize this experience, which means experiencing the city through certain images of it.[4]

Lynch's writing suggests that the freeway has been the driving force in the structuring of the city right from the start. Without the freeway, there was hardly any specifically Los Angeles-related urban identity, just as the freeway has shaped the corporeal experience of the city right from its origins. The freeway brought Los Angeles to itself. Lynch (ibid: 42) writes that driving constituted "the daily experience, the daily battle – sometimes exciting, usually tense and exhausting". Many Angelinos experienced driving as a "challenging, high speed game". What might at first be mistaken for an unambiguously positive urban experience in fact points to profound difficulties that such an urban experience poses. If experiencing the city is a high-speed game, then not participating in the game implies emptiness and disillusionment. Also, the game is one that does not lay its rules open. Hence, the experience of Los Angeles is always characterized by a sense of ambiguity.

This ambiguity in the urban experience is a parallel between Los Angeles and Wolfsburg. It is the ambiguity of an urban experience intimately connected to the car, and to driving. In order to understand Los Angeles, one has to be in the driver's seat. The same holds true for Wolfsburg. Los Angeles and Wolfsburg are, in very different ways, car cities. However, the Wolfsburg experience is complicated further by the fact that the car here is not only a consumer good, but also the abstract core of the connection of the urban experience to the specific economic grounding of the city. Wolfsburg would never have been built without the technological advances and economic necessities of the car industry; this presence of the need for economic productivity makes the experience of the city by car an even more profound, and ideologically charged one.

Wolfsburg can also be compared to Los Angeles in that it reflects the higher degree of flexibility and change brought to the city by capitalist globalization (which is one central factor allowing for both cities' virtualization in the sense developed in this work). As Zukin (1991) describes, the Los Angeles landscape has been shaped by the quick movements of capital and capitalist production into and out of certain areas of the city. Its urban fabric, she points out, constantly reinvents itself, thereby becoming the stage of the working of flexible capital. Like Wolfsburg, Los Angeles can and does change so quickly and to such a significant degree because it has little structure, permanence, or identity to confront capitalist flows with. What is more, its centrality for the film industry makes Los Angeles a paradigmatic place of Postfordist production. Through Hollywood, Los Angeles is the place where the global fantasies of capitalist consumer culture are produced. Hence, the permanent transformations of Hollywood (and of Los Angeles as a whole) reflect the history of capitalism; it is the materialization of capitalist phantasmagoria, the form of the formless.

In this way, it is a parallel to Wolfsburg. Just like Los Angeles, Wolfsburg as a city has been completely adopted by capitalism. In terms of Norman Klein (2004), urban life here is immersing itself in the abstractions of capitalism. Interestingly, in this case, it is none of the hypercapitalist megacities that are subject to this capitalist immersion, but a rather small town in social welfare-focused Germany. This immersion might also be a clue to the unease one might feel in Wolfsburg. It can be argued, albeit speculatively, that this unease has less to do with aesthetic judgements than with the unpopular realization that the history of capitalism is in fact the history of Germany, too.

## Hybrid history

The ambiguous historicization of Wolfsburg outlined at the beginning of this chapter leads to a city image that is rather opaque – because it makes it difficult to develop fantasies about the city. Such fantasy development constitutes processes that, according to Hetherington (1997: 189), make a city space knowable. Wolfsburg does not trigger this fantasy development – at this point a difference from Los Angeles, the latter being virtually present in the films it produces, as has been shown in the documentary *Los Angeles Plays Itself* (Andersen 2003) and is reflected in the films of David Lynch, particularly in *Mulholland Drive* (Lynch 2001). The lack of ability to create fantasies or stories about Wolfsburg, to "tell" Wolfsburg, and the lack of knowability of the city, also lead to rather limited tourist flows, at least before the Expo 2000 and before Autostadt (Marbach *et al.* 1998: 6). Apparently tourists want to be able to "know" a city by exercising their tourist gaze (Amin and Thrift 2002: 124).

However, the question is to what extent this lack of knowability must be seen as a deficit – or, more precisely, whether the deficit of a lack of knowability and straightforward identity cannot also be seen as a strength. One can argue that it links Wolfsburg with certain debates about hybridity and syncretism that have become relevant in cultural studies in the 1980s. Hybridity here means that elements from very different cultural contexts are recombined, creating the hybrid as a new cultural entity (Hepp 2004: 221; see also Gilroy 2003).

If we apply the same concept to a place, such as Wolfsburg, then hybridity takes on different, more fluid features. What is parallel to the notion of hybridity put forward by writers like Gilroy, however, is that also, in our understanding, hybridity is created by several very different sources of influence fighting for dominance. In Wolfsburg, historical discourses about German mid-sized towns, about the relationship between capital and political representation, and about technological and social progress come together. There is, however, no sense of the contradictions at some point merging into a new meta-story. No one even expects one strong, overarching and largely non-debated history to be told about Wolfsburg. This lack of expectation, rather than the clash of different histories alone, constitutes the hybridity of the historical in Wolfsburg. Even the story of economic progress does not and cannot go uncontested, despite the relevance of technology for the formation of the city's self-image.

This openness as enabler of hybridity refers to the question of authorship. Several sources are fighting for the dominant role in the telling of any Wolfsburg history, one being the company Volkswagen. This is where brands come into play. The relevance of the company for the development of Wolfsburg endows it with a capacity to influence what counts as an element in Wolfsburg's history. There is no counter-discourse questioning the company's role, simply because it is accepted that Volkswagen *is* Wolfsburg's destiny. In this sense, capitalism is writing its own hybrid history here.

The argument about the hybridity-influenced history writing can also be applied to Munich and BMW Welt – in a very different way. As city, Munich can be seen as the opposite of Wolfsburg: 800 years old, rich, usually considered beautiful, with an apparently "intact" architectural inner city structure. In the city centre, BMW Welt presumably wouldn't develop any significant urban reality of its own. But as outlined, it is positioned at the Northern outskirts of Schwabing, just north of the inner city ring. I explained how the area is made up of several large-scale architectural structures (Olympiapark, Olympic Stadium, Schwanzer Tower). It is this architectural context that creates hybridity and hybridity-influenced history writing around BMW Welt. The impact of the "city history" as displayed by the inner-city, traditional Bavarian building complexes has lost most significance in North Schwabing, as the area becomes self-reflective. I outlined how the construction of BMW Welt pays reference to, but also frames the experience of the architectural monoliths that surround it, including design features that seem to suggest a common history of the area, like the icons mentioned from the 1972 Olympic Games. In this way, the area highlights certain historical key moments specific to itself, thereby deconstructing any sense of historical continuity pertaining to Munich as a whole.

This hybrid history is haunted by its own black spots. The 1972 Olympic Games had their own dark side with the "Schwarzer September" terrorist attack (the kidnapping and eventual killing of Israeli sportsmen by Palestinian terrorists). What is more, any German engagement with this topic has to be interpreted with reference to the Second World War and the following effort of Germany to rebuild relationships with the State of Israel. Therefore, any architectural reference to the Olympics simultaneously implies an involuntary engagement with this highly charged political background.

However, to a certain extent the architectural setting around BMW Welt can also be read as an almost strategic engagement with the German Nazi past. The 1972 Olympic Games were to be the counterpart to the 1936 Olympics in Berlin. They were to be the "friendly" Games, displaying a version of a new, internationalized and internationally open Germany. In this context, the whole area can be argued to function as an urban screen; it is screening the version of the better Germany, as opposed to the one visible in central Munich. After all, Munich was the "Hauptstadt der Bewegung", the capital city of the Nazi movement (Nerdinger 2006). The Feldherrnhalle, an infamous monument to the Nazi movement, is the end of the major street "Leopoldstraße" that starts in North Schwabing.

If we take the screen approach one step further, then the screen in the Munich case is the broad street "Ring". The Ring can be seen as the screen that separates Munich from BMW World and at least from parts of the Olympic area (the stadium itself, however, is on the south side), but that also manages its visibility – from the city centre, but also from the car.

The "Olympic Village", one of the prime Olympic icons for international understanding, is directly north. Until recently, it was still used in an international context – as student village mainly for international students. In terms of the expressway as screen, the international students can be argued to have been "on display", just as the athletes were in 1972. It is this counter-historical frame of reference that BMW Welt puts to use for itself. Hence, one can argue that BMW Welt is part of a larger urban context apparently involved, if not in a rewriting of German history, then at least in screening processes that emphasize certain historical reference points. The area as a whole does not necessarily have to be seen as autistic and inward-oriented, which might be the first impression when driving through it. It is subject to very different historical forces, aiming at a particular display value for the construction of history; here is modern Germany, not haunted by the (Derridian) ghosts of the past.

Of course, this logic is bound to fail, which was not only shown by the 1972 Olympic terrorist attack (effectively bringing the ghosts of history back), but also by the feeling of a certain abstractness or coldness one develops when walking through the area. It is the very concrete coldness of being pulled into a screen.[5]

What this architectural screen effectively creates in brand space is a situation of a parallelism of past and present, yielding what Bonomi (2002: 455) calls a "hyperpresent". Deleuze effectively takes this one step further, tracing this hyperpresence primarily within the conceptual frames of cinema and the time image (Colebrook 2002: 33). For Deleuze, the medium of cinema is capable of showing us time itself, disjoined from space and movement.

## *Hybridity and the uncanny: Argento's Suspiria*

The experience of a history-related hybridity is arguably constitutive of the modernist urban experience, which I have argued with Vidler to involve a loss of orientation and order. Efforts to get away from the chains of history create a sense of being pulled back. This relationship is reflected medially in an interesting way with reference to the BMW Welt area. The Schwanzer tower itself has become an actor in a classic horror movie: Dario Argento's 1977 *Suspiria*. The film is about a witch chasing and killing an international crowd of young girls attending a ballet school. The appearance of the tower is a short shot, and the building does not play itself, but an anonymous modernist environment. In fact, the film itself does not play in Munich, but in Freiburg. Nevertheless, Argento uses several Munich locations, apart from the BMW Tower, also the Hofbräuhaus and the Königsplatz. (The Königsplatz is another place at which a Nazi appropriation of urban space blends with the urban fabric.) The clashing of modernist architecture with an involuntary presence of the Nazi past in Munich seems to be perceived by Argento as relevant, and as suitable material for a horror movie.

Regarding the tower itself, Argento apparently thought that its modernist environment has the capacity to enhance the uneasiness the film creates (mainly through references to the past; a hidden history, a history that runs counter to the stories of cosiness and Gemütlichkeit often associated with old Southern German towns). Argento's use of the tower illustrates the uncanny potential of modernist architecture through the ghosts of the past that haunt it, and the voluntary and involuntary engagements modernist architecture creates with the past (Klewer 1999).

Hence, the problem of modernist architecture is not the "emptiness" of modernism as such. The problem is that it does not stay empty, but that there is always a threat of it being filled with hidden memories. This modernism haunts itself. And capitalism adds to this problem, Argento seems to think. In this way, one can interpret his use of the prominent BMW building as an indicator of the uncanny potential of the hybridization of history through brand architecture (exemplified for him by the Schwanzer tower). Urban space here tells historical stories to hide its own involuntary past, but is at the same time continuously haunted by it – especially in a film dealing with witchcraft. On a meta-level, the witch in the film can be argued to represent German history itself.

### *Virtual urbanity, urban life and architectural heterogeneity*

The complexity of the hybrid history that brand space as media space is staging points to a very specific mode of temporality. This temporality is part of the virtual urbanity I see as characteristic of the media spaces I analyze here. This virtual urbanity is characterized by a distinct lack of certain elements normally considered central to the urban sphere. It has little to do with the gradual, centuries-long growth of city spaces that urban historians like to describe (Peter Ackroyd's *London* perhaps being one of the most impressive examples; Ackroyd 2000).

City "life" in brand spaces is limited; no one actually lives in Autostadt, apart from people who make the mentioned hotel their home, as is often the case with the top players and managers of the ambitious, Volkswagen-sponsored football club VFL Wolfsburg. BMW Welt is also free of conventional "living". With Anting New Town, of course, things are different, for it is a planned urban environment destined to be a home for people. At the time of writing, however, the place had not yet managed to develop any sense of being "busy" or "vibrant". Only a few people had actually moved there.

Hence, brand space is providing us with a rather peculiar impression of urbanity. And yet, brand space as media space is more than the mere simulation of certain elements of cities in non-city environments. Autostadt, BMW Welt and Anting New Town are all part of distinct cities – geographically, legally, and also in terms of city planning. They are not theme parks in no-man's land. What is more, in very different ways all three places function along principles we would call urban. Specifically, the role of architecture is a distinctly urban one. Architecture has a presence not entirely defined by corporate strategy, nor by the events that might or might not be taking place. Rather, it is one key force in the creation of a spatial complexity and heterogeneity that is seen by thinkers like Amin and Thrift (2002: 30) as distinctly urban.

If Autostadt creative director Maria Schneider complains in our interviews that marketing decision makers failed to make creative use of the pavilions, then what she has in mind is that fun events won't work here. This illustrates the independent life the architectural structure in Autostadt plays; it is stubborn, permeating a sense of resistance as pertains to a one-dimensional, fun-event-focused controllability. This independence, this capacity for creating lines of escape is part of what distinguishes the urban from artificial environments. Urban architecture is defined by a certain stubbornness. Autostadt architecture is indicative of that stubbornness in brand space.

With BMW Welt, the lack of controllability holds true to a lesser extent. The place seems more controlled, also because there is no significant "outside" which apparently invites the visitor to simply dwell. Hence, in this respect, BMW Welt is more theme-park-like. Nevertheless, architecture plays a very distinctive and complexifying role also here. It draws its own connections to its architectural environments, as we have seen in the last chapter. The architecture of BMW Welt interacts with the city, thereby becoming part of it, even if not seamlessly merging with the surrounding urban fabric.

The architectural reality fostered by brand space is characterized by an internal heterogeneity. Two antagonistic forces are at work, the relationship between which is constructed by two different kinds of buildings (Uhlig 2000). On the one hand, there are the structural large buildings: piazza, ZeitHaus, hotel. These give structure to the whole setting, their "role" apparently rather predefined. On the other, there are the pavilions, whose function seems to be less structurally fixed. Indeed, as explained, those responsible for their activities initially found it difficult to develop a strategy of what to do with them. It is not that they do not have any predefined sense, that they are the result of pure chance, but, as Uhlig (2000: 10) puts it, their sense is defined not by the Autostadt itself, but by external, somewhat larger paradigms. Each of the pavilions is an individual statement of heterogeneity, an inherent opposition to any homogeneity in the spatial structure. This points to a tendency of media architecture to open up itself to externalities, thereby creating a heterogeneity that has the capacity to deconstruct any sense of local urban coherence.

The heterogeneity of Anting New Town is, due to its own characteristics, even more fundamental. As a "German town", it has been conceived as an internal contradiction to the eclecticism of Shanghai. Inwardly, it is harmonious – modernist architecture, Bauhaus-influenced, just what master planner Albert Speer Jr. considered as typically German. The building blocks of different heights and colours indeed bear close similarities with mid-size German towns; "it nearly seems to be organically grown" (Siemons 2006: 41). Even significant parts of the urban technology have been imported from Germany – for instance, environmental protection measures such as an elaborate energy-saving program.

Externally, however, Anting New Town is producing a new layer of heterogeneity in Shanghai – simply by being explicitly "un-Chinese". It confronts the Chinese people with the ultimate outside, thereby evoking a sense that being Chinese is combined with a certain lack. However, from an urban viewpoint, the fact that this lack is transformed into a competitive advantage (as I have explained in Chapter 4) renders all questions of urban authenticity irrelevant. Everything that exists in Anting does so as an image in the Deleuzian sense. With the domination of the image, Anting is not so much a deviation from Autostadt Wolfsburg and BMW Welt, but rather develops their functional mechanisms further (rhizomatically). Autostadt Wolfsburg also plays with stereotypes of national identity, pulling national characteristics of Czech or Spanish architecture and city-building into its gates, thereby undermining all potential notions of national purity.

*Inside/outside*

In this sense, Anting New Town is also indicative of a new relationship between the notions of inside and outside. Its sense of inside/outside is unique, and at the same time puts a new twist to Sloterdijk's idea of "foam city" as a hyper-interior.

Foam city, one of Sloterdijk's core concepts of the urbanization processes implicated in his Schaum metaphor of the post-globalized world, pulls everything inside its own premises. It is thereby creating a "Makro-Schaum" which functions in urban space as a collector and connector (Sloterdijk 2004: 655). It collects and connects people – while at once limiting their opportunities for social participation. In this respect, Sloterdijk is critical of the utopian architectural models of the 1960s and 1970s, in particular of the situationists (the ideas of which have been employed by other poststructuralist cultural thinkers, such as Tschumi or Derrida). Sloterdijk's vision of the urban sees potential for creativity, but is sceptical regarding many situationists' expectations of the revolutionary effects of the urban model. He outlines this scepticism by orienting to the ideas proposed by painter and architectural visionary Constant. In his model "New Babylon" Constant develops a vision of the urban that essentially envisions what Sloterdijk (ibid.: 662) calls a "kollektiven Fließraum", a space of the free flow. In this space, everybody is an artist, an installation artist, and at the same time an element on a grand, overarching installation.

Sloterdijk does not believe in this utopian optimism. His global inside rather poses a universal threat: the threat of exclusion. The idea of a threatening outside enables, but also limits, internal creativity. The relationship between repetition, mimesis and innovation remains unclear (ibid: 663). In this sense, Sloterdijk's conceptualization of a collector-connector space also points to limitations of notions of the creative city, which have informed a lot of urban politics in the 1990s (Doevendans and Schram 2005: 29–37). This network space of unlimited creativity, miraculously at once creating an economic surplus, seems naïve to him.

Sloterdijk's processes of collection and connection work through pulling the most diverse elements inside (collecting and connecting) as much as through constantly redefining what is the outside. Thereby, inside and outside can coexist on one level, even in one physical space. In Sloterdijk's perspective, the permanent redetermination of what is inside is the core of capitalist urban development. Branding in particular has the capacity to include and exclude.

Anting New Town is indicative of this process. It is inside and outside at once. On the one hand, it is the outside of Shanghai. It is clearly positioned at its suburbs, indicatively set away from the famous hypercapitalist inner city places such as the Bund. What is more, by displaying an artificial Germanness, it is emphasizing its distinctively non-Chinese, extra-Chinese character.

But at the same time, it is supposed to function as an initiator of real change (inside). With change being the very core of today's Shanghai, Anting New Town's unique character makes it on a process-based level very much a part of the city. It is supposed to offer certain change-enabling functions for the whole city and its people (Siemons 2006: 41). Apparently, the officials' idea is to transform and "educate" Shanghai's citizens through the assumed features of Germany or of German cars (reliability, etc.), and the creation of a proto-German showcase helps spread this idea.

In sum, there is an ambivalence in Anting New Town between openness and closure, between its orientation towards its inside and its outside.

This double characteristic of inward- and outward-oriented buildings, conceptualized by Uhlig (2000) as one of structure and event, distinguishes brand space from classical modernity. There is no longer one formula of construction, one overarching urban principle that drives the way every building is built and works. Instead, there is an interplay of forces of inclusion and exclusion, which bears the possibility of conflict. And the contrast between the two perspectives is made obvious by the design of individual buildings.

An example of the peculiar arrangements of notions of inside and outside within Autostadt is the spatial position of the restaurants. They are inside buildings, but at the same time outside the concepts of the individual pavilion. They are internal disruptions of the stages the pavilions create. This is particularly evident regarding the Italian restaurant in the ZeitHaus. Positioned on the ground floor, its walls left and right are formed by the exhibition spaces of the two worlds of the pavilion (analogue and digital). The visitor has to leave the exhibition space to enter the restaurant, which nevertheless is in the same building. One is outside the exhibition area and inside the restaurant. But at the same time, this creates an uncomfortable feeling, for the exhibition content is almost "lurking", leaving the restaurant with an almost claustrophobic atmosphere. The visitors I talked to all complained that the restaurant was "too loud". And loud it was; but this noise came significantly from the exhibitions. It was, one could say, the noise of the content that lurks just around the corner.

In this way, when content becomes physical as is the case in brand spaces, this transforms the relationship the visitors have towards this content, ultimately creating a specific kind of "intensive space" (Lash and Lury 2007: 30). Intensity here is generated by the visitors – through their perception of, and affection by, content. They do not just read content, but perceive it – potentially even as a threat. This notion of a content as threat is part of what Kwinter (2001: 15) analyzes as new forces in contemporary architecture. For him, architecture from modernism onwards is being properly understood in connection with "a system of force that give shape and rhythm to the everyday life of the body". The visitors and their entire capabilities to be affected become part of the process set in motion by the building and by the "content-ionality" *of* the building.

The functioning of this content-ionality depends on the personal time of the visitor ("seen this already" vs. "first-time visitor"). Furthermore, brand space indeed applies a system of rhythm to concrete bodies here, through the intense use of music, sound and other audiovisual elements. Brand space is about moving as much as about seeing; it combines perception, affection and movement. This is why it is possible, as I will do in the next chapter, to conceptualize brand space as a space of the mass ornament. It creates ornamental structures that drag bodies or body parts into an assemblage that supposedly carries, or rather develops, a specific relevance for the brand. The actualization of brands in space takes place *through* the creation of such mass ornaments.

## The topology of competition

The architectural initiation of these mass ornaments effectively results in a new abstract paradigm for urban reality and development: the paradigm of competition. This paradigm evolves in the first instance topographically; the Autostadt pavilions are built in more or less equal distance from each other. This topographical starting point, however, develops topological reality (Günzel 2008b: 9). It is as if each pavilion is given its own force field, the opportunity to develop a life of its own, its own ornamental features, and a residual order not to conflict too drastically with another pavilion. But this does not neutralize potential interactions. Their position in relative proximity towards each other forces the visitor to compare, and to see each pavilion as a contrast to all the others. In a Foucauldian setting of hyper-visibility, almost every pavilion can be seen from every other pavilion. What is more, the outline of Autostadt as a whole provides the power play between the pavilions with a frame. ZeitHaus, hotel, piazza are like visitors at the outside of the game of powers between the individual brand pavilions. One gets the impression of viewing a kind of sports event.[6] The space where the pavilions are positioned is the playing field. Within it, every pavilion tries to capture as much attention as possible.

Competition in this way actualized in urban space is indicative of the topological relevance of Sloterdijk's Schaum concept (cf. van Tuinen 2007: 48–50). In Chapter 3, I have outlined why the idea of Schaum is a suitable tool for the analysis of the interaction of different capitalist companies. With the Autostadt pavilions this thought can be extended, showing that Schaum allows for a more thorough grasp not only of capitalist activity, but in particular of capitalism's desire for spatialization and the strategic role it assigns to architecture; architecture is the way in which companies compete in a capitalism that is defined by the functionality of Schaum.

This leads to an understanding of the city that is informed, but influenced, by the capitalist paradigm of competition. Autostadt brings competition to the city. The idea of a coherent urban structure is broken up by juxtaposing different architectural bases, resulting in a collision of perspectives. Autostadt is a playground of different architectural monoliths. Similarly, BMW Welt is an architectural statement within an area made up by architectural monoliths.

This idea of an "architecture of competition" puts significant pressure on the managers involved in brand space. Maria Schneider of Autostadt, for instance, claimed that right from the start she wanted the managers responsible for the pavilions to start their own cultural initiatives. Also, Schneider told me that visitors are supposed to engage with the pavilions in as active a way as possible. A similar program is at play in BMW Welt, where different business units had to develop their own architectural and design-focused representation concepts. One might argue that there is a vague idea that the claim "stadt" is not only an interesting statement, but also awakes social expectations. The problem is not so much that brand spaces are simulations right from the start, but that if they don't develop their own dynamism, something one might call urban "life", then they will be seen as pseudo-urban imitation. Even from a poststructuralist, process-based urbanist perspective, one can argue that if process makes reality, then the degree of process is what distinguishes reality from mere simulation.

The pressure put upon the marketing managers implies in terms of topology that each pavilion is the actualization of a strategy developed in respect to the other pavilions. The pavilions thereby spatialize the competitive capitalist spirit in general, and even more so as structures of competition are not limited to the city builders, but are understood and enacted by visitors as well. The visitor, different from the citizen of a traditional city, will compare. When I asked a visitor who just left Autostadt the (rather neutral) question "What do you think?" he immediately started to compare: "I liked Lamborghini most". Hence, this kind of competition-informed city-building is a central feature that brand spaces integrate in the development of the urban sphere. In as much as brands become prevalent as city-building forces, this will transform the way in which cities develop and are being perceived.

## *Urbanity of counterforces and the mediatization of decay*

The urbanist presence of the notion of competition points to an intense play of counterforces in brand space. This pertains not only to architecture as such. If the engagement of visitors is what makes the difference between successfully and unsuccessfully competing pavilions, the content offered *and* the interactive processes allowed for are other levels of competition, or of the clashing of counterforces in space. And also the aforementioned antagonism between architecture and content can be reread in this respect. Uhlig (2000: 11) claims that the "architecture parlante" of brand space defines a middle ground between "Ausplaudern und Verschweigen", between telling everything and remaining silent. This middle ground, however, is not always kept, but makes way for a parallel presence of both, *Ausplaudern* and *Verschweigen*, noise and quietness – in a very concrete sense; there is an inherent contrast between the relative quiet and peacefulness of the outskirts of Autostadt and the sometimes loud, always intense goings-on in the pavilions. With BMW Welt, this contrast works differently because the architecture is more expressive. Still, in both places, architecture seems to be questioning the content and thereby also the concept of content. Vice versa, one can argue that through the confrontation of display and architecture, brand space turns into what Read (2000: 324) calls *liminal space*, reflecting upon the limits of architecture, and upon the fact that architecture today is always inherently connected to process.

This *liminal* and *conflictual* character of brand space, or space of new media, is becoming even more evident if we look at the ultimate outside of conscious architecture: decay and dirt. In order to understand this, we have to recapitulate that this work aims at treating space as a new medium in

Kittler's sense. For Kittler, noise and disturbance are integral parts of new media. In brand space, these disturbances obtain a visible presence, although many caretakers ensure that, compared to a normal inner-city place, Autostadt and BMW Welt appear to be clean and aseptic. There are, of course, trash bins at every corner. But the cleanliness is never complete; there is always the abandoned Coke can or wrapping-paper.

In brand space, the fact that no one expects it there provides the individual piece of litter with a stronger, symbolic presence, turning it into what Lash and Lury (2007: 166) call an "object-event". Similarly, the fact that parents might ask their children not to throw things away actually draws attention to the existence of litter. The same holds true for the pavilions as soon as they show even the slightest signs of decay, or get dirty. As with litter in general, the dirt or the occasional missing brick in a façade has a stronger presence than dirt on buildings in general. It is becoming the white noise that interferes with the mediation processes the brand-building companies aspire to.

In this sense, dirt, mediated through its very character as *the outside*, is part of the overall mediatization of brand space. It is to new media space what the virus is to the internet: an anti-force that at the same time obtains a perverted role as a productive element.[7]

In Anting New Town this "virus" has obtained an even more significant presence. Despite being so new, the city is full of architectural mistakes and cracks in all kinds of walls. The place is already ageing catastrophically, although it is not even fully inhabited. In our interview, Johannes Dell explicitly complained about the missing sense of quality in China. When we follow his interpretation of poor quality as a sign of Chinese-ness, then this adds a new level to the internationality of the image of China developed in Anting New Town. This internationality is so bound on change that it does not bother to really "build like" Germans; it is satisfied that the results of the building process look vaguely German. From this perspective, this architectural "freedom of low quality" is not a problem, but proof of the strength of the "new China".

Hence, litter or other disturbances have their place in brand space, by obtaining a mediatized hyperpresence. Just as objects in brand space become media, so do these kinds of counter-objects or small-scale object deformations.

*Iconic abstraction in brand space*

The abstraction strategies transformed by the presence of dirt in brand space are mirrored on another level by a very different spatial force of abstraction: the logic of iconization. The main driver of the architectural iconization in brand space is the logo. The idea of the logo reflects the problematic relationship between content and matter in architecture. Here, architecture is turning more abstract, in a way very different from the abstractions created by the implication of symbolic meaning carriers. The abstract (the logo) is becoming part of the concrete (the building).

106  *Virtualizing the actual of space*

The logo is the link between product and brand world. It is the transcendent that is connecting the consumer to the world outside her physical experience, and also to a whole history that has not been her own before, but is now (Lury 2004, Chapter 4). In brand space, the logo becomes a step towards a new understanding of architecture. This is particularly true when the logo becomes form and obtains a physical reality by being transformed into a concrete building.

An early example for this was the former NatWest tower in the City of London (Wright 2006: 135). Seen from above, the skyscraper, completed in 1981, resembles the corporate logo of NatWest. With the three chevrons in a hexagonal arrangement, British architect Richart Seifert effectively documented the transformation of the City of London from a rather secluded place to a prime spot in the global finance industry, an industry that can be seen as a twin industry to branding, driving global capitalism just as much as the activities of the big advertising conglomerates.

In Autostadt, there is another example of such logo-becoming-architecture. The Audi pavilion is three-dimensionally playing with the motif of the ring, a central feature of the brand Audi. The pavilion uses the company's logo as a background for an architectural project. The building *is* the logo, and visitors entering the building now know that they are an integral part of the branded mass ornament.

The question is what this means for the concept of the logo. I have outlined earlier that in terms of Peircian semiotics the logo is on the one hand a symbol, while at the same time constantly working on the levels of the index and the icon, through qualities and similarity as well as through existential connections between sign and object (Lury 2003: 78). Hence, what exactly the logo as symbol "means" is permanently changing. This points to a very specific way in which different semiotic levels are combined by this new architectural actuality of the logo. Through becoming actualized in a physical building, the logo as symbol *is becoming* at once indexical and iconic. Parts of the indexical and iconic processes that make up the logo as symbol are now happening *in the logo itself*, because they are taking place in an architectural setting. The three levels of the sign are thereby collapsing together. More radically, one can even see this as a collapsing of the world of the symbolic altogether. The logo as symbol is somehow becoming a ruin, with "the real" entering it. The real is conquering the symbolic.

### *Logo and ruin: pop art and Ed Ruscha*

Understood in this way, logos have the capacity to thoroughly shape urban life. In order to understand the ways in which they do so, I will now deploy insights from art, in particular from certain core paintings from pop art. Pop art was the first artistic style to reflect intensely the three-dimensionality of logos and in particular their tendency to obtain ruin-related characteristics. Since the early 1960s, pop art has engaged with logo's ever-increasing presence in the post-war landscape, particularly in the US (Osterwold 2003: 12). In the present context of the transformations of urbanity through spaces of new media, this engagement demonstrates on the one hand the strong impact logos have on urban experience when replicated. It also indicates logos' particular capacity to weave themselves into the urban fabric. Their two-dimensionality is always on the verge of becoming three-dimensional. And the mediation of the urban sphere makes the city even more prone to become subjected to the spatialization processes of logos.

From an arts perspective, this has been visible in a lot of pop art works (Andy Warhol, Jasper Johns, etc.). Perhaps more than any other artist, Californian painter Ed Ruscha developed an intensive engagement with the spatial qualities of logos. In particular logos from the world of Hollywood and the film industry are the material for many of his works (Schwartz 2010: 99–100).

One of the best-known examples is certainly the 1962 oil on canvas work *Large Trademark with Eight Spotlights* (ibid.: 66–67). The logo of iconic film studio Twentieth Century Fox is presented in this work in an equally hyperreal and spatial way. Schwartz (ibid.: 68) points out that the logo here obtains an unusual monumentality. It does so because it conveys qualities of a painted building, a large-space architectural structure three stories high that can be walked through, or rather, climbed, and that offers shelter as much as shadow in the shining light of the spotlights at the back of the logo-building.

The spatiality in this picture is contrasted with an equally present spirit of movement. The logo develops a very peculiar relationship with notions of speed and stillness. On the one hand, its monumentality evokes a sense of heaviness, stability and inflexibility. On the other, its diagonal tail on the right of the picture can be seen as an infinite street, which would then make the logo itself the carrier of this street structure (reminiscent of a Los Angeles freeway, most of which in fact run one level above ground). Or it can be interpreted as the result of the logo's extremely fast movement forward. Then the whole scenery would be reminiscent of the movement of a high speed train. Both interpretations point to a close connection between the logo and the notion of movement. From Ed Ruscha's (and, by extension, pop art's) viewpoint, the logo seems to be an element in the reconfiguring of space in which movement remains the only invariant.

At the same time, Ruscha's use of the logo of a film company is of course not a coincidence. As an Angelino, he was intrigued by the culture of the Hollywood system, and like other LA pop artists reflected on this culture in many of his works (ibid.: 69). Furthermore, he seems to be intent on developing an understanding of the relationship between branding and the Hollywood system. To him, branding seems to be connected to the functioning mechanisms of Hollywood. The permanent creation of fantasies by the Hollywood system is presented in Ruscha's work as the foundation and inner core of the workings of brand culture and the brand-driven economy.

From this perspective, it is merely consequential to present as the paradigmatic brand that of a film studio. If brands are striving on the dynamic production and reproduction of human fantasies, Ruscha seems to imply, then the ultimate brand is that of a firm that is producing nothing but these fantasies. The Hollywood studio is a brand that thrives on the strength of these fantasies alone. It is the brand behind all branding.

In order to investigate the power of these meta-brands, and the power of the logo, Ruscha, who also has been working repeatedly with photographic representations of West Coast vernacular architecture, looks at their engagement with space. It is by creating concrete spatial structures that Ruscha manages to demonstrate how logos are defining and structuring the urban real. At the same time, certain details in his paintings, like the strong presence of the spotlights in the 1962 work, show that urban reality is unreadable without laying open what defines perspectives and the gaze of the viewer. It is the spotlights (perhaps a symbolic reference to the film industry as such) that define visibility and readability. But all that these spotlights see and therefore make readable are signs. These signs exist only in order to be found by the spotlight. They are signs that do not signify.[8] Hence, Ruscha is clearly interested in developing a critical perspective towards Hollywood and branding – while at the same time being sceptical regarding the degree to which this kind of criticism is still possible.

All this notwithstanding, the ways in which Ruscha presents logos in many of his works engage with the logo's spatiality by clearly searching for their dark sides and for their inherent contradictions. Spatiality for Ruscha is a tool to convey these contradictions. The most poignant demonstration of this is offered in some of his works focusing on the most iconic of all Hollywood-related signs: the Hollywood sign itself. While not really a corporate logo, the sign is arguably the most powerful and iconic of all logos, setting the limit for the possible power of logos. The Hollywood sign is the meta-logo. Ruscha presents this meta-logo not in the two-dimensional matter-of-factness in which it is usually conveyed in photos or movies (seen from central Hollywood or downtown Los Angeles). Instead, he often offers a perspective from which the sign's spatial structure becomes visible: the scaffolding, the pipes (for instance, in the 1969 *Hollywood Study #8*; cf. Schwartz 2010: 102–110). In other works, he looks at it from the back (*The Back of Hollywood*; ibid.: 109). Each of these works, besides their obvious critical undertones regarding the shallowness of the Hollywood industry, is also intrigued by the spatiality of the logo. Each of them investigates the three-dimensionality of the Hollywood sign. Hence, painting as a two-dimensional medium here manages to engage with the three-dimensionality of a sign that in three-dimensional reality is always seen as a two-dimensional being.

Through spatializing the perspective on the Hollywood sign, the latter is derived of its overwhelming and over-lit iconic clarity. It is questioned and demystified. Just as spatial reality demystified the logo in the 1960s through material decay and logistical lack of sufficient care, and in 1932 by actress Peggy Entwistle committing suicide by jumping off the "H" of the sign, Ruscha demystifies it by pointing out its unglamorous and fragile spatial structure. Through the use of dark colour, Ruscha investigates the ruin-related character of the sign, which might be read as an indication of a tendency towards ruin in any spatialized logo.

If we follow Ruscha on this, then it indicates that spatialized logos have an inherent tendency to become ruin.[9] The cases of brand space I analyze here offer vivid examples for this. Particularly, this ruin-ization process seems to be reflected by the way in which Autostadt deals with the Audi logo. The logo is not exposed 1:1. From above, one does not see the four rings that form the Audi logo, but three (two bigger rings at the edges, a smaller one in the centre). From the perspective of the visitor, one sees one or two rings. The logo is deconstructed, "ruin-ed" architecturally. Thereby, the association "Audi logo" is irritated. The visitor is alienated and thereby made to live and feel the complexity of the virtual–actual relationship of brands.

The connection of logo and architecture is one of experiential abstraction. The logo as such is an abstraction of the physical product and the consumer. The latter's experience is enhanced, but also derived from its matter-of-factness. "Abstract experience" (Goffey 2008: 15) is created through the absence of the ultimate end of all brand work: consumption. The visitor to brand space is no longer just consuming any one product, which is the process in which capitalism would normally become concrete. In fact, not much is consumed in BMW Welt or Autostadt at all. It is rather difficult to buy much there. There are souvenir stores, but one does not get the impression that the whole visit is directed towards a culmination in shopping. Autostadt in particular is about brands, but it wants to avoid any impression of being a shopping sphere. Creative Director Maria Schneider repeatedly emphasized this in our conversations (Schneider 2007). The closest it gets to actually engaging with a purchasing process is when buyers pick up their cars, but the handing-over process above in fact seems intent on avoiding anything resembling a sales procedure. What is more, only a minority of the visitors to Autostadt or BMW Welt actually come to pick up their new car. The majority are just visitors. For them, the visit is in no way connected to shopping, which effectively creates a vectorial experience (Goffey 2008: 24) – the experience of an absence, of even of the capitalist abstraction process itself.

## The subjectivities of brand immersion

By creating such an abstract and in a sense post-consumerist urban setting, brand space has strong transformational effects on the possibility of human subjectivity. It creates affects, thereby changing everything (and potentially everyone) it connects through them. We can understand this through Klein's "immersion" concept (Klein 2003). Essentially, immersive spaces suck the human in, using multiple perspectives (spatial as well as historical) to create irritations, but also to affect us (ibid.: 59).

In immersive space, perspectives are continuously going awry, and there is no distinction between foreground and background structuring of the human experience and creating a sense of topological knowing and security. For example, the idea to transform London's former Millennium Dome, today an entertainment district sponsored by telecommunications provider $O_2$, into a huge $O_2$ logo (Kleinman 2005) would clearly have had shattering effects on learned urban perspective. If the tent had become the "O", this would have reproduced the logo in vast and *shocking* dimensions (Lash 2001: 219). What is more, different from the Audi pavilion in Autostadt or the NatWest tower, the "$O_2$", as the arena is simply called, also undermines any notion even of an explicitly capitalist urban perspective by occupying an area formerly run down and explicitly non-symbolic (therefore, one should guess, not fit for capitalist hyper-expressive building). In this context, the presence of strategically motivated brand architecture necessarily develops unsettling effects.

At the same time as irritating, however, immersive space is highly addictive; it not only offers the comfort of entertainment, which makes people effectively want to be tricked (Klein 2003: 97). It also develops a strange promise of bodily transformation. People seem to be willing to immerse themselves, linking their own body to a larger structure, even if it means losing control, as this is perceived as a way to corporeal self-extension. Immersive space is satisfying this desire for self-extension through being immersed.

An example of how brand space integrates the idea of immersion into its construction right from the start is the complex way in which the Skoda pavilion in Autostadt has been constructed (explained in Chapter 2). We need not discuss here whether the mental model that was the basis of this design process is simplistic, or whether it can be generalized. What should be noted is that the pavilion architecture is the reflection of an intellectual process. By becoming-architecture, this process is broadened in its effects, now encompassing the whole of the visitor. They are not just asked to "think about" experience, nor simply invited to "make" the experiences laid out here (learning, experience, reflection). Visitors are forced to "immerse" themselves into this process and the abstract categories that lie at the heart of it, because these categories are adopting architectural form. They immerse themselves into an intellectual abstraction.

The idea of an architectural immersion in Klein's writing is connected with another highly complex concept – that of the "frame" (Klein 2003: 60). In a logic similar to Deleuze and Guattari's de- and reterritorialization, immersive space works in close interaction with the frame as a conceptual counterpart that is also producing illusions (ibid.). Framed space works through creating a situation of architecture-induced media consumption, including a screen or a monitor. As I have shown in the previous chapter, brand spaces and in particular BMW Welt create situations for a thoroughly architectural media consumption. The subsequent immersive experience has the capacity to occupy the subject's entire sensory field (Mitchell

2005: 184). All bodily as well as psychological human functions are pulled into the situation.

These immersion frames have the potential to transform spatialized or urbanized human subjectivity. A central media-architectural tool in this context is the screen. In framed space, the individual is subject to an omnipresent screen-ization. It is impossible to determine precisely where a screen ends and sheer physicality begins. The architectural surface is one huge potential screen. This creates what Mitchell (ibid.: 185) calls a situation of "endless shifts of attention and engagement throughout the reaches of space and time".

In BMW Welt, the immersion of the visitors is taken to a new level through a framing of the visitor by screens. Monitors and screens are creating a sense of walking through (a landscape of) monitors. One is not standing in front of the screens, but is always inbetween them. There are countless explanation monitors, many of course interactive, where the visitor can get answers to questions he presumably has. Their omnipresence doubles the immersion through the architectural setting. First, the visitor is confronted with a process of immersion, thereby being sucked into the architectural and design-related setting. Then, this situation is transformed by the presence of the screen, pointing towards a world of knowledge that is not one of the concrete space that immersed the visitor. The screen is pointing to the presence of an outside. Hence, its almost brutal presence leaves the visitor in a disposition of permanent insecurity.

This disposition is increased by the fact, outlined in Chapter 4, that many screens deliberately refrain from performing the basic mediation task of informing. At the time of my visit, many offered stills of technological details, like paintings. What exactly is shown by these stills remains unclear to the visitor, just like the perspectives and the size of the objects. All this is what Klein calls the monumentalization of "technology through wonder" (ibid.). Technology is not explained, but treated as an aesthetic fact. And the visitor does not seem to expect more. When I asked visitors what they saw, they could not explain. Responding to the question whether they were satisfied, they answered yes, irritated by my question.

In terms of information, screens in BMW Welt can be argued to be deliberately under-performing; they do not *in*form – but form. The monitor and screen are not present as an informational element on top of architecture and design, but rather built-in; it is pure design. In terms of medium, it can be described as a media icon, representing the idea of media as such, rather than tools for the distribution of information. The non-informational screen is primarily a physical object, matter. It is on a small scale repeating the logic of brand space as such: that medium and matter are collapsing together, are becoming one. In this sense, brand space can be seen as the combination of Klein's concepts of immersion and framing. What is more, it also refers back to Kittler and his concept of all media becoming material in a world of new media.

## Normalization and openness

The question of what this idea of an immersive urban activity means for the possibility of subject creation is a political one, relating to issues of social and individual control. Klein understood his work on the electronic baroque as a political contribution. He is critical throughout, even if obviously fascinated by the creative and imaginative ways through which the electronic baroque becomes a producer of scripted places. For Klein, spatialized immersion and framing as two forms of what he terms "scripted space" are significantly elements of social and political control (Klein 2003: 19). Scripted space "gives us the illusion that we have control over our entertainment, while it encourages us to give up control" (ibid.: 65).

In brand space, this logic is applied. In all three spaces, there is an element of control and of expected human behaviour, made visible by the omnipresence of cameras and of service people. In Autostadt, the entrance fee is an additional element of social control.

In this sense, they are in line with developments of city branding as analyzed by Moor (2007), in that both "intervene in the visual and material culture of a place in order to work on the feelings, perceptions, attitudes and self-image of the existing population" (ibid.: 76). And yet, as Moor has also shown, the normalization taking place in brand space is always incomplete. It depends on the degree to which, and the sense with which, visitors are immersed at a given moment. This relates to the topic of attention. Crary (1999) develops a political theory of attention, showing how modernization and the management of subjects' attention went hand in hand and were co-productive in the shaping of subjectivities. Similar to Klein, Crary offers a political perspective, based on a notion of the political founded on "non-coercive forms of power" (ibid.: 74). Central to these power forms is the breakdown of an experiential whole into different individual, isolated elements. Hence, the "normative conceptions of attention intersected with problems of cognitive and perceptual *synthesis*" (ibid.: 79, italics in the original). What is created through this partial breakdown of the sensual and identity-related synthesis of the modern subject is a subjectivity that is, by means of certain sensual offerings, dragged out of its inwardness as conceptualized by Hegel ("in sich gehen"). The modern subject is always characterized by an externalized subjectivity.

In order to understand the incomplete normalization of the subject in brand space it makes sense to look at the offerings of interactivity. Interactivity there pertains to all ways used to create links between visitor and space beyond the purely visual. Even though brand spaces are clearly less interactive than classical fun parks, interaction is a conceptual element there. For instance, visitors to the ZeitHaus had the opportunity to grow their own small plant for a while. There was a laboratory-style arrangement with a small flower bed. Visitors were invited to type in their names, whereupon a small robot arm would automatically plant a new seed into the bed. Back home, one could follow the growth of the personal flower online.

Of course, this kind of interaction is a strongly regulated one, and transports notions of *good behaviour*. What is more, such offerings of interactivity also create a symbolic link between the visitor and (the brands of) Autostadt even after the visit. The visitor has to *check back* later to see what his productive activity at Autostadt did afterwards. He is *part of* Autostadt now, he is thereby implicitly told.

And yet, the externality of the subject in media space and the social control pattern established by interaction offerings involuntarily allow for counter-strategies. The poststructuralism of brand space also implies an inclusion of both a strong play of power *and* opportunities to escape this power momentarily (Amin and Thrift 2002: 106). Specifically, turning back inward is one way of not being completely normalized by strategies of subjectivity externalization. This behavioural pattern of resistance is based on the mechanism of partial psychological closure. What is more, even the connection of an external, say, design-related, offering with something unforeseen by the external agency is a permanent opportunity to develop modes of resistance (one can simply counter a design strategy by confronting it with different designs). And finally, as much as a potential normalization effort pertains to one particular sense, the inclusion or activity of another sense can also be seen as subversive.

What is more, even though this might sound trivial, the visitor has the opportunity not to engage in the forms of interaction offered. He can say "this is not for me", or not pay attention (Crary 1999). Just as any representation strategy or strategic imaginary is subject to contestation by those who feel excluded or "at the margin of the dominant imaginary" (Bridge and Watson 2001: 351), brand-space offerings are sometimes refused, thereby allowing for processes of momentary self-definition through not supporting a certain representation or an invitation to participate.

This points to patterns of subversion initiated by not paying "proper" attention. Similarly, in terms of Crary, one can also pay "too much attention" thereby disrupting any normalization system. In Autostadt, the sometimes far from clean sight and smell of the ponds drew the attention of the visitors, who photographed them. Apparently, their heightened level of attention with its willingness to accept everything in Autostadt as a medium in this case turned against the spatial strategy. All these are of course not big time "system disruptions", but instances of the unforeseen, bound to occur once such an experience-promising architectural area is constructed.

Another factor in the context of normalization is the incomplete exclusionary system at work. As all mass-market-directed consumer activities, brand space is democratic in a limited way in the sense that in principle everybody can enter. BMW Welt and Anting New Town are accessible for free, Autostadt asks for a modest if not insignificant fee. There are no obvious control mechanisms preventing, say, poor people, or any kind of nationality or ethnicity. However, Autostadt's formally dressed service ladies and the entry gates greeting the visitors may be seen as exclusionary, as creating what Bridge and Watson (2001: 357) call the "tacit rule of contact". So do the guards in Anting New Town, part of a private police, positioned at the entry to the area. They are exerting a Foucauldian control power by simply watching.

In terms of nationality or race, there is no apparent exclusionary regime. During my visits to both Autostadt and BMW Welt, I always encountered numerous young guides or service people of Asian or African-American background. The presence of these multiethnic guides actually appears to emphasize a certain forced internationalism, creating a hyper-multinational model world. Compared to the not particularly multinational city of Wolfsburg, Autostadt appears to be a transnational dreamland. Hence, the virtualization of urban space through brands is also a trans-nationalization. This of course holds true to an even greater extent for Anting New Town. There, in the German town, trans-nationalization is an explicit part of the concept.

## The creation of brand citizens

The complex normalization regime outlined above implies questions regarding the levels of self-expression or self-transcendence media space allows for. As Bridge and Watson (2001: 358) write, quoting Sennett, the role of the city is "to provide a credible space for performative encounter without threat in which self-identification can be transcended". Hence, urban space is the space of individuality-transcendence and change more than of finding and living a fixed individuality. In this context, it can be argued that brand space is developing a very specific urbanity, triggering different expressions of individuality. People who enter Autostadt or BMW Welt are promised an outstanding (and therefore potentially self-changing) experience. Regarding Anting New Town, the allusions to German culture might be interpreted as an offer to transform the national identity of the Chinese inhabitants as well as the expats. They are offered the idea of Germanness as a background for personal transformation. On the other hand, their national identity (as well as that of potential German inhabitants) is openly put into question.

If brand space creates a version of the urban as proto-capitalist expressive and identity-changing space, then the landscape design of Anting New Town and Autostadt seems to support this point. Both areas are characterized by a lot of empty open space, free to different expressions of momentary individuality. This specific spatiality seems to articulate a social expectation for such expressions. In Anting, there are park areas and small squares, a structure very untypical for Chinese town planning, which invites citizens to be part of what is apparently considered typical German mid-town life. Autostadt is criss-crossed by paths and narrow streets that provide ample space for different behavioural modes. This highly artificial space is also a space of highly artificial communicative encounters.

My empirical observations indicate that such communicative processes indeed occur. These are places where, to quote the well-known Sennett idea, strangers do meet. When observing some of the Autostadt alleys for an hour I noticed several conversations between complete strangers. When I asked members of one family what they had discussed with another family, they explained to me that they exchanged views on the Lamborghini cars, and on the question whether one would actually want to own a Lamborghini. "We all agreed that this kind of car is not for us", a father of two explained to me. Autostadt seems to create a social setting in which a) social interaction is possible and encouraged by the setting, b) social interaction even with strangers takes place and c) social interaction is directed towards a discourse on products and brands.

But of course, after temporarily adopting the identity of an active brand citizen and brand critic, visitors return home. Hence, the possibility of individual expression and communication between strangers should not be seen as an argument for a strengthened new subjectivity. Rather, branded capitalist urbanity should be analyzed regarding its capacity to change and desubstantialize subjectivities.[10] This permanence of subject transformations in contemporary urban space makes brand space indicative of a distinctly poststructuralist geography (cf. Murdoch 2006: 10).

## Subjectivity and conflicting modes of experience

As a thoroughly mediatized urban phenomenon, brand space is creating a new way in which urban space is *experienced*. Specifically, the idea of a new, light and temporary (pseudo-) brand citizenship is characterized by a high degree of *experiential potentiality*. It is the potentiality of experiences as existing somewhere within the consumer that is given new space through the concept of the brand when played out physically. An offer is made to intensify, and intellectually enrich, physical experiences in urban space, to create opportunities for affects. The same experience now means more, or promises to mean more. Every sound, every view, every individual piece of steel suddenly has the potential, and indeed is expected, to trigger an affect.

Affect in this context is connected to the production of what I want to call "synaesthetic abstraction". Contrary to theories sympathizing with the social appeal of an "everyday life", it would be wrong to assume that we are increasingly resistant towards urban influences of the nose, ears and eyes of the body. On the contrary: media space actually makes us *want* and *expect* them. We open our body fully to the urban, in order to immerse ourselves *by* acting on a synaesthetic register. Capitalism has taught us to be ready for the urban to communicate with us through our senses. Architecture becomes a medium not so much for information, but for physical impact.

This reconceptualization of experience can be understood even better when we think about what brand space does to our senses. Affect, Massumi writes, is "synaesthetic, implying a participation of the senses in each other" (Massumi 2002: 35). Such an interplay and interaction of different senses without any physical object necessarily in the centre of the attention is what brand-space strategies are aimed at. In the former Bentley pavilion in Autostadt, the visitor was confronted with the smell of leather before seeing it, which caused a sense of contradiction, as the general visual atmosphere in the pavilion was technology-focused rather than earthly. This is the contradictory sensuality that Massumi refers to.

Hence, the synaesthetic experience in media space is not only *abstract*, but also *conflicting*. Brand space creates conflicts between the individual senses. In Anting New Town the smell of Chinese industrial suburbia nearby disturbs the visual impression of a cosy German town. In BMW Welt, the contrast between inside and outside creates an irritation of the visual by a differing regime of visuality.

This permanent possibility of sensual contradiction is a new reality for the mediatized urbanity. Urbanism, then, is arguably moving beyond one core feature of the politics of capitalism: the dominance of the visual (cf. Buck-Morss 1989; Gilloch 1996; Keith 2000). Different senses become dominant at different times. During the many experiences in brand space which effectively isolate one or several senses – from each other, but also from the product as object – it is not the car we perceive and feel, and perhaps not even the brand alone. It is capitalism itself. This generates a very peculiar contradiction; through certain processes of abstraction and of virtualization, capitalism as sensual abstraction itself becomes concrete, and in a way actual.

*Mirror and screen as urban reality*

As a force of externalized cultural intensity, Autostadt seems to be an abstract reflection on what a city can, might or should be. Its concrete topology adds to this. It is piling up along the canal and the rail tracks, with the city centre, including the railway station, shopping district and the new museum Phaeno by Zaha Hadid, starting south of the canal and the tracks, right at the north end of the city. Especially the Phaeno has actually shifted Wolfsburg's centre of gravity north. Apparently, the city is almost *drawn to* the canal, as if attracted by Autostadt as a force of urban magnetism.

North of the railway station, there is the "Mittellandkanal" itself, a completely straight, artificial water line connecting the central German cities of Magdeburg and Brunswick with Hanover and the Ruhr. The canal is the dividing line that draws a clear distinction between the vernacular urban reality (Wolfsburg) and its mediatized counterpart (Autostadt). It thereby functions as an element of mediatization itself; with its straightness and its appearance and history of artificiality, it can be argued to function as a screen. It effectively creates a screening, a display of urban life.

And as urban screen, it is at the same time also functioning as a mirror. In cultural theory, a lot of emphasis has been put on the functioning of the cinema screen as a Lacanian mirror (cf. Elliott 2009: 102–104). In these readings, it has been shown how cinematic representation positions our sense of identity and even constructs subjectivity. This can be said also of Autostadt, which is developing a very specific sense of identity in brand capitalism and brand space. The difference between cinematic mirroring in films and spatial mirroring in brand space is that the latter not only constructs the identities of individual human beings, but that of an urban space. Space itself is negotiated through the spatialized screening and mirroring in Autostadt.

What is more, in the urban context of Autostadt, the screen does not exist a priori, like the cinema screen. Rather, through the construction and positioning of Autostadt the canal is effectively redefined, now functioning as both mirror and screen; it shows to the city of Wolfsburg a version of the ideal city. What this means is that the screen now *is* the mirror; screen and mirror are collapsing together. This is the virtualization effect and at once the very specific shock effect of brand space – it constructs urban structures that function as screen and mirror at once. It thereby actually *extends* the relevance of the concepts of screen and mirror for an understanding of contemporary cultural processes.

The way in which Autostadt realizes its screen and mirror function is not the same as Scott Brown's and Venturi's concept of city-as-mirage (Venturi *et al.* 1972). Even though Venturi and Scott Brown were sympathetic towards Las Vegas, their reading of this paradigmatic urban space always had an element of illusion to it. In Autostadt, the screen is not creating pseudo-urban illusions. Rather, Autostadt is demonstrating to Wolfsburg what certain city processes look like from the distance. It has integrated urbanist concepts fashionable at the time it was built, for instance the idea of a "piazza". (Every large real estate project in the 90s that wanted to be seen as architecturally and socially acceptable had to integrate a piazza of some kind.) It displays to Wolfsburg what an ideal city life would look like (screen). At the same time, it also makes Wolfsburg realize just how far away the city is from this ideal life (mirror).

However, this reflection process is not focused on Wolfsburg alone. Autostadt's play with piazzas and areas of urban hyper-communication is a reflection on the principle of urbanity as such. Brand space as screen-mirror introduces a distinct capitalist subjectivity to the urban sphere. It derives conclusions from what it reflects – from a distinctly capitalist viewpoint. As far as it wants to engage with the concept of city planning, it shows what concepts of "good" and "effective" city planning look like to the capitalist institutions that built the brand space in question. As far as we take the corporation responsible for a brand space as a representative of capitalism as a whole, it exposes what cities look like and are supposed to look like *to the eye of capitalism*. Consequently, this screen/mirror function has very real effects in Wolfsburg. Creative director Maria Schneider mentioned, and seemed to complain about, the fact that the city of Wolfsburg observes closely what is happening in Autostadt, and tries to imitate it. When Autostadt started a certain innovative Christmas market, the city soon did likewise in various other locations. The idea spread virally.

What is more, it can be seen as a reaction to Autostadt's complex, meaning-laden architecture that the city of Wolfsburg had Zaha Hadid build the Phaeno Centre. Positioned directly at the other side of the canal, in an area that used to be more or less empty public space, the Phaeno is a grand architectural gesture, one through which the city of Wolfsburg seems to want to say "I am capable of such gestures, too."

In terms of their architectural principles, the Phaeno engages with Autostadt, but does not imitate it (Meyhöfer 2006). In the latter, the diverse architectural forms in the different pavilions create a sense of heterogeneity and discontinuity. Hadid counters this with an architectural form and building process that is pure continuity. The building is a single entity, made mainly from one material – self-compacting concrete. It appears to be a frozen movement, condensing time towards one eternal moment, whereas Autostadt engages with temporal discontinuity proactively and expressively.

Another comment on Autostadt can be seen in Hadid's use of the ground level. Autostadt architecture emphasizes the ground level as an important place for communication. The walkways outside the pavilions are at ground level, as are most of the displays within the pavilions. Hadid, on the other hand, puts the entire 12,000 square metre exhibition space one level higher. The ground level is dominated by ten conical pilotis. It is deliberately dead space. Gregory (2006) reads this architectural gesture as a criticism of modernist use of ground space in general. More specifically, it can be seen as a scepticism regarding the assumed democratization of the ground level in Autostadt. Hadid seems to challenge the assumption that there could be permanent open communication and free exchange.

It seems arguable that this criticism is not only provoked by the architectural principles dominating Autostadt, but also by the fact that it is brand architecture. Hadid here is developing a critical perspective on any notion of a democratization through capitalism and its emphasis on markets. However, in order to formulate this critique, Hadid has to adopt certain architectural principles from the spatial setting she wants to criticize (a mechanism that is part of many viral media processes).

What this shows is that brand space does not necessarily run the danger of remaining architecturally isolated. More than most other urban spaces, it has the capacity to cause reactions. Its specific virality is defined by the counter-gestures it provokes, like that of Zaha Hadid. It does so not despite, but because of its character as capitalist.

*Architecture image and urban transformation*

As I argued before, brands trigger the production and consumption interaction of images. By doing so, they develop the capacity to change the rationale behind the process of building, initiating a new kind of architectural *controversy*.[11] When becoming urban reality, the presence of brand images in a city alters the character of the urban by pulling individual buildings into an interaction with the brand. While doing so, these buildings become images – in the sense not of meaningless superficiality, but of Tschumi's more thorough understanding of image as a combination of space, action and movement, leading to the generation of substantial (individual and urban) shock (Tschumi 2000: 176). In this sense, then, the brand actually *transforms* urban architecture into an image. This makes it possible for Deleuze to claim that there is no difference between images, things and motion (Deleuze 1995: 42). Brand-influenced urban space is not just proof of this Deleuzian claim; it actually makes it stronger.

This image-driven transformation of the city is connected to the permanent change of subjectivities I described above. For Deleuze, the "human" is no longer the instance that constructs or perceives images, but rather an element *in* the flow of images; it is pulled to the level of the image itself. Images are passed on or stopped; but it does not matter who does this; what matters is always the image as such (Deleuze 1986: 58).

This corresponds with the role Kevin Lynch sees for the subject in the city. He argues that in an image-based urban reality, the individual chooses to work with certain images while rejecting others (Lynch 1960: 11). According to Collins (1995: 35), the "excess of images which makes imageability more complicated than ever before also means that the activity of the perceiver is not simply a matter of recognition of formal contours but a choosing between semiotic alternatives". In the context of a brand city, this choice can be seen as a decision about how to combine the images of certain urban elements with that of the brand. The individual might contrast them, developing some kind of nostalgia for the lost brand-free city of old. She might try and reconcile them, developing an understanding of the urban as not much changed. Or she might develop a new version of the city, one in which the brand is a central key element, thereby accepting the constitutive reality of the brand city. And in this sense, taking Lynch further, I want to acknowledge that the image simultaneously creates the observer and has the capacity to deconstruct her – by allowing for the aforementioned choice-process.

## Shanghai, Anting and the process of "global citying"

It has been claimed above that brand spaces such as Autostadt have the capacity to spread virally. This virality (and virtuality) can certainly be seen in Anting New Town. On the one hand, the place copies certain elements of German living that the arising Chinese middle class apparently finds valuable. On the other hand, Anting is brand space with lines of continuity towards Autostadt Wolfsburg. Anting is virtual, post-national, mediatized space just as is Autostadt. It is often also referred to as "Autostadt Shanghai" or "Autostadt Anting".

The connections between Autostadt Wolfsburg and Anting New Town are interesting in the context of the idea of competition between global cities. Usually, the hyper-energetic urban development of Shanghai is interpreted as sign and even a natural outcome of the Chinese economy's boom. But there is a different way to look at it. Olds and Yeung (2005) argue that Shanghai is a national project, targeted at making the city part of the network of global cities (and of the discourse around global cities, which can be seen as constitutive of the identity of urban spaces, cf. Sassen 1991; King 1991; Brenner and Keil 2005). Olds and Yeung (2005) argue that Shanghai's showcase projects exist primarily to theoretically qualify Shanghai as global city. This thinking reverses the traditional global city argument; it is not that a place is part of so many economic flows as to naturally become a global city and lose its national identity; instead, a place aims at *being seen* as a global city, hence actually strengthening the creation of a transnational identity that perhaps has not even been there before.

Olds and Yeung argue for a culturally grounded understanding of different kinds of global cities. Rather than following them in that direction, I want to take the idea of Shanghai as theoretically global city further. For if becoming a global city is a process, if a kind of "global citying" is at stake, then any kind of global multiplicity in the sense introduced in the introduction of this work will presumably be considered by the initiators as an opportunity. Hence, it does not come as a surprise that Shanghai appears to be taking up the idea and terminology of an "Autostadt" without the original Autostadt actually initiating this. A partial becoming-Autostadt brings Shanghai closer to an identity and public perception as a global city.

In this context, it is interesting to note that the city deals with notions of history in ways similar to Wolfsburg. For Shanghai, notions of historical continuity seem to have become irrelevant (Prakash and Kruse 2008: 5). The only value of the past is to become a source of productive development, as it can be a source of justification for the frantic creation of the new. The fact that Shanghai was a nodal point for global trade in the nineteenth century, for instance, is appropriated a lot in the construction of a narrative of Shanghai's history that is supportive of the image-development of today (Long 2004). This history "has been resurrected as the foundational myth for a new global city" (ibid.: 434). Hence, the past is sucked into the present to be productively appropriated. The new hypercapitalist façade of the city, this permanent look into the future, is adopting a notion of pastness in order to be linked to the present. The promise of a future of economic success and cultural and political as well as economic world relevance is based on a notion of just this relevance to the past.

This appropriation of the past and the future to the needs of the present is one main element providing Shanghai with an arguably virtual character. Brands play a vital role in this process, as they are generating a sense of national pride by demonstrating China's involvement in the word of globalized consumption. In this way, however, they also link the country to the post-nationalization processes of globalization.[12] All current media images and other representations of Shanghai are beaming with logos and corporate signatures. Chinese consumers appear to be longing for brand names while lacking all rhetoric of critical distance by which Western consumption is increasingly characterized.

Anting New Town can be seen as a radicalization of this brand-driven creation of a post-national identity. Given that other than Germany/Wolfsburg, China/Shanghai can still be seen as an industrial place, Anting as a place for real production is also a setting where the (in itself identity-constructing) production of mass products and the creation of brands converge. The production of cars in Anting is part of all car brands' identity and history. Vice versa, the presence of an urban area dedicated to the simultaneous production of cars and car brands becomes an integral part of the identity of the hyper-rapidly changing nation.

However, Anting New Town's impact on the Shanghai people goes even further. Particularly its assumed virtual "Germanness" is an element in the government-strategic project to change Shanghai and its people. Brand space and post-national space is a way of weakening the idea of a national character, while at the same time changing this character. For example, an article in the newspaper published to promote the ideas of Anting New Town reports proudly that a higher awareness of quality issues has already been produced by the German character of Anting and, connected to this, by the way it has been built (Siemons 2003). Hence, Anting's virtuality, its non-identity, actually becomes a vehicle for a new kind of transnational engagement with notions of national identity.

# 6 The rise of the global mass ornament

The emphasis on the viral aspects of brand space in the last chapter points to the notion of the global as essential for brand space in general, but also for the interaction of virtuality and actuality (as developed in the last two chapters). Globalization and virtualization are, on the one hand, co-developments driven by contemporary capitalism. On the other hand, globalization has also created new actualities and actualizations. I want to take this idea further in this chapter, linking the concept of the "mass ornament" as put forward by Siegfried Kracauer with the understanding of both globalization and the post-globalized world put forward by Peter Sloterdijk. The main argument will be that brands' search for actualization opportunities (Chapter 4) and the virtualization of urban space this creates (Chapter 5) together generate a situation in which the urban is being transformed by a potentially global process of mass ornamentalization. The idea of mass ornament thereby, I want to argue, is the concept most substantially capable of describing the mechanisms in which Peter Sloterdijk's concept of "Schäume" becomes physical. Hence, I will use Kracauer's mass ornament concept to concretize Sloterdijk, while at the same time introducing Sloterdijk's concept as a mode of spatial thinking that can be seen as a useful extension of the Deleuzian virtualism that has guided much of my previous analysis. In this sense, this chapter can be seen as a conceptual bridging of the previous two chapters.

By developing this conceptual bridge, I want to arrive at a new understanding of the virtual–actual interaction and of the current state of the world as one of post-globalization. Regarding Kracauer's writing, this will necessarily involve a significant broadening of his original theoretical project, which had been written in a very different historical and cultural setting. Specifically, the concept of the "global mass ornament" will come out as a radical extension of the mass ornament as conceived by Kracauer in the 1920s. In certain respects, it will even appear to be the latter's inversion. However, I hope to show that this stretching of the mass ornament concept will prove justified, laying the ground for a further analysis of contemporary capitalism as an arrangement of the interaction of different kinds of such mass ornaments.

## Sloterdijk: synchronizing the globalized world

In his *Sphären* trilogy and in *Weltinnenraum des Kapitals*, which is sometimes referred to as the fourth book of the Sphären project (Jongen et al. 2009: 15), Sloterdijk distinguishes between three phases of globalization (Thrift 2008: 234). The metaphysical globalization of Greek mythology (phase one) is followed by the nautical globalization that started in the fifteenth century (phase two). The third, current phase of globalization can be termed, in the broadest possible sense, relational, or interactive. Sloterdijk (2005: 258) calls it the "global age", emphasizing that the process of globalization as a large-scale process of conquering the earth is finished. Now, the process the globe is subject to is one of a permanent creation and recreation of the most diverse, semi-relational micro spheres. These micro spheres create a spatial setting that Sloterdijk presents as the basis for cultural process today.

To describe how these micro spheres relate to each other, Sloterdijk introduces the concept of "Schäume" (foams). I have described in Chapter 3 that Schäume as the processual and structural basis of contemporary culture are relational without being based on an interaction model that gives a superior role to the idea of meaningful "communication". Other than Habermas, and even unlike Luhmann, Sloterdijk is sceptical regarding such communication as the basis of the interactive spheres he drafts (Borch 2009: 376). The interactive dimensions making up Schaumsphären have little to do with the rational, logic-driven interactions the term might be associated with. In fact, even the notion of "interaction" might imply more intentionality than is characteristic of the micro spheres Sloterdijk envisages. The central link that makes his Schäume the constitutive model for current cultural and social process is not intentional interaction, but sheer proximity: spatial proximity and proximity through the existence of shared walls (of whatever kind).

The concept of Schaum implies a rather distinct understanding of cultural or social change. The change process taking place within a Schaum sphere is based on permanently shifting positions or sizes. Schaum is made up of "Blasen" (bubbles). If one Blase alters its position or size, then this has a direct impact on the other Blasen within the Schaum. The relationality of the Blasen towards each other is also what makes possible or hinders the exchange of images or even substances (such as human bodies). The exchange processes occurring are not, however, based on intentional communication or intentional action (Sloterdijk 2004: 59). Hence, his concept of the third globalization wave (the first wave after physical globalization has been completed) fits into my analysis that has also pointed to a spatial deconstruction of communication.

As the essence of how cultural process and social interaction are taking place today, Schaum is a substitute for notions of "society", "religion" or "nationality", in fact for any kind of people-organizing totality, which for Sloterdijk ceased making sense. The idea of an all-encompassing meaning sphere is imploded, substituted by the multiplicity of micro spheres (Borch 2009: 276). For Sloterdijk, one central problem with the old totalities is that they underestimate the spatiality of cultural process. The Schaum concept does not use the spatiality of Schaum as a mere *metaphor*. Rather, it is by being spatial, by spatializing, that this level of cultural process gets its *very real* social effectiveness.

What is more, the mentioned totalities develop an insufficient understanding of individuality as being isolated through media. They fail to offer a notion of the individual that is, by means of media, isolated just as much as connected. For Sloterdijk, the density of the many connections that encapsulate individual life today at the same time creates a form of isolation. Also, the combination of human, physical and image-driven or informational elements potentially engaging with each other in a constructive way, on a micro- just as on a macro-scale, needs a concept that is more open than, say, "nationality". Schaum is this concept. It can be made up of many different essences, and engages with another Schaum structure, thereby creating a new, broader Schaum sphere.

The ambiguous relationship between isolation and connectivity is central to the concept of Schaum. Schaum separates and connects us; in fact, it separates *by* connecting us. Sloterdijk (2004: 255) calls this a connected isolation. This also explains why he uses his Schaum idea to understand modern architecture, and why architecture is such a central vehicle for him to understand social reality. Social reality and social structure is for Sloterdijk always architectural because anything social can be understood only by determining the specifics of its spatial embeddedness (Borch 2009: 277). It is an architectural analysis (of modernist living, and in particular of Le Corbusier's "Wohnmaschinen") that leads Sloterdijk to an interpretation of the immersion of individual human beings in the social spheres around them through understanding their sharing of what Sloterdijk calls "cell walls". These walls divide the individual space (cell) from the cell of at least one other person. We are part of many cells at once, because individual cells are the different micro spheres that make up social life: couples, households, companies, unions, etc. (Sloterdijk 2004: 59).

Sloterdijk's micro spheres theory is significantly based on a distinct understanding of media, and the presence of media messages and images. Such messages do not create or distribute meaning, but rather create a permanent sense of semi-isolation. For Sloterdijk, we are connected and isolated at once by the circulation of modules of communication, surrounded by media, and therefore locked up. Brands are a constitutive element in this process. This is the other side of Lury's concept of the brand as interface (Lury 2004, Chapter 3): That the interface of the brand can disconnect and isolate people, just as much as it can be a tool of social togetherness.

The spatial regime suggested by Sloterdijk is characterized by a very peculiar concept of urbanity. As a whole, urban structure, including its architectural elements, is characterized by a weak physicality that never quite reaches the physical stability and stasis that we used to associate with the urban sphere. This is the soft physicality of Schaum. It is physical, but always subject to change, permeation, mutation, or simply disappearance. Also, it allows for the fast and, in Deleuzian terms, rhizomatic creation of three-dimensional structures, particularly those structures apparently aimed at abandoning any sense of gravity. Very concretely, this is exactly what Coop Himmelb(l)au's BMW Welt does, as I have shown before. The building is aimed at creating an architectural space that substitutes gravity with the pure dynamism of asymmetrical shapes.

By making Schaum the core of his third spheres concept, and by defining it as constituted significantly by a broadened notion of media, Sloterdijk suggests a new regime of visibility and of sense-making (Sloterdijk 1998). Schaum creates dense connections, but also makes it impossible to see much. Constituted by the presence of a hyper-mediatization, Schaum connects us physically with the environment, potentially over long distances, but also limits our view (and our capacity for understanding). The critical theory implications of this are significant; in order to understand what keeps people from realizing a situation's potential for liberation or knowledge, it is mandatory to offer a perspective capable of understanding in which way media are used to allow for, but also to potentially hinder, this realization.

However, Sloterdijk does not aim at a universal critique of "the media" and even less at developing a new sense of politics through such a critique. Rather, he wants to unveil the foundations and limits of how any kind of sociality is generated today. These foundations and limits are characterized by a partly media-induced structure that can be conceptualized as foamy.

There are significant implications in this for the history of philosophical thought. The foam concept fosters an abandonment of any notion of linearity – even if the guiding idea were the concept of a linearity ultimately heading towards a higher degree of complexity. The radicalism of Sloter-dijk's thinking, and the criticism he often provokes, are connected to his refusal to believe in the idea of a permanent progress towards "more complexity". The logic of his three globalization stages is not so much one of a permanent "further". Rather, for the logic of spheres he suggests, complexity is a variable. From this perspective, Sloterdijk interprets the current stage of (post-)globalization not as necessarily *more* complex than other stages. This can be seen most clearly with regard to his application of an analysis of the first World Exhibition's Crystal Palace as the basic mode of existence in the Western world. This world is significantly based on boredom, generated by permanent efforts to *reduce* contemporary cultural complexity. This happens *by means of media*. Similarly, when he suggests that in our times globalized capitalism is not so much driven by a heightened cosmopolitanism but by a kind of global provincialism, then this can be translated, in terms of the history of thought, into a notion of a world that is actually *less complex*. Complexity is merely a variable to be managed.

## Sloterdijk: the virtual and the actual

This figure of thought can be linked to what has been argued in the previous chapters with regard to the Deleuzian concepts of virtual and actual. The argument there was not "from actual to virtual" but rather "from virtual to actual to virtual–actual". Sloterdijk effectively extends this logic. A world made up of micro spheres that together form a Schaum structure is characterized simultaneously by virtualities *and* actualities, by sudden outbursts of mediatized intensities and by the spatial emptiness of a building that simply exists, without carrying any obvious messages – even if it has been designed at some point for the transportation of those messages. Sloterdijk's spheres can therefore be read as a model to describe the virtual–actual interaction of contemporary media culture without being restricted to a concept of juxtaposed binaries.

I want to follow this idea through further, for there is also a more concrete and direct effect of applying the Schaum idea to Deleuzian categories. Schaum can be used as a conceptual device to derive a concept of a multiple spatial globalization from Deleuze's thinking. I will now outline the relationship between virtuality and actuality on the one hand and Sloterdijk's globalization theory on the other in more detail.

One could argue that the world of the ancient Greeks, metaphysical and meta-spatial as it was according to Sloterdijk, was quite succinctly focused on the virtual of the human existence. Then, in phase two, came what can be expressed in Deleuzian terms a new orientation on the actual. The process of nautical, spatial globalization (which Sloterdijk sees as finished since 1945) has been very much involved in the creation of an earth-bound actuality. For Sloterdijk, the globe as key orientation category is the actual of globalization.[1]

The conquerors, in Sloterdijk's thinking taking over from ancient Greek philosophers, who had assumed and constructed a metaphysical take on the world, actualize global thinking just as the thinking about the global. For the Greeks, there was not one globe that counted, but many; one was in a way "virtually" represented in the other. This changed with the advent of what Sloterdijk conceptualizes as terrestrial virtualization (with the conquerors around Columbus). They started a process of conquering the earth, drawing maps of it and deciding which part belonged to whom. This process, I want to argue, can very much be seen as an actualization of human nature. The new orientation of the large, but limited, physical space of the earth can be seen to have reduced the globe's capacity to be part of a larger, multidimensional, metaphysical – *and virtual* universe. Also, the capacity for change, which I have described above as a central element of the virtual, has been reduced. Drawing maps of an object only makes sense under the assumption that the object will not fundamentally change soon. Hence, when Sloterdijk writes that the globalized world is a synchronized one, he claims at the same time that it is converging in actualities ("ihre Konvergenz findet sie in Aktualitäten"; Sloterdijk 2005: 221).

However, this notion of convergence is simultaneously the starting point of the third wave of globalization, because it is driven by difference, established through the flow of bits of information and images (the Schaum phase). This regime of difference-creation is once again connected to processes of virtualization. Hence, through the actual process of terrestrial globalization coming to an end, humans are once again left in a situation of confrontation with virtualities.

This, however, does not render the actual of the globalized world irrelevant. The extended world is a permanent source of actualization; this actualization presents itself as a means for the exchange with the virtual of information and images. Physical globalization and the physical (and architectural) as such cannot be ignored, as they are the source of images. The actual is now reflected in the virtual. This means that the third wave of globalization is neither actual nor virtual, but is creating a new intensity of permanent interaction between the two. There is a complementarity of actual and virtual experiences in Sloterdijk's globalized world (cf. Chaplin 1997). And just as the experience of the same physical or architectural element can be at one moment virtual, at another, actual, essentially every piece of architecture has the capacity to function as virtuality or actuality, depending on the external forces it is confronted with.

In times of an omnipresent drive for a society dominated by developments in information technology and new media, this means that there is a permanent quest for a voluntary – and physical – proximity. The actual is always close, and its relevance for the virtualization of the hyper-mediatized world means that there is a desire for proximity, for neighbourhood, for the local. What is more, the drivers of globalization themselves also create physical connections; globalization really brings the world physically close to us, for instance, through internet order systems like Amazon, but also through the physicality of atmospheres and the climate. Global climate is physical in a Schaum way. Vice versa, climate change is actually part of a Schaum-induced change process.

Sloterdijk develops his notion of global proximity further in the concept of a global "Innenraum" (internal space). The realization of this Innenraum is, for Sloterdijk, necessarily mediated. The media create the impression of a globalized internal space. In this sense, although McLuhan's idea of a "global village" is implied in Sloterdijk's theory, Sloterdijk is lacking the media-affirmative optimism of McLuhan. Media do not constitute the global village by allowing for a "free flow of information" within the village. Rather, they create the *image* of this global village by producing stories of how we are living in it.

In terms of the new degree of a virtual–actual interaction, the question then is whether the concept of "the medium" can still be dealt with in exclusively virtual terms. It seems as if in Sloterdijk's concept of a "Weltinnenraum des Kapitals" the medium is not so much virtual itself, but rather an instrument of the *mediation between* virtual and actual. Whether an element of cultural reality, be it a political process or a work of art, is virtual or actual, is structure or change agent, is decided by how it is reflected in the media.

Also, as I have described in the earlier chapters, with the time of actualized, physical globalization coming to an end, the physicality of space, particularly that of built space and architecture, is itself subject to an interaction between virtual and actual. In particular through spatialization, then, media develop a capacity to switch between virtual and actual. Whether a medium is virtual or actual has to be decided anew at any given moment by looking at the medium in question, and its spatial and spatializing effects.

If we apply at this point once more the Schaum concept in concrete terms, then what distinguishes between virtual and actual is perhaps the density of the Schaum in question. High density would then mean that a virtuality is actualized; but never permanently. Any high-density actuality threatens to, or rather has the capacity to, get back to the virtual status of before.

### Kracauer: the mass ornament as cultural form

In the next step, I want to link Sloterdijk's understanding of the current stage of globalization to Kracauer's concept of the mass ornament. The result will be an extended concept of mass ornament: the mass ornament going global, or the global mass ornament. Before doing so, I want to briefly outline certain key aspects of the mass-ornament concept with which my argument will start.

With the mass ornament, Kracauer offers more than a piece of architectural analysis. It is a vehicle for providing an understanding of the cultural and political situation – of his times, but also of modernism per se. By doing so, he suggests, like Brecht or Benjamin, a conception of modernity that can be described as materialist rather than metaphysical. In the first sentences of *Das Ornament der Masse* Kracauer lays open his methodological basis (Kracauer 1963: 50). He wants to focus on the surface, on "Oberflächenäußerungen", to understand the presence in relation to its position in history. This is a methodology of the visible, but unlooked-at, grounded in an interest in phenomena otherwise ignored by sociologists and cultural critics (Giles 2001).

Central for the development of the mass ornament concept have been the performances of the dance combo the Tiller Girls in the Berlin of the 1920s and 1930s. By means of a theoretical writing embodied in essayistic miniature, Kracauer derives from their performances his theory of the mass ornament. For him, modernist spatial reality is very much made up of such ornaments. The ornaments transform this spatial reality by laying on its surface the spatial ornament structures that include architecture, images, and human beings. These ornaments work by means of a certain capitalist *magic* (Kracauer 1963: 51). It is a central feature of modernity that ornaments magically link people and spatial structure through a peculiar "meaning"-driven cultural process.

This meaning, however, has nothing to do with individual rationality. Rather, it is the rationality of capitalism that is reflected in the mass ornament. Kracauer saw the ornaments he identified as *representative of* a new form of capitalism. The mass ornament, he writes, is the "ästhetische Reflex" of the abstract rational capitalist production system (ibid.: 54).

The mass ornament is physical as well as conceptual. On the one hand, its entire logic is thoroughly physical, because it is architectural. It creates structures that consist of buildings as much as of human beings (as spectators, for instance, or as performers). What is more, the way in which Kracauer treats the human bodies yields an architectural concept; human bodies become part of the ornament essentially as building elements (the masses are "eingesetzt", literally "inserted" as stones; ibid.). This means that the mass ornament is an architectural structure. At the same time, however, particularly through its immersion of the human body, it is not static, but constituted by a high degree of fluidity. The mass ornament is involved in permanent movement, and is subject to change. The application and integration of human beings is a central element in "fluidizing" capitalist architecture.

Concretely, Kracauer links the performance of the Tiller girls to the architecture of the stadium. In the stadium, human bodies and physical architecture form a unity (which is certainly still true today). Together, they become an element in the production of what can be termed a concrete cultural form. They are part of this cultural form that is created on the basis of a partly emptied-out subjectivity. Human beings, deprived of their individuality, are driven into an ensemble with architecture, and the result is the mass ornament (the term "ornament" provocatively implying that there is a certain kind of aesthetics involved in this modernist phenomenon).

## The global mass ornament: deterritorializing megastructures

If we link Kracauer's mass ornament with Sloterdijk's understanding of spatial globalization connected to the spatial formation of Schaum structures, we see that in Sloterdijk's Schaum stage, we are still confronted with the creation of actual cultural forms. This creation, however, now works differently from the form creation prevalent in times of "terrestrial globalization". That globalization, and this includes even the colonial activities of transporting the building traditions of one place to the environment of a completely different culture, still meant that "places" as such were capable of providing the physical and cultural material for the completion of this transfer. Cultural artefacts were local, even if transported; they would always be re-localized, or, in Deleuzian terms, reterritorialized. This also implied an ongoing and meaningful existence of "the local" as such.

In the world of a completed terrestrial globalization, the basics of cultural form-creation have fundamentally changed. It can be argued that now, bodies as much as psyches or human desires (or affects) enter into a mass ornament that is in fact a global set of deterritorialized metastructures; structures made up of corporate strategy, of cultural change and of flows of products, money and images – on a global scale. Individual brand spaces such as Autostadt or BMW Welt are the result of these processes. And they do not exist in isolation, but are rather part of a larger set of interdependencies. Territorialization now is always temporary, and the exception. On a more abstract level, "brand space" is replicating globally, but is also subject to permanent transformations and subversions. The result is a certain connection between images, individual desires, products, and architectural ensembles on a global scale. This connection is what I call the "global mass ornament".

For this ornament, globality is a potentiality (a virtuality), but not necessarily a permanent fact. In times of global capitalism, the concrete ornament can obtain a small size as well as extend to a huge scale. The logic of the ornament is multifaceted and potentially virtual (Moussavi 2006: 8), yet not necessarily mediated. When looking down at the countryside while flying over a cloudless country, we recognize a completely unmediated ornamental pattern – that of large-scale farming, the ornament of capitalist-managed agriculture.[2] Beyond the specifics of this example, the ornament of agriculture is indicative of the fact that ornaments can reproduce indefinitely; on a long-haul flight, one can actually read agricultural management systems through the global patterns of agricultural space.

Spatialized branding is readable as another example of such a mass ornament that can start small, but also extend to a global scale. Brand-based mass ornaments might involve only one brand, and more often than not they will. But it is equally possible for different brands to form a relation with each other, creating a multi-brand mass ornament. Put in a Kracauerian way: the individual patterns of different ornaments always have the capacity to morph into one another.

From Sloterdijk's perspective, global mass ornaments can be seen as that which make up the Schaum structure of capitalist society's micro and macro interiors. The connection between Schaum and ornament is twofold. On the one hand, the ornament is focused on surfaces, and yet it is three-dimensional and deep, like Schaum. Schaum is carried only by surfaces, by the infinitely thin and the immaterial. And yet it has a certain stability and depth. This is why architecture is so relevant for Sloterdijk's thinking – because architecture is the primary model that functions through thin materiality (walls). And so one could extend this thinking; the thinner and more fluid a built environment is, and the more porous it becomes, the more effective it is for Sloterdijk's world system.

A key term in the functioning of such a "thin" architecture for Sloterdijk is his concept of "Atmosphäre". It is the capability to create and contain distinct atmospheres that makes architecture so relevant today – because the atmosphere has become a very real, cultural fact (Borch 2007: 379). Böhme (2006: 16) defines atmosphere as architecturally designed, quasi-objective emotions ("räumlich ergossene, quasi objective Gefühle"). It does not seem too far-fetched to claim that we might replace "emotions" in our context with "affects". From this perspective, we can use Sloterdijk's and Böhme's thinking to point out that the development of atmosphere has constructive social *effects* by creating social *affects* (Böhme 1995: 97). Following up on this, the unique relevance of brand architecture can be described along Sloterdijk's lines as an atmospheric architecture, an architecture the very function of which is to create a certain atmosphere. One example is the atmosphere of British leather-ness generated by the former Bentley pavilion; another the German calm in Anting New Town.

Atmosphere here is an ornamental category. Or rather, the ornament functions on an atmospheric level. It creates atmospheres. Anting New Town is the ornamental surface providing this concrete space with an atmosphere of Germanness. And this atmosphere-producing surface is also the category that makes it possible to link this space with the "original" German spaces, which are characterized by a similar atmosphere. In terms of atmosphere, the differences between "real" Germany and "simulated" Germany in Shanghai vanish; the mass ornament effectively includes both.

On the level of the individual building, the atmosphere this building produces is its link to the outer environment, one could even say its "function". This is, on a micro level, the specific cultural significance of architecture (Borch 2007). And this is, on a macro level, why the ornamentality of brand spaces brings them right to the core of Sloterdijk's philosophy of space – because they allow for the transfer of this functionality to the globality of mediatized Schaum structures.

Connected to this, the second connection between the ornament and the concept of Schaum is the specific combination of locality and globality. Ornaments are local and concrete as well as potentially global, just as Sloterdijk's interiors, which are strictly limited (one cannot see further than the concrete blade), and yet also interconnected on a vast scale. Ornamentalization is the mechanism by which the local extends to potentially world-spanning dimensions. Obviously, the global presence of certain logos, in micro-form as stickers within the structure of certain products, as globally flowing advertisements, and realized in the architecture of brand-space buildings, is an ornament of particular strength and perseverance. It is actually an enabler of an increasing globalization of ornaments, thereby also driving the globality of a certain Schaum structure.

The adaptation of the ornament concept to the global stage thoroughly transforms Kracauer's understanding of capitalist spatiality. His ornament represented capitalism, but always within one concrete architectural-social place, such as a cabaret, or a sports arena. Now, the stage is the globe. This means that, for instance, sports arenas and their function as what Sloterdijk (2004) calls "collector/connector" are delimited. The collector/connector process in one football stadium is linked to all the other branding activities surrounding the brand of global football clubs. Old Trafford is not only a temporary collector and connector of football fans, but also a central element in the functioning of the global mass ornament "Manchester United".

The capitalist framework within which football clubs act, the transfer market, TV rights, etc., simultaneously supports, channels and undermines the spirituality of the stadium experience. Hence, the notion of a pseudo-spiritual one-ness that Sloterdijk pointed out regarding the sports arenas he described becomes fragile. The one-ness in the football stadium is always inherently threatened.

We can see that by being taken to the global scale, the mass-ornament concept develops new analytical strengths. Vice versa, the notion of the global brings us closer to the core of what the ornament "is": a rhizomatic structure. As a rhizome, they are not spatially limited. Neither are they destroyed by any part being cut out. And, very importantly, they do not have a centre; or rather, the many centres and nodal points they have depend on the patterns they convey. These characteristics are part of what I developed in Chapter 5 as key elements in the rhizomatic character of globally spatialized brands. Therefore, the mass ornament is an analytical tool suitable for offering a better understanding of the rhizomatic functioning of such brands. And vice versa, branding is a field of capitalist activity that drives the cultural presence of mass-ornaments that are no longer, as was the case with Kracauer, spatially bound. Brands drive the globalization of the mass-ornament concept.

As an analytical construct, the mass ornament is able to explain capitalist efforts of affect-creation on and over the global stage (Moussavi 2006: 9–11). In this relation, it is superior to certain lines of thought that could be seen as an early example of postmodernity, such as the writings by Robert Venturi and Denise Scott Brown, which also aimed at understanding proto-capitalist space, but which were the result of a methodology focused on tracing messages distributed by architecture. In comparison with this, the concept of ornament has a different focus. It is an effect of architectural efforts to build expressions out of an internal order that maintains stability *even if the stability given by language-based meaning ceased* (ibid.: 7).

As Moussavi points out, ornament is not the same as décor. Rather, it is creating and managing what has often been called, also in this work, the origination and alteration of human and trans-human "affects". Ornament "is in line with non-representational thought and the creative actualization of the virtual" (ibid.: 8). This actualization, as I have shown earlier, is not a dissolution of the virtual, but rather the creation of a new intensity in the exchange between actual and virtual. It is also, and this is why I quote Moussavi at this point, connected to affects. Without affects, there were no global mass ornaments; there could not be. Affects are what keep the concrete ornament together. And they create a significant cultural productivity. Affect can even be seen as a driver of cultural progress. From this perspective, then, it becomes clear why the ornament maintains its centrality in much cultural writing, despite having been condemned as backward-oriented as early as 1908 by modernist Adolf Loos.

In this sense, what could be termed the "affectivity" of the ornament provides us with a new concept of the workings of both urban space and society in general. Both initiate process and change no longer through what is happening "within", but at the outer shell, the surface. The surface is the centre of productivity in this concept – just as in Sloterdijk's Schaum model (and, of course, in this work, which aims at understanding brand space primarily through its architecture – the outside – not through the exhibitions – the inside). This mode of urban and social productivity is architectural as much as it is cultural; as Moussavi points out, the surface is what relates a concrete building to its wider environment and therefore to culture. From a perspective that sees culture not as static, but rather as prone to, and made up of, permanent change, the more flexibly a building can adapt to the cultural transformations at play at any time, the less it is threatened with being disconnected from culture. It needs to build an internal consistency (ibid.: 8) that at the same time adapts to differing cultural conditions.

In an abstract way, this process pertains not only to the architecture of an individual building, but also to the collections of buildings, flows and embodied human activity that I refer to as the global mass ornament. They have to develop both internal consistency and external cultural connectivity. In this sense, the way in which ornamentalization is treated here extends Moussavi's engagement with the ornament; for me, ornament has an architectural actuality, but is itself not purely architectural. Following Kracauer, I see the (mass) ornament as the combination of matter, form and human activity and "affectivity". The inclusion of the human into a concrete (branded) mass ornament lends additional relevance to the concept of affect in this context. For the strength of affect, as outlined earlier with regard to the topic of driving, is that affects are not intra-human, and also not only trans-human, but also include matter. Matter can be part of an affective intensity, too.

One central strength of the concept of ornament with regards to an analysis of branding in space is that it makes it possible to see the brand not just as the effect, but also as the driver of spatial practice. Moussavi and Kubo (2006) demonstrate this by demonstrating concretely that branding can be the very material of an ornament strategy in architecture. They show how the two Tokyo Louis Vuitton stores in Roppongi Hills and Nagoya use the brand as "material" for the creation of ornament effects and affects (Moussavi and Kubo 2006: 116–123). In Roppongi Hills, for instance, a circular pattern derived from the Louis Vuitton logo is extruded into a deep screen made up of layers of glass, glass tubes and perforated stainless steel (ibid.: 118). The logo is thereby materializing *by* becoming ornament.

It has to be clear that the ornamentalization of space through brands does not imply that only the visibility of logos can be part of an ornament. Companies with logos less iconic than Louis Vuitton might use different means of spatializing their brands. The products might become more central, and so might a certain architectural style (a method often employed by retailers, for instance).

Even if logos are the core of a branded mass ornament, the strength of the ornament concept is that size does not matter. As is the case with the Tokyo

Louis Vuitton megastores, the logo is often spatialized through a method of small size and infinite repetition. Audi, on the other hand, uses its logo only once in the construction of its pavilion in Autostadt, and in a radically blown-up and simultaneously provocatively deconstructed form (see Chapter 5). This illustrates that with ornamentalization, absolute size does not matter. What counts is not the size of objects, but the relations between them.

The last thought is what links the theory of ornament with certain lines of topological thinking; the latter is also engaged with developing an understanding of contemporary spatial practice and allowing for an understanding of spatial structure *without* focusing on absolute size. Its mathematical roots yield an analysis of spatial forms that I want to term at this point "hyper-transformational"; the core idea is that these forms remain "topologically" unchanged through spatial transformations such as stretching or blowing-up (Günzel 2007: 21). This method can prove useful here, for in my understanding the individual mass ornament is also not threatened by the taking-away of individual elements or by the spatial transformations of these elements. To make this concrete: the mass ornament of the brand of Audi is not threatened by the building in Autostadt blowing up the logo. Even the effect of laying two of the four rings on top of each other, which can be interpreted in topological terms as an extreme case of *bending*, is actually rather a sign of the strength of the logo and the brand. These qualities make the Audi building an example of a topological architecture of branding. Vice versa, topology seems to be one central process to allow the brand to become spatial.

The application of topological categories to my analysis of globally spatialized branding helps dissolve an apparent contradiction between other uses of the concept of ornament and the one I am putting forward here. On the one hand, I am deliberately taking the concept to new dimensions, compared for instance to Moussavi, arguing that an ornament might stretch over up to the whole globe. I thereby also divert perspective, focusing on the horizontal as much as on the vertical. And yet, from a topological perspective, this operation is not that huge a step. Topology is capable of transforming perspective from the vertical to the horizontal, too. Connections count, and these are playing out through horizontal linkages. In fact, topology means that vertical and horizontal are increasingly indistinguishable. Therefore, topology allows for an understanding of the ornament in all its spatial dimensions.

The dominance of the surface renders Kracauer's idea of mass ornament thoroughly topological, and highly relevant. Kracauer was looking at the surfaces of spatial and social activity. At this point, the category of surface helps me explain why from a topological viewpoint, one would search for ornaments that also play out horizontally rather than those functioning purely vertically. And of course, the focus on surfaces is a necessary effect of the idea of a "global mass ornament", for the globe is treated in this perspective as the ultimate surface spanned by these ornaments.

The question though is what "playing out" or "spanning" in this context means. Put differently, what is the relationship between change and structure within a mass ornament going global? From the perspective of this work, the global mass ornament is understood as change and structure at once. On the one hand, it is functioning topologically, creating certain spatial permanences. It is characterized by specific aesthetics, by specific images and other sensual (for instance, architectural or design-driven) elements, which create a certain permanence. In this way, it creates a frame for the otherwise frameless globalized world and makes it readable. Thereby, it fits into the thinking of Sloterdijk. When we take Sloterdijk's concept of a global internal space literally for a moment, then the internal space is a room to which the mass ornaments provide the "aesthetic patterns" of a "wallpaper" (and aesthetic patterns are essentially what the term "ornament" implies). They define the aesthetic reality to this "Weltinnenraum".

On the other hand, the global mass ornament is characterized by a permanent spatial process. New elements might link to its structure, thereby transforming it. In terms of brand-driven global mass ornaments, for instance, new products or economic transformation processes such as the takeover of one company by another mean that the mass ornament changes its character. As soon as Volkswagen sells any of its brands that Autostadt stages, the concrete brand pavilion necessarily becomes part of a different ornamentality. In an extreme case, a capitalist change process can mean that a mass ornament effectively disappears. For instance, during a merger of two companies, the mass ornaments created and upheld by them melt into each other, creating one completely new ornament, which then has further, real, spatial effects: different products, different spatial arrangements in terms of production facilities and office blocks, different retail strategies. This example makes clear why the ornament is a suitable term to describe capitalist reality: because it shows that the same elements, be they buildings, products or logos, can impose different effects and fulfil different functions, depending on the ways in which they are moulded into an ornament.

This combination of permanence and change is why the global mass ornament can be seen as a realization of Sloterdijk's third stage of globalization, described above as a closer interaction of virtual and actual (Moussavi 2006: 8). In this interaction, physical space and architecture are no longer elements of stasis. On the one hand, when entering the ornament as platforms where ornamentalization processes might solidify, concrete buildings might become key elements, or nodes, in the ornament. They are, however, also active producers of images that might be replicated in architecture elsewhere. This is particularly obvious when looking at branded spaces (not just the brand spaces we are mainly focusing on here, but all architectural systems that are the outcome of branding processes). These spaces are all system spaces. That is, their shapes can be replicated wherever necessary. This holds true for car showrooms, for football stadiums or other sports arenas, for airports, Starbucks coffee shops, as well as for all kinds of event spaces. These spaces are spaces as concepts, easily transferable from one place to another. In this sense, architecture and design are vehicles for very real economic and cultural change processes.

Significant part of such concept spaces, as well as of any kind of mass ornament, is that their individual elements cannot be captured with terminologies of "the original" and "the fake". The individuality of the concrete building or distinct part of a building is not as strong as its immersion in the mass ornament in question. A concrete Starbucks coffee shop is not primarily this one unique shop, but is at least as much defined by being part of the Starbucks coffee chain (which is the ornament here). Without its link to the ornament, it would be a completely different entity. It has to keep up its link to the whole through architectural or design gestures. Visitors come in order to satisfy their desire to consume, but also in order to immerse themselves in the ornament. In fact, consumption and immersion can be seen as closely related processes now. At the same time, by *entering* and by *wanting* to be part of the ornament, they are *strengthening* the concrete coffee shop's immersion *in* the ornament.

The way in which what I understand as the global mass ornament keeps together different architectural spaces (concept spaces) undermines the specifity of individual buildings; a clear extension of Kracauer's original concept. For Kracauer, architecture was the built foundation for the integration of human beings into the concrete ornament. In fact, the concrete building was extended through the integration of human bodies. Now, the building is sucked into a larger whole, just as human bodies were in the original mass ornament (and are still). One can argue that this is still architectural; this process is still following a logic of building. But the notion of building now is different; more abstract, poststructuralist. Building in one area of the world can be seen as a change of the built reality elsewhere. (To illustrate this, I have shown in the earlier chapters that Anting New Town is in a way an extension of the concept of the German town and, simultaneously, of the concrete place of Autostadt Wolfsburg.) Understanding the deterritorialization of the urban now always needs a tracing of the extra-local effects of a concrete city (Amin and Thrift 2002).

This trans-local, deterritorialized understanding of architecture is thoroughly Sloterdijkian. It is paralleled by Sloterdijk's concept of a deterritorialized living (Sloterdijk 2005: 405). In this concept, modern nomads seek for a reterritorialization of their lives *in the process of deterritorialization*. Heidegger's desire for a "dwelling" is thereby taken to the global scale – as is, in my argument above, the practice of building, of creating something local. This is the architectural essence of Sloterdijk's Weltinnenraum; by building the concrete building, a global mass ornament is built at the same time. Thereby, the "Weltinnenraum des Kapitals" is effectively concretized and extended.

The process of transportability of the mentioned concept spaces is creating its own momentum; it is making itself bigger. The replicability of an individual Starbucks coffee shop is a step towards the replicability of a whole street, a quarter, or even a city. This is where Anting New Town starts. With its many hints towards the town of Weimar, Anting is an extension and intensification of Weimar, this quintessential German city. And what is more, Anting even intensifies and rewrites the concept of what is means to be "a German city", "a modernist city" or "a Bauhaus-influenced city". It is proof that the idea of a whole town can be replicated through the mediatization of space. But the degree of Shanghai or Anting's becoming-medium means that even the *idea of the city as such* becomes a concept space that can be replicated.

## The surface and Zerstreuung

The argument above implies that brands are drivers of the becoming-concept-space of the urban sphere, in this sense extending Kracauer's pre-globalized understanding of capitalism through the concept of the mass ornament. Brand space is no longer only what Kracauer called an *aesthetic reflex*. Every brand space has to fight for its position in the new capitalist production system. Critical analysis no longer has to look for clues as to the hidden capitalist functionings. Instead, capitalism here demonstrates itself simply *by* functioning. Architectural reality is no longer the area where one can detect certain hidden capitalist mechanisms; it is instead a central element in these mechanisms. Capitalism exposes itself and its use (one could even use at this point the Marxist term of exploitation) of the human. It does so in brand city through the very mass ornaments it creates to keep up its productivity.

In this sense, the concept of mass ornament is transformed when applied to Sloterdijk's third stage of globalization. For Kracauer, the mass ornament was still working on a basis of representation. It was "reflecting", partly aesthetically, the spirit of capitalism (the mass-ornament structure "spiegelt die der gegenwärtigen Gesamtsituation wieder", Kracauer 1963: 53). The fact that this spirit was one of an increased abstraction simply meant that representation had to make use of aesthetical categories; it could not rely only on physical qualities. These physical qualities had to carry an aesthetic value. Hence, the fact that it engaged bodies like those of the Tiller Girls represented for Kracauer the way in which capitalism exploits human beings in its production processes. Kracauer read the Tiller Girls show as a form of art; this art was reflecting involuntarily capitalist reality.

With the going-global of the mass ornament, such reflexivity no longer exists, and is no longer necessary. Brand space as the core of global mass ornamenting does not simply reflect capitalist production outside itself. Rather, it is the core of this production. The surface is not merely mirroring something that is going on deep down. Everything there is on the surface.

This surface is the place on which movement can take place seamlessly and uninterrupted. Sliding on the surface means sliding fast – and far. This is why globalization has a lot to do with what one could call "surfacization". It creates surfaces. In terms of architecture, the collection of architectural ornaments presented by Moussavi and Kubo (2006) shows that entire buildings increasingly function only by means of their ornaments. This means that the surface here has strategic relevance. This strategic relevance of the surface has been understood by Sloterdijk's conquerors. Effectively, what they did through their conquests was create surfaces. They made the world a surface, fit for all kinds of travel. They made it possible for worldwide movements of all kinds to take place – on the surface.

In this way, the globalization of the mass ornament takes Kracauer's surface processes from the local to the global level. Specifically, cultural analyses from local and global perspectives both offer insights into the same kind of movement. This can be shown by a reference to another Kracauer essay, in particular by the German original. The text "Cult of Distraction" has the original title "Kult der Zerstreuung" (Kracauer 1963: 311–317). The German term "Zerstreuung" is based on the word "Streuung", which means, in a very concrete sense, to sprinkle, to spread, or to scatter. What it alludes to is, apart from the psychological notion of the word, is a process of physically spreading out something that had been a homogeneous one-ness before. This is what for Kracauer the experience of the new technological art form of cinema does to every individual city dweller (local level) (ibid.: 313). The modern metropolis causes the end of community. People are dispersed in the urban landscape, their attention in a state of permanent distraction through the influence of cinema and other image machines. They are part of the metropolis, but only as an amorphous "mass", no longer as members of a "community".

My argument is that on an abstract level, this movement, this "Streuung", is repeated through what I call the global mass ornament (global level). The global mass ornament tears apart what used to be one, and spreads its elements out. All around the globe, there are flows of human beings, images, bits of information, products or architectural styles that are all part of the same ornament. All these elements lose their local embeddedness, instead now being part of this global and extensive ornament as a new, scattered entity.

This process cannot be imagined without the workings of media. Through mediatization, the global mass ornament is erected and can initiate its effects of Streuung. At the same time, media also ensure ornamental coherence; products, images, acts of communication, architectural ideas or references are all spread out on the same plane, on the same surface (Sloterdijk 2005: 343). This surface is that of the mass ornament going global.

The idea of media as devices of distraction and of scattering not only challenges the understanding of media as devices of communication and information. More significantly, everything that is *able* to create such scattering, and the unity of the scattered, can now be called a medium. Media do not simply "exist"; rather, they are created performatively. This creation of media is a dynamic, nonlinear process – and a process that is not spatially limited. For example, architecture in Autostadt is performatively transformed into a medium partly by goings-on elsewhere (for instance, the ways in which Autostadt is reflected in other media, or even in this work). The Goethe and Schiller memorial in Weimar also becomes a medium *through* its replication in Anting New Town. This kind of media creation builds on Kracauer's original concept of "Zerstreuung"; extending it, but also showing the intellectual potential it (still, or perhaps for the first time) has.

In this way, brand space points to a thorough reimagination of urban reality. Being urban today means being part of this global structure of Streuung. This, in turn, implies a partial reconfiguring of the spatiality of the city, as has been argued by Chaplin (1997). Chaplin calls this new mode of spatiality the *distributed city*. One can argue that this distributed city is an urban sphere that defines its city-ness *through* the global mass ornaments it is part of. It should be understood not so much as the spatial alternative to a form of nucleated centrality, but rather as a result of the infiltration of capitalist societies by a kind of new media neo-realism.

This mediated realism, as I have shown before, transforms the understanding we have of the relationship between the city and the media. The city is not just a medium because it is filled with media. Rather, it is a medium that might or might not make use of content-communicating media objects. Architectural urban structure is not so much "invaded" by media technologies, as demonstrated by McQuire (2008). Instead, as Kittler (1996) has argued, the physical itself is the medium. The presence of screens or other media devices within this city is relevant, and involved in the de-localization of the city space. But the architecturalized screens should not be interpreted as contrasts to physical city structures. Rather, as I have shown above regarding BMW Welt, they are an integral part of its very physicality, and therefore of its city-ness.

## The pavilion as global cultural form

Sloterdijk (2005, Chapter 35) finds for this hypermediated physicality of contemporary space the metaphor of the Crystal Palace. The palace is sucking everything in, functioning on a global scale, thereby destroying the possibility of a geographic outside. As global interior, the Crystal Palace is the result of a world that has internalized (almost) everything. It is a descriptor for the all-inclusiveness of contemporary capitalism. For this capitalism, there no longer appears to be any geographical outside (that conquerors could explore, cartographers draw, etc.). The outside is an image produced by media. Sloterdijk implies that the deconstruction of the spatial, actual outside needs the outside as image. Thrift (2009: 124) calls this a "gynaecological" understanding of space: a space that gives its inhabitants the ability to produce and permanently reproduce their world – by creating new insides and outsides.

This is the sense in which also the inside-ness of the Crystal Palace is not static. Within the palace, new insides and relative outsides are created, relationships that one could in fact interpret as micro-replica of the palace itself. Once again, micro and macro perspectives converge. Therefore, it makes sense to combine the spatial metaphor of the Crystal Palace with yet another architectural form to understand what I have called the globalized mass ornament. The form that I see as relevant at this point has played a major role throughout this work: the pavilion.

As an architectural principle, the pavilion has its roots in the ancient Egyptian and Oriental societies (Bußmann 2009: 35). In the seventeenth century, European architects began experimenting with this building type on a large scale (Leydecker 2009). The pavilion is the most temporary form of building; it is associated with experiment, a potential for complete architectural redefinition or even abandonment. Leydecker (ibid.) reads it as a laboratory for new static experiments (see also van Berkel 2009: 81). Also, the pavilion thrives more than other buildings on a close connection between architecture and function.

What is more, the pavilion is the architectural form that captures the complex micro-mirroring processes of the globalized world as conceptualized by Sloterdijk most succinctly (Hirsch 2009: 53). It mirrors on a micro scale the functioning of Sloterdijk's Crystal Palace. Whenever a temporary world fair, an arts biennale or a trade show takes place – that is, whenever the world condenses in a certain place, and globality becomes an issue – the pavilion is the building type of choice. The original Crystal Palace in nineteenth-century London was essentially a pavilion. Now, the palace as a cultural principle in Sloterdijk's sense is creating its global inside through the logic and working of pavilions. If we consider the palace as the role model for the global inside, then the macro perspective here replicates features of the micro perspective. More than any other architectural form, the pavilion has the potential of replicating and (re-)presenting the whole world, or any part of it, in its own confines.

This capacity for flexible and encompassing representation holds significant attractiveness for brand- and message-driven capitalism. And yet, the pavilion is not just a real-space concept that drives either capitalism as a whole or spatialized branding. Just as much, it can be seen as a model for the abstract mechanism within the globalized mass ornament that reflects how as media, brands are always local and global at once. In this sense, any pavilion is not just "a building". Autostadt Wolfsburg not only *has* pavilions, but features an interplay of symbolic forces that the pavilions *initiate*. It is in this sense that the pavilion seems to be the proto-capitalist building form, and a capitalist driving force.

What makes the pavilion so relevant for this work is that it is also an inherently global form, actualizing the virtual of globality in a physical place. Many pavilions on World Exhibitions or Trade Fairs imply the architectural style of another country. Also, very practically, they are often flexible, can be transported and re-erected at will. Some of the pavilions at the Expo 2000 in Hanover have indeed been transported elsewhere. The Serpentine Pavilion built every summer in front of the London Serpentine Gallery is always temporary, after some weeks often being bought by wealthy architecture fans and rebuilt in their gardens. The London Crystal Palace has also proven to obtain pavilion-style qualities in this sense; even if unintended when built initially, it was rebuilt twice. These examples show that the pavilion is the globalization role model because of its capacity to endure globalization even in its most disturbing effects (the availability of human beings, products, and even architectural structures on a global scale).

At the same time, the character of the pavilion is that it is always semi-open. The prototype of the pavilion as architectural role model, the Barcelona Pavilion by Mies van der Rohe from 1929, is a demonstration of an extreme transparency and physical openness. (In fact, it is possible to enter the building without opening any door.) This implies a peculiar combination of inside and outside, which is typical of pavilions in general (Campbell 2006: 38–39). As is the case with the Mies building, the (display) function of many pavilions starts at their outside, as they are supposed to lure people inside. Also, often they are displaying large, transparent entry areas.

This impression of a semi-openness makes the pavilion highly attractive for capitalism. It means that the flows of capitalism run through it more seamlessly than through other buildings. Bußmann (2009: 48) points to the flow-related capacities of pavilions. Elaborating on this viewpoint, pavilions can be interpreted as means of managing and channelling flows. It is arguably through this vicinity of the notion of flow that the pavilion develops a very specific mode of mediality. It can be seen as a building type for which "functioning" means functioning *as medium*, and on a supra-local level, connecting the elements of capitalist flow – products, images, tourists or money – and spreading them out (along the lines of Kracauer's concept of Streuung). Thereby, as a cultural model, the pavilion is effectively dissolving the locality of architectural form (ibid.).

The mediated and mediating actuality of the pavilion fosters a rather ambiguous relationship with the notion of the national. On the one hand, being global, the pavilion clearly transcends the thinking in categories of nationality. On the other hand, architectural engagements with notions of the national are often realized today through pavilions, rather than through castles or representational government buildings. The pavilion is, as Penelope Harvey (1996: 81–85) demonstrates with regard to the pavilions on the 1992 Seville World Exhibition, the paradigmatic building form for the negotiation of national identity (see also Bußmann 2009: 40). Thence, an engagement with architectural representations of what is "German" today would sensitively not start with visiting castles in Germany, but with getting immersed in the spatial representations of Germany in a pavilion, say, during an Expo (which will usually not take place in Germany, but anywhere around the globe). This is where the country's (and of course any country's) idea of itself is reflected through the lens of its image in the world. This is also where this image construction is contrasted to other countries' image constructions. Expo pavilions are together staging a runway of image constructions. They are thereby defining how the notion of the national is simultaneously constructed and deconstructed today.

## Beyond temporal totalities

In this way, the modality of the pavilion questions certain temporal assumptions prevalent in Lefebvre's differentiation between representations of space and representational spaces. The logic of the pavilion changes the way in which representations of space create meaning. The notion of temporal totality that used to be connected to nationalist architectural representations is substituted by the idea of temporal relativity and spatial totality. Even and especially buildings of strong historical significance can be rebuilt anywhere and any time.

The logic of the pavilion therefore can be argued to potentially extend to very much any kind of building that would in earlier days have been described as a representation of space. The city of Berlin is currently demonstrating how this works by rebuilding the old Berlin castle. The Stadtschloss, severely damaged in WW2, was torn down by the GDR regime soon after the war. Now, decades later, it is erected again, at the very place where the GDR Palast der Republik used to stand (which has been torn down by the reunified Germany, an action arguably replicating the architectural logic of the GDR regime). There has been a lot of critical debate in Germany about this effort of writing history through architecture, a process based on the imitation of an old building as a reference point for national sentiments (cf. von Boddien and Engel 2000). From the perspective of the building as medium, however, the fact that it is not the original building that is becoming medium here, but an imitation, is the very essence of this mediatized identity-creation, or nationality-building. The imitation of the old castle then functions along lines similar to the imitation of a whole German city in Anting New Town.

National identity, then, is no longer produced *in* a country or *by* that country. Rather, the mediatization of its representations of space implies that these spaces can be built anywhere or by anybody. The city as medium in this sense means that the creation of media for the construction of identity is completely delimited. In Anting New Town, German national identity is built and thereby mediated in Shanghai, by Chinese government officials and through the construction of an urban space that has the capacity to function as a medium. From this perspective, McLuhan's optimism regarding new media transforming old ideas of nationalism no longer seems as over-enthusiastic as contemporary critics thought (cf. Kloock *et al.* 1997:

59–68). Nationalism is indeed changing. However, it is not disappearing for some kind of harmonious global village. Rather, the construction processes of individual national identities are becoming significantly more intertwined.

Not all countries find it equally easy to participate in those negotiations of each other's national identity. Today, the new urban China or the city state of Dubai seem to be more heavily engaged in such processes of bilateral identity-formation than others (Klingman 2007: 2). This might indicate that these countries are specifically inclined towards this kind of transnational identity-creation. The fact that they are at the same time among the countries with the highest economic growth rates worldwide can be taken to indicate that the category of the national has become a tool for the generation of economic growth. And as a source of economic growth, it does not pertain to one nationality only, but to the interaction of different images of nationalities (as is the case in Anting New Town).

And yet, regarding China in particular, the argument specifically around the notion of pavilion is even more complex, offering analytical support for the claim that the logic of the pavilion as proto-capitalist building form seems to be particularly applicable to contemporary Chinese architectural thinking. Pavilion architecture has a long tradition in China. More generally, Chinese architecture is principally characterized by a rationale of permanent reinvention and reconstruction. In traditional Chinese wooden architecture, the original wood is assumed and made to be perishable and reproducible. In this way, each building element can simply be replaced as needed, and the building permanently changes – actualization as change (Pang 2008: 123; see also Stille 2002: 40–42). Chinese architecture therefore can be argued to be pavilion architecture to a certain degree, because it is an architecture permanently in the flux of becoming.

From this perspective, it does not seem to be a coincidence that the first major Expo after the 2000 event in Hanover was the Expo 2010 in Shanghai. (There have been others, but they seem to have fostered significantly less public attention.) In this work, I have shown through the example of Anting New Town that the mediation of spatialized identity engagements is a process that the city of Shanghai apparently provides fertile ground for. It brings my argument full circle now that Shanghai is also a driving force in the negotiation of national identity through the principle of the pavilion on a major World Exhibition.

And indeed, the Expo gives the impression that it is negotiating not so much national identity, but rather the degree to which, and the ways in which, national identity can be negotiated at all in the urban sphere today. The overall title "Better City, Better Life" points to the role of the city already, even if in PR jargon. The more complex pavilion concepts seem to explicitly deal with their own role in the construction of images of the national (de Muynck 2010). The Australian pavilion is playing architecturally with the social imaginary of the scenery of the Australian landmark

Ayers Rock. It transforms this imaginary into a distinctly urban shape, thereby pointing to the fact that natural national landmarks need to be reworked through media to become this landmark. The Brazilian pavilion by Fernando Brandao seems to pay homage with its rectangular design to the "Bird's Nest" Olympic Stadium from the 2008 Olympic Games in Beijing. Hence, the building lays open the process of nationality construction by the interaction of different nations' images – and different events. It is perspectives like these that arguably make the Expo 2010 a *Meta-Expo* (Lagerkvist 2010).

From today's perspective, the Shanghai Expo seems to have been the culmination point of a development that started long ago (the idea that a sense of national identity can be developed through pavilions). As mentioned before, the pavilion principle already signified the first World Exhibitions in the mid-nineteenth century, which clearly had the role of constructing national identity images. Through the arts show Biennale in Venice, the pavilion principle is linked to artistic production. In the original area of the "Giardini", built in the late nineteenth century and still the core place of today's Biennales, the pavilion principle allows for an idea of national representation through artistic production. Each country is expected to present its best in art, which would then have identity effects (Martino 2007). There are national pavilions, managed by their "home" countries during the Biennale, usually with an installation by an artist from that country. However, by today, this principle has turned on itself, becoming a topic for artistic reflection, with many artists engaging with grand and visibly outdated efforts to represent a country through architectural styles.

In terms of the cultural effectiveness of the pavilion, the undermining of classical processes of national representation on the Venice Biennale once more underlines the capability of the pavilion as building type to thoroughly transform its own assigned functioning principles. This flexibility is what makes the pavilion a paradigmatic medium – and a realization of the globalized mass ornament. The pavilion's ornamentality is connected to what can be called their "atmospheric thinness". They are, in Sloterdijk's terminology, the pure "Blase". One does not quite feel secure, or "at ease" in there. And perhaps one is not supposed to. The undermining of Autostadt's Skoda pavilion with water creates a voluntary feeling of unrest. The pavilion is permanently at risk of not only changing its "meaning", or function, but also of being transformed very physically by the outside entering in. The walls of the Blase are infinitely thin, and porous.

It is this feeling of unease writ large that seems to be a central feature of Anting New Town. It is the prototypical place of the replication of the Crystal Palace/pavilion principle. It is porous space; the poor quality of the individual buildings threatens to peel off the polished shell, unveiling an architecture of low-quality sameness. Anting is also porous because the non-Chinese is invited in. It is the application of the notion of porosity to the national, constructing a porous nationality. In this context, its porosity can also be seen by the surprising fear of its planners and management of being copied. Anting New Town can be seen as *a town turning pavilion*. Its porosity is connected to its thinness, and to its being-medium. Everything there seems to have a strange kind of display value; everything seems to claim that it should be read, rather than just lived with. Everything here is an element in a mediation process.

In this sense, Anting New Town is productive in the creation of a global mass ornament, employing the "real" bodies of its Chinese inhabitants as well as those of the workers in the factory, which we can assume (as the developers of Anting New Town do) to come largely from abroad. It is the replication of building principles invented and originally built elsewhere. It is itself copied. It is also part of a rhizome of satellite towns around Shanghai (English, Italian Town).

The Anting case allows for a deeper appreciation of the ambiguity of what Sloterdijk sees as the central feature of the Crystal Palace: that it is perceived as a comfort zone. On the one hand, life in the palace is comfortable, which has a lot to do with the permanent presence of the promises of a brand-saturated lifestyle. At the same time, however, the lack of any way to leave the comfort zone creates a distinct aggressiveness (Sloterdijk 2005: 269). The individual is involuntarily present in the global ornament. The permanent presence in the ornament is creating comfort, but also the discomfort of not *joining* the ornament, but rather *being immersed*, merged and trapped in it. Also, the omnipresent possibility of the creation of new ornaments provides the urban space with a strong sense of insecurity. This insecurity is not based on the potential for architectural destruction, displayed in urban horror film visions such as Godzilla or King Kong, but on the possibility that something new might be created – a new mass ornament that once again pulls subjectivities in, or transforms the existing ornaments.

The outlined transformation and undermining of the idea of human subjectivity performed by the mass ornament (and conceptualized by Kracauer) connects Anting New Town *and* Kracauer to my main argument regarding brands. The momentarily actualized brand might allow for a more thorough understanding of the lack of any stable subject position that is characteristic of brand users, even while driving this loss of identity *through* offering thinned-out versions of national identities. In this way, brand space as global space also transcends the learned distinctions between (capitalist) emptiness and (pre- or supra-capitalist) space as more meaningful, deeper. In the essay "Die Hotelhalle", Kracauer himself had developed this distinction in his comparison of the cultural significance of the (early) modern hotel lobby with that of the church (Kracauer 1963, pp. 157–172). He outlined that both churches and hotel lobbies were places that function on a post-local level. Both connect the present human beings to a larger logic by dissolving existing notions of individuality. But the logic of the hotel lobby is that of an overarching nothing-ness, whereas the church creates links to a metaphysical entity.

The way in which Kracauer theorizes the actions of humans in hotel lobbies can be interpreted as a spatial foundation for the physicality of brand engagements to be seen in the West from the mid-1950s. He calls them de-individualized "mannequins" engaging in a meaningless conversation that does nothing but confirm their belonging to the same logic of zero (ibid.: 168). Their conversation is intended not to exchange information, nor to get to know the other's individuality. Its function is to make clear that all belong to the same logic of the pure "Oberfläche" (surface). This focus on the surface can be seen as a precursor of the ways in which brands, when carried, when worn, define the individual *by doing away* with individuality.

The difference, however, is that the brand creates a new sense of content, and of affective significance. Surfaces are no longer the dimension of the exotic as with Kracauer, but carry a sense of the intimate. The sense of a duality between the *rich* post-individualized being in a church and a *poor* post-individualism in the hotel lobby is substituted by a sense of a post-individualized intimacy of those carrying the same brand logos on their bodies, driving them around, or using them otherwise. From this perspective, the term "mannequin" that Kracauer suggests proves prophetic. Because today, all the functions of the mannequin, the working in a condition of "künstlicher Dauerbeleuchtung", in permanent crass artificial lighting, are fundamentally met not by models, but by all of us. Hence, branded product and brand space work together. The carrying of brands makes us mannequins in Kracauer's sense, and the creation of brand space implies the permanence of artificial lighting.

What is interesting from the perspective of a mediatization of space is that Kracauer identifies the logic of the hotel lobby with that of the number zero. The term "null", core element in all concepts of digital media, is present throughout the essay, and it seems to condense everything that distinguishes hotel lobby from church. However, for Kracauer, the zero is not pure negation; it is also becoming productive. The zero is creating a "Schein der Gestaltenfülle" (Kracauer 1963: 165). From what this work has argued, this "appearance of the fullness of shapes" can be interpreted as the presence of the virtual. This presence, and this productiveness of the zero, indicates a new relationship between new media and space. From this perspective, new media is not so much entering space from outside, transforming functioning spatial arrangements. Rather, space is developing its inherent potentialities by means of the virtualization of the zero. If space is obtaining a logic of new media, as has been argued in chapter 5 and as seems to be supported by Kracauer's intensive use of the term null, then this means primarily the permanent possibility of restarting, constantly reconfiguring spatial relationalities.

Kracauer presents the relationship between lobby and church in a dualistic way. With the urban becoming subject to processes of brand spatialization, this duality can be argued to be overcome. It is the notion of *the global* as developed in this chapter that transforms the extra-religious emptiness of the hotel room as capitalist space. In the brand spaces capitalism creates, mediatization offers the global the opportunity to become a productive presence, a place-intensifying entity. The differentiations pure locality allowed for, those of concrete humans and of strong nature (ibid.: 163), lose significance through the global creating a post-local spatiality. The global then obtains almost metaphysical features, employing human bodies and human subjectivities, engaging them in the creation of an affective globality.

# 7 Conclusion

I started this work by considering the changing character of capitalism. Coming back to this angle now, I want to conclude by asking what relevance the observations in this work hold for the concept of capitalism as such. What conclusions can be drawn regarding the current transformation of capitalist reality, and, if there is such a thing, a specifically capitalist culture? More concretely, I will ask whether the spatial argument of this work simultaneously allows us to identify a novel understanding of the *temporality* or *temporalities* that capitalism is capable of producing. My point will be that through the new regime of spatial productivity that has been the topic of this work, the multiple temporalities that capitalism is staging are subject to a process of permanent change as well as processes of an inherent undermining. "Time" is no longer a primary category, but rather an effect of the spatialities of media, and of the brand.

Many past analyses of the temporalities of capitalism have focused significantly on the issue of consumption. Frantic consumption and capitalist ways of reorganizing life around how we consume were seen as a core to an encompassing capitalist time management (Featherstone 1991: 18). Consumption had been the prototypical capitalist process, and it needed a regime of reconfiguring human lifetime strategically for its desire-employing strengths to unfold. Consumption time was maximized by longer opening hours and by tools such as home shopping or internet purchases. Classical consumption time was essentially following a modernist, almost Fordist, model, developing its own stringent linearity as a resource (Lash and Urry 1994: 234).

If the brand spaces discussed in this work are an element in capitalism's quest to increase its own productivity, then one could expect them to get hold of this Fordist and modernist temporal regime, perhaps intensifying it, adding more lines of flight, but still being thoroughly focused on the temporalities of consumption. One could expect the brand spaces – which are, after all, developed by capitalist desire for actualization – to imply temporalities that are concentrated even more thoroughly on allowing for a flawless process of permanent consumption. However, brand space and brand urbanism did not turn out to be drivers of a blunt consumerism, creating an intensity of shopping that deprives urban culture of all sense of diverse and unique urban localities (as has been claimed, for instance, by Miles and Miles 2004). The temporality of a "consuming city", or a "city of consumption", often presented as the product of a myth that our society has convinced us to consume, is not what brand space is about. Rather, the myth that is consumed is that of a consumption-free brand essence. The implication is that it is no longer necessary for capitalism to manage consumption time; it even seems as if capitalism no longer needs any time for consumption at all.

What the liberation from consumption time through brand space suggests is a novel abstraction of capitalism; a capitalism that is not about shopping, not about the exchange of money against goods. This capitalism is about brands alone, developing a desire for a "pure" engagement with a brand by performing certain patterns of behaviour in a given architectural set. What turns up at this point is a thoroughly new, different regime of capitalist productivity. To understand this productivity and its impact on the relationship between space and time, I want to engage with another recent effort to understand the capitalist regime of productivity: the current concepts of immaterial labour. These concepts suggest a new dominance of a capitalist temporality. I want to reconsider this suggestion, asking whether the transformation brand space imposes upon the capitalist real also implies a transformation of its temporalities.

Although, or by, being spatial, the concept of brand space I have introduced affects the sense of time featured in a place. Massumi (2002: 30–31) describes these effects as the creation of a "lived paradox where what are normally opposites coexist, coalesce, and connect". The virtualization of space in capitalism is connected with the confrontation of different regimes of temporality. Places are deprived of their original, one-dimensional system of time.

This deprivation process has been an undercurrent of this work. In Chapter 4 I have shown how the brand-induced use of space, through business-strategic concepts such as history marketing, works through the idea of a virtual co-presence of past, presence, and future, and by demonstrating how brand space effectively challenges all notions of a relatively stable temporality and historicity. The brand, I have argued, is turning spatial through a search for stability and actualization, because the isolated management of consumption-related temporalities is no longer sufficient to generate competitive advantage. The argument I made around this process has then become the foundation for an analysis of the transformational capacities of capitalism in space. I have argued that the spatialized capitalist regime of brand space creates a new possibility for capitalism to actualize, thereby also generating new intensities of virtuality and actuality. I have outlined the degree to which this transformation can occur, but also shown the potential for a catastrophic outcome that this process, which from a critical perspective almost appears to be a spatial and architectural gamble, entails. Effectively, I have traced the dangers inherent in the architectural "making-productive" of ideas of the historical, showing how history develops into a force of hauntology.

Chapter 5 has linked this media-capitalist thinking to the idea of a new, mediatized regime of urban space. I have shown that brand space as media space, and specifically as space of new media, is transforming any possibility of the constitution of a stable "urbanity", and even more that of an "urban public sphere". The city is entering into a mode that has been described as virtual urbanity. In this process, architectural urban structure has been shown to be forcing the historical into space – in a way that brings out its colliding forces. This again implies the dimension of the temporal mainly as a problem, because what I called "hybrid history" effectively means that different temporalities create different strands of history, and these collide in space.

These colliding temporalities have been demonstrated to be part of what I called processes of "viral urbanism". The mediatization of urban space has been demonstrated not to occur in a linear way, but virally, paralleling the flows of information in the spaces of new media. The result of this is a new intensity of global urbanity; the world is not becoming, as McLuhan thought, a global village, but rather a space for the constitution of potentially conflicting global urban force fields.

The workings of these force fields have been treated in more detail in Chapter 6. Here, I have extended the primarily Deleuzian perspective by integrating it into Sloterdijk's spheres. These have been argued to allow for a thoroughly spatial understanding of the Deleuzian interactions of virtuality and actuality. Simultaneously, Sloterdijk's philosophy of a Schaum sphere also afforded the development of an understanding of the specific spatiality of mediatized spaces; they are connective and disconnective, rather than informational and disinformational. Or rather, even informational elements constitute primarily spatial, and even architectural, categories; they create connectivities and disconnectivities, rather than shared meanings.

This is also the sense in which I have linked Sloterdijk's thinking to the concept of the mass ornament suggested by Kracauer. I have argued that the mass ornament, as a spatial key category of modernity, has itself been thoroughly transformed, and that brand space is a central figure in this transformation. I suggested the notion of a *global mass ornament*, of which brand space would be a driver and a key example. What I have shown is that these global mass ornaments feature a permanent redefinition of dimensions, with verticality and horizontality permanently engaging with and merging into one another, thereby demonstrating the feasibility of approaching the spatial development of branded reality with concepts suggested by topology. It can be seen as an addition to the approaches of topological thinking that I have managed to show how creating spaces of surfaces allows even for a "surfacization of intimacy"; the surface can be "intimate", and so can the global.

From the arguments of this work, then, a notion of capitalist reality can be derived that makes the temporality of today's cultural conditions understandable only when combined with the complex spatialities at play within the capitalist realm of an extended, in fact increasingly limitless, cultural and economic production. This concluding argument engages critically with a post-Marxist understanding of capitalism as primarily temporal. In this, Kittler's mediatization theory once more becomes productive. The historical development of media that Kittler demonstrates is also very much a development of the nature of capitalism. From this viewpoint, this techno-capitalist development features an increasing complication of the cultural role of time. Time is becoming a variable to be manipulated (Krämer 2006: 96). Real time can now be stored and processed. Furthermore, the whole temporal order is turning into a variable that can be changed and manipulated. This entire process is triggered by the experience of space (Kittler 1997: 130–146). I hope to have offered some insights as to how such an "order-reversing experience of space" can be created. For future research, determining where else such reversals of the temporal order take place might prove a worthwhile undertaking.

Such analyses will have to deal with the question of what kind of capitalist production process is concerned. In order to understand the degree to which these processes are Postfordist, it makes sense to end this book with a reference to Lazzarato's work on the concept of immaterial labour (Lazzarato 1996b). For Lazzarato, this concept is central to his understanding of time, just as time is for him one central category to any engagement with capitalism. In this account, capitalism is moving away from a notion of power that is based mainly on a logic of prescription or ideology. This new regime of power is intimately related to the very specific temporalities of capitalism beyond Fordist control of the temporal. In this sense, Lazzarato (1996a: 117) is right to point out that the making-productive of the temporal for the productivity processes based on his notion of immaterial labour does not rely on any specific time, like the Marxist "labour time". Any kind of time can be subsumed in immaterial labour processes. However, from the perspective of this work, this thought has to be extended. The contradictory production situation is characterized by an encompassing materiality of the immaterial; immaterial labour needs the material and architectural. It is in space that brands develop their own strategy of multi-temporality; it is in brand space that they create different time regimes. The active employment of micro-histories that has been described in Chapter 4 means that the presence of numerous different temporal implications is itself an architectural productivity factor for capitalism. In immaterial labour regimes, capitalism is becoming more effective to the degree that it manages to integrate as many temporal shifts, and the confrontation of as many temporal differences as possible, into one plane of immanence. This plane of immanence has been conceptualized in this work as a *global mass ornament*.

From this perspective, the political construct in Lazzarato's work of multitudes undermining immaterial labour processes by setting their own time regimes has to be questioned. If multitudes develop their own time regimes, then this does not mean that capitalism won't employ them for its own purposes. Whether it manages to do so is a matter of its own competitiveness and flexibility. In principle, however, it would seem as if a capitalism that has at its very heart the employment of as many different regimes of time as possible has the capacity to exploit all imaginable temporal settings. Hence, all escapes from capitalist production, and all malfunctions within the capitalist employment of time, some of which I have described in this work, are in themselves temporary.

Beyond this power-related argument, however, it needs to be stated that contemporary capitalism, especially when entering the urban as its main playground, is at the same time a battleground for what can be called, without overstating, "time wars". If "technologies of time" are at work which "allow the exteriorization of intelligence" as the foundation of immaterial labour (Toscano 2007: 85), then the question is per se open to what extent intelligence is indeed exteriorized, and in which cooperative context it eventually finds itself. This is a radical openness in Lazzarato's thinking, and there is no need to argue against it as a whole – as long as one is aware of the potential short-term-ness of any escape from the employment of a certain temporal setting through capitalism.

The concluding remarks above position this work in the context of the current trend towards a cultural analysis of capitalist space. One of its strengths was hopefully to develop a more precise picture of some of the inherent ambiguities of contemporary capitalist productivity. What I have tried to do is shed light on one particular spatial process of capitalist self-reinvention and on the transformations this induced for the ways concrete physical urban places are perceived and mediated, and for the degree to which they can indeed still be argued to be "lived", as cultural theorists used to call the appropriation of space. But the working of multiple (de- and re-)temporalizations, which much of this conclusion is dedicated to, transforms these possibilities thoroughly. Vice versa, the (de- and re-)temporalization of space by and beyond capitalist strategies is in itself temporal. This suggests some directions for future research. For the transformation of special time regimes through brands is just one possible impact of what I called mediatization. There can be many other mediatization processes, also evoking other particular regimes of time and other processes of time destruction. To trace the spatial configurations of these (de- and re-)temporalizations and the capitalist self-identifications they create is a meaningful approach to the cultural study of the presence. In order to understand capitalism, one has to take into account the way in which it transforms space by trying to develop its own temporalized regimes of space.

Perhaps the most difficult approach to the effects of the new, mediatization-driven capitalist space-time, or rather, times-space, would be to trace its effects on the concept of human subjectivity, on its disappearance (as noted by many poststructuralist writers), but also on its surprising reappearances where one might not expect it. The question is what kind of anthropology can still record what is happening within individuals and their social interaction when the self is, as Sloterdijk calls it, "light", and when the subject cannot depend on its own temporality, but rather encounters time merely as a permanently changing force? Can one talk about the human condition without locating it in spatio-temporal coordinates? Lury (2004: 96) points to the direction such an analysis would have to take as far as the effects of branding are concerned. She describes how brand logos worn by people create situations in which multiple frames of time are at work simultaneously. These time frames will have to be traced on a recurring basis for any subject of, to speak once more with Sloterdijk, "Schaum" that is at stake.

In terms of space, this research would always imply a search for spaces or places that are simultaneously *in* and *at a distance from* (Amin and Thrift 2002: 41). As this work has argued, the degree of multiplicity is even stronger in situations where brands or branded logos are no longer worn by passers-by, but are physically around at a place as is the case in brand space; any conventional sense of place is broken up, place becomes near and distanced at once, and gets connected to a larger temporal regime, the centre and functioning of which remain unclear to the visitor. The concrete place itself becomes an actor in a process of inhibiting and extending the possibility of traditional concepts of place and time. Again, this leads to further questions for future cultural analyses: how to pinpoint human subjectivity in this process? And what is the role of the mentioned concept of "dark space" in this (Vidler 1992)? As outlined, Vidler describes space as a category inherently characterized by objects of fear and phobia. But to what extent is this phobia caused by the de-temporalization of space itself? And can that de-temporalization create a subjectivity based mainly on negative sentiments? Is fear the main driver of subjectivity in capitalist space? These questions point to one conviction that was present in all the arguments of this work: that the mediatization of urban space is always both – threat and productive change.

# Glossary of German terms

| | |
|---|---|
| Ästhetischer Reflex | aesthetic reflex |
| Blase | bubble |
| Emporgehobene Meta-Städte | elevated meta-cities |
| Große Installation | great installation |
| Gruppenbehälter | group container |
| kollektiver Fließraum | space of collective flow |
| Innenraum | internal space |
| null | zero |
| Oberflächenäußerungen | surface expressions |
| Schaum | foam |
| Schichten | strata |
| Sphären | spheres |
| Streuung | spreading |
| Unbehagen | the uncanny |
| Verdichtungsräume | spaces of densification |
| Weltinnenraum des Kapitals | inner world space of capital |
| Wohnmaschine | dwelling machine (French original "unité d'habitation") |

# Notes

## 1 Introduction

1 The term used in many texts dealing with capitalist spatialization strategies is that of "brandscape" (cf. Klingman 2007). However, "brandscape" often signifies a marketing-strategic concept, referring to an assumed strategic appropriation of space. Therefore, applying the brandscape terminology might limit the analytical perspective. Hence, it makes more sense to refer to corporate space-related brand building efforts more neutrally as "brand space", which I will do throughout this work.
2 Kittler, too, has been employed in this respect, although, as I will show later, he can also be read in a spatial way.

## 2 The cases

1 This de-naturalization of atmosphere links Coop Himmelb(l)au's architectural philosophy with Sloterdijk's understanding of atmosphere as a creation of architecture. For Sloterdijk, atmosphere is the outcome of the nineteenth-century process of making globalization a mediatized phenomenon; atmosphere is what is created, in hothouses or botanical gardens, to mediatize globalization (Sloterdijk 2004: 338–358).
2 This urbanist dominance of the stadium points to the cultural (and factual) power of the stadium as a prototypical modernist architectural form, constituting the architectural frame for the effectiveness of cultural or political movements (Sloterdijk 2004: 626–645) or, in the current context, reflecting movement and the dynamics of modernity itself in an architectural way, creating a structure that almost appears to be made out of pure movement. This abstract force of movement is taken up by the dynamic architecture of BMW Welt, a process that indicates a significant proximity between the stadium as the classical modernist "collector" as suggested by Sloterdijk – and brand space as discussed in this work – as an extension of the collector function into a world of a thorough globalized hypermediality.
3 For an argument pointing out the necessity of developing a postcolonial critique of contemporary capitalist urban space, see King (2006).
4 Of course, we are dealing with a glorified version of the medieval town here, unaware of medieval backyards as they actually were: dirty, smelly and loud rather than harmonious and green.

## 3 Branding and the spatialization of capitalism

1 Analytically, it is also a way of bringing business discourses into closer relation with certain arguments stemming from complexity theory (cf. Thrift 1998 and 2008).

2 Despite being treated as paradigmatic model village, the level of concreteness of Cadbury's spatial-social idea is contested today (see Bryson and Lowe 2002).
3 Similarly, Deleuze and Guattari do not talk about territories so much as about territorialization. For Deleuze and Guattari, the space of the city is not based on strict organization and striation only (a certain form of territorialization), but also on deterritorialization – and on chaos (Deleuze and Guattari 1987: 481). This is relevant, also, as we will see later, with regard to branding. Brand city building takes a part of the capitalist system (the brand) and confronts it with what it is not. This opens up opportunities for new processes of deterritorialization. Whatever reaction of capitalism to that process my analysis will define, it can be said already at this point that the reaction will go beyond a mere logic of attack and counterattack, of domination and resistance. The smooth-striated opposition "gives rise to far more difficult complications, alternations, and superpositions" (ibid.).
4 I do not see the virtual as the all-encompassing concept to describe "our world". Virtuality is a quality that might be a tendency in contemporary cities, but is also confronted with counterforces that are completely actual or territorial. Virtualization even triggers actualization. This is relevant because when I suggest brands to be virtual, then I contrast branding with other concepts in contemporary capitalism that are not adequately described as virtual.
5 Sloterdijk grants the notion of the bubble (Blase) ontological status as one of the three dimensions within which he analyzes reality (aside globes and foams). In terms of capitalism, then, the bubble is not a term for criticizing the artificiality of certain boom phases without real economic substance, as it is in the language of economics. The world is essentially always creating bubbles, and linking them to foam structures.

## 4 Actualizing the virtual of capitalism?

1 The image effects of car crashes have been demonstrated by David Cronenberg in *Crash* (Cronenberg 1996). Therein, the crash develops a higher reality beyond destruction or pain. It seems to promise a richer way of life.
2 At the same time, a more negative reading would also be possible. From that perspective, such pseudo-architectural imitations can also be read as a deconstruction of any imaginable "alternative" urbanity. The massive presence of such poster buildings in today's metropolises would then imply that urban space does not even need this alternative to be built. Perhaps its simulated form is sufficient in itself.
3 Nevertheless, copyright infringements are a significant issue for all major producing industries. In this respect, it is interesting to see how China itself is applying and extending the – originally Western – concept of brand space. For a discussion of notions of the copy in Chinese culture and capitalism see Pang (2008).
4 Consequently, Toyota is also among the car companies defining space through the values and ideas of their company. Their headquarters and seven of their twelve Japanese factories are all based in an artificial, mono-structural town called "Toyota City" (Saiki 2003).
5 This, of course, holds particularly true for companies such as Volkswagen, the history of which cannot be understood independently of the German Nazi past. The Nazis are the "ghost" haunting German history-writing, and with the history of Wolfsburg and the Volkswagen company, it is "spooking around" in the area where Volkswagen built Autostadt.
6 The German Kaiserreich was present in China as a colonial power by occupying the province of Jiaozhou until 1914.

## 5 Virtualizing the actual of space

1 Von Borries (2004: 78 ff.) claims that the event-based urban intervention achieved by Nike in their Niketowns and in the basketball playgrounds they create in urban environments goes further than the urban engagement of Autostadt. By contrast, from the perspective of this work, both Autostadt and Nike basketball courts are urban engagements aimed at delivering their own version of contemporary urban process. Comparing the two, the Nike-style creation of urban sports playgrounds makes it easier for the participant to "understand" the event that is taking place, and thereby also to understand the city. The Nike events allow for an easy creation of a mental picture of what the constructed cityscape is; the city is what I experience when I engage in the event. In Autostadt, on the other hand, the visitor is left unaware what exactly the place "is", and how to deal with it, how to "experience" it.
2 For the specific regime of productive abstraction as a feature of contemporary capitalism see Toscano's comments on the Marxian concept of "Real-Abstraktion" (Toscano 2008).
3 The degree to which German post-war society can indeed be charged with not having faced its Nazi guilt is subject to significant controversy (cf. Graml 1990: 169).
4 The experience of images through movement can be read as the counterpart to the Deleuzian concept of the movement-image (Deleuze 1986), where the movement was *in* the image.
5 Recently, the dread of being pulled into screens became a major motif for horror movies.
6 It is in this sense consequent that the football arena of VFL Wolfsburg has been built only 200 metres away. On matchdays, the noises from the arena are heard in Autostadt. And of course, this building of another big solitary architectural structure creates a new competition – for attention, for spatial dominance and, ultimately, the flow of visitors.
7 Viruses are, after all, deliberately produced, often quite smart, computer programs, and are praised for their capacity to unveil security problems. For an actor-network-theoretical discussion of the computer virus, see Parikka (2007: 11–20).
8 From the viewpoint of this work, this can be interpreted as a link between Ruscha's work and the excessive use of lighting in BMW Welt outlined earlier.
9 For a discussion of the notion of the ruin in twentieth-century cultural thinking, see Lash (2001: 152–153).
10 Even though subjectivity created in brand space is weak and temporary, the change effects of brand space on subjects do not necessarily vanish with the end of a visit (even if only because we take the merchandise t-shirts home, thereby being marked as brand citizen). Moor (2004) outlines the way this works when developing the notion of the brand as a "mask or framing device for the subject" (ibid.: 64).
11 This distinguishes them from Baudrillard's concept of simulacra (Baudrillard 1994).
12 The contradictory character of these two different approaches is demonstrated by Wang (2008, Chapter 3).

## 6 The rise of the global mass ornament

1 At the same time, it remains the object of virtualizations in terms of the dreams of the conquerors.
2 It would be an interesting project, but beyond the scope of this book, to investigate whether it is possible to argue for a mediatization even in such apparently media-free areas as large-scale farming. Can agricultural activity be analyzed through a media-theoretical framework?

# References

Aaker, D.A. (1996) *Building Strong Brands*, New York: Free Press.
Ackers, W. (2000) "Lernen von Wolfsburg? Der EQ als Standortfaktor", in Deutsche Akademie für Städtebau (ed.) *Wer plant die Stadt? Wer baut die Stadt? Bericht 2000*, Berlin: Edition StadtBauKunst.
Ackroyd, P. (2000) *London: The Biography*, London: Chatto & Windus.
Alison, J., Brayer, M.-J., Migayrou, F. and Spiller, N. (eds) (2006) *Future City: Experiment and Utopia in Architecture 1956–2006*, London: Thames & Hudson.
Allais, L. and Rock, M. (2004) "Wired is History", in R. Koolhaas (ed.) *Content*, Cologne: Taschen.
Amin, A. and Thrift, N. (2002) *Reimagining the Urban*, Cambridge: Polity.
Andersen. T. (2003) *Los Angeles Plays Itself*, Los Angeles: Thom Andersen Productions. [DVD].
Ang, I. (1999) "Radikaler Kontextualismus und Ethnographie in der Rezeptionsforschung", in A. Hepp and R. Winter (eds) *Kultur – Medien – Macht: Cultural Studies und Medienanalyse*, 2nd edn, Opladen: Westdeutscher Verlag.
Appadurai, A. (ed.) (1986) *The Social Life of Things: Commodities in Cultural Perspective*, Cambridge: Cambridge University Press.
—— (1996) *Modernity at Large: Cultural Dimensions of Globalization*, Minneapolis: University of Minnesota Press.
Argento, D. (1977) *Suspiria*, Los Angeles: Blue Underground. [DVD].
Armitage, J. (1999) "From Modernism to Hypermodernism and Beyond: An Interview with Paul Virilio", *Theory, Culture and Society*, Vol. 16 (5–6): 25–55.
Arvidsson, A. (2005) "Brands: A Critical Perspective", *Journal of Consumer Culture* Vol. 5, No. 2: 235–258.
—— (2006) *Brands: Meaning and Value in Media Culture*, London: Routledge.
—— (2007) "The Logic of the Brand", *European Journal of Economic and Social Systems*, 20 (1): 99–115.
Arvidsson, A. and Peitersen, N. (in press) *The Ethical Economy*, New York: Columbia University Press.
Assheuer, T. (2005) "Die Werk-Stadt", *Zeit Wissen* 13: 64–67.
Attridge, D., Bennington, G. and Young, R. (eds) (1987) *Post-Structuralism and the Question of History*, Cambridge: Cambridge University Press.
Augé, M. (1995) *Non-Places*, London: Verso.
Autostadt GMBH (2007) *Automobile Erlebniswelten in Deutschland: Wettbewerbsanalyse*, Wolfsburg: Autostadt GmbH [unpublished internal report].
Badiou, A. (2007) "The Event in Deleuze"; trans. J. Roffe, *Parrhesia* 2, 37–44.

Ballard, J.G. (2006) *Super-Cannes*, London: Harper Perennial.
Barthes, R. (1972) *Mythologies*, New York: Hill & Wang.
Baudrillard, J. (1973) *Le miroir de la production;* trans. M. Poster (1975) *The Mirror of Production*, St. Louis: Telos.
—— (1981) *Simulacre et Simulation;* trans. S. F. Glaser (1994) *Simulacra and Simulation*, Ann Arbor: University of Michigan Press.
—— (1968) *Le Système des objets;* trans J. Benedict (1996) *The System of Objects*, London: Verso.
Beaverstock, J.V. (2005) "Transnational Elites in the City: British Highly-Skilled Inter-Company Transferees in New York City's Financial District", *Journal of Ethnic and Migration Studies*, 31(2): 245–268.
Beckmann, J. (2004) "Mobility and Safety", *Theory, Culture and Society* 21(4/5): 81–100.
Beller, J. (2002) "KINO-I, KINO-WORLD: Notes on the Cinematic Mode of Production", in N. Mirzoeff (ed.) *The Visual Culture Reader*, London: Routledge.
Benjamin, W. (1925, new edn 1972a) "Neapel", in W. Benjamin *Gesammelte Schriften* (R. Tiedemann and H. Schweppenhäuser eds) (vol. IV), Frankfurt/Main: Suhrkamp.
—— (1929, new edn 1972b) "Die Wiederkehr des Flâneurs", in W. Benjamin *Gesammelte Schriften* (R. Tiedemann and H. Schweppenhäuser eds) (vol. III), Frankfurt/Main: Suhrkamp.
—— (1983) *Das Passagenwerk*, Frankfurt/Main: Suhrkamp.
Bentele, G., Großkurth, L. and Seidenglanz, R. (2005) *Profession Pressesprecher: Vermessung eines Berufstands*, Berlin: Helios Media.
Berg, D. (2010) "Die zwei Türme" [Online]. *manager magazin online*, 28 March. Available from <http://www.manager-magazin.de/lifestyle/auto/0,2828,682648,00.html> [Accessed 8 November, 2010].
Bernhart, W. and Dressler, N. (2008) *The Next Wave: Emerging Market Innovation, Threats and Opportunities*, Munich: Roland Berger Strategy Consultants.
Bieber, C. (2000) *Die Sneaker Story*, Frankfurt/Main: Fischer.
Bingham, N. and Thrift, N. (2000) "Some Instructions for Travellers: The Geography of Bruno Latour and Michel Serres", in M. Crang and N. Thrift (eds) *Thinking Space*, London: Routledge.
Böhme, G. (1995) *Atmosphäre: Essays zur neuen Ästhetik*, Frankfurt/Main: Suhrkamp.
—— (2006) *Architektur und Atmosphäre*, Munich: Wilhelm Fink.
Bonomi, A. (2002) "Smooth Space", in R. Koolhaas, S. Boeri and S. Kwinter (eds) *Mutations*, Barcelona: Actar.
Borch, C. (2009) "Schaum-Organizationen: Über das Management von Atmosphären", in M. Jongen, S. van Tuinen and K. Hemelsoet (eds) *Die Vermessung des Ungeheuren: Philosophie nach Peter Sloterdijk*, Munich: Wilhelm Fink.
Borgelt, C. (2005) *Architecture in Wolfsburg*, Berlin: Stadtwandel Verlag.
Bourdieu, P. (1979) *La distinction: Critique sociale du jugement;* trans. R. Nice (1984) *Distinction: A Social Critique of the Judgement of Taste*, London: Routledge & Kegan Paul.
Brayer, M.A. (2006) "the spirit of experimentation", in J. Alison, M.A. Brayer, F. Migayrou and N. Spiller (eds) *future city: experiment and utopia in architecture 1956–2006*, London: Thames & Hudson.
Brenner, N. and Keil, R. (eds) (2005) *The Global Cities Reader*, London: Routledge.

Bridge, G. and Watson, S. (2001) "Retext(ur)ing the City", *City* 5(3): 350–362.
—— (eds) (2002) *The Blackwell City Reader*, Oxford: Blackwell.
Brownlie, D., Saren, M., Wensley, R. and Whittington, R. (eds) (1999) *Rethinking Marketing: Towards Critical Marketing Accountings*, London: Sage.
Bruhn, M. and Ahlers, M. (2004) "Der Streit um die Vormachtstellung von Marketing und Public Relations in der Unternehmenskommunikation: Eine unendliche Geschichte?", in *Marketing*, 1st Quarter: 71–80.
Bryson, J. and Lowe, P. (2002) "Story-Telling and History Construction: Rereading George Cadbury's Bournville Model Village", *Journal of Historical Geography* 28 (1): 21–41.
Buck-Morss, S. (1989) *The Dialectics of Seeing: Walter Benjamin and the Arcades Project*, Cambridge, Mass.: The MIT Press.
Bull, M. (2004) "Automobility and the Power of Sound", *Theory, Culture and Society*, 21(4/5): 243–260.
Bussmann, K. (2009) "Der Pavillon: Eine Geschichte der beständigen Vergänglichkeit", in P. Cachola Schmal (ed.) *Der Pavillon: Lust und Polemik in der Architektur*, Ostfildern: Hatje Cantz
Cachola Schmal, P. (ed.) (2009) *Der Pavillon: Lust und Polemik in der Architektur*, Ostfildern: Hatje Cantz.
Callon, M. (ed.) (1998) *The Laws of the Markets*, Oxford: Blackwell.
Campbell, C. (2006) *Icons of Twentieth-Century Landscape Design*, London: Frances Lincoln.
Carrier, J.G. and Miller, D. (eds) (1998) *Virtualism: A New Political Economy*, Oxford: Berg.
Castells, M. (1977) *The Urban Question*, London: Arnold.
—— (1989) *The Informational City*, Oxford: Blackwell.
—— (1996) *The Rise of the Network Society*, Oxford: Blackwell.
Cai Y. and Bo, H. (2004) "Anting Neustadt: Die Transposition europäischer Raumformen nach China", in D. Hassenpflug (ed.) *Die aufgeschlossene Stadt: Öffentlicher Raum in China von Anting bis Zhuhai*, Weimar: VDG.
Caygill, H. (1998) *Walter Benjamin: The Colour of Experience*, London: Routledge.
Chaplin, S. (1997) "Report to the Virtual HQ: The Distributed City", *The Journal of Architecture*, 2(1): 43–57.
Chikamori, T. (2009) "Between the 'Media City' and the 'City as a Medium'", *Theory, Culture and Society* 26(4): 147–154.
Christmann, G.B. (2004) *Dresdens Glanz, Stolz der Dresdner: lokale Kommunikation, Stadtkultur und städtische Identität*, Wiesbaden: DUV.
Chung, C.J., Inaba, J., Koolhaas, R. and Leong, S.T. (eds) (2001) *Harvard Design School Guide to Shopping*, Cologne: Taschen.
Cochoy, F. (1998) "Another Discipline for the Market Economy: Marketing as a Performative Knowledge and Know-How for Capitalism", in M. Callon (ed.) *The Laws of the Markets*, Oxford: Blackwell, 194–221.
Cohen, S. and Taylor, L. (1992) *Escape Attempts: The Theory and Practice of Resistance in Everyday Life*, London: Routledge.
Colebrook, C. (2002) *Gilles Deleuze*, London: Routledge.
—— (2004) "The Sense of Space: On the Specificity of Affect in Deleuze and Guattari", *Postmodern Culture*, 15(1). [Online]. Available from <http://muse.jhu.edu/login?uri=/journals/postmodern_culture/v015/15.1colebrook.html>.

Collins, J. (1995) *Architectures of Excess*, New York: Routledge.
Cova, B. (1999) "From Marketing to Societing: When the Link is More Important than the Thing", in D. Brownlie, M. Saren, R. Wensley and R. Whittington (eds) *Rethinking Marketing: Towards Critical Marketing Accountings*, London: Sage.
Cova, B. and Cova, V. (2002) "Tribal Marketing: The Tribalization of Society and Its Impact on the Conduct of Marketing", *European Journal of Marketing*, 36: 595–620.
Crary, J. (1999) *Suspensions of Perception: Attention, Spectacle, and Modern Culture*, Cambridge, Mass.: The MIT Press.
Cronenberg, D. (1996) *Crash*, Toronto: Alliance Atlantis. [DVD].
D'Aveni, R. (1994) *Hypercompetition*, New York: The Free Press.
Dalan, M. (2008) "Autokäufer entdecken ihre Liebe zum Phaeton", *Die Welt*, 15 April: 24.
De Bertodano, H. (2006) "Willkommen in Marthasville", *Welt am Sonntag* 50: 89.
De Muynck, B. (2010) "Hard Facts: The Shanghai 2010 World Expo in Numbers", *Mark*, 27: 170–181.
—— (2012) "Eine Stadt, neun Städtchen", *Bauwelt*, 7: 22–30.
Debord, G. (1970) *La Société du spectacle*; trans. D. Nicholson-Smith (2002) *The Society of the Spectacle*, New York: Zone Books.
Delanty, G. and Jones, P.R. (2002) "European Identity and Architecture", *European Journal of Social Theory* 5(4): 453–466.
Deleuze, G. (1982) *Cinéma 1: l'image mouvement*; trans. H. Tomlinson and B. Habberjam (1986) *Cinema 1: The Movement Image*, London: The Athlone Press.
—— (1966) *Le Bergsonisme*; trans. C. Boundas (1988) *Bergsonism*, New York: Zone Books.
—— (1983) *Cinéma 2: l'image temps*; trans. H. Tomlinson and R. Galeta (1989) *Cinema 2: The Time-Image*, London: The Athlone Press.
—— (1969) *Logique du sens*; trans. M. Lester and C. Boundas (1990) *The Logic of Sense*, New York: Columbia University Press.
—— (1968) *Différence et Répétition*; trans. P. Patton (1994) *Difference and Repetition*, London: The Athlone Press.
—— (1990) *Pourparlers 1972–1990*; trans. M. Joughin (1995) *Negotiations 1972–1990*, New York: Columbia University Press.
Deleuze, G. and Guattari, F. (1972) *Capitalisme et Schizophrénie: L'Anti-Oedipe*; trans. R. Hurley, M. Seem and H. R. Lane (1977) *Anti-Oedipus: Capitalism and Schizophrenia*, London: The Athlone Press.
—— (1980) *Capitalisme et Schizophrénie 2: Mille Plateaux*; trans. B. Massumi (1985) *A Thousand Plateaus: Capitalism and Schizophrenia 2*, London: The Athlone Press.
DeLillo, D. (1995) *White Noise*, London: Picador.
—— (2003) *Cosmopolis*, New York: Simon & Schuster.
Dell, J. (2005) "Anting New Town: 'German Town', A Case Study", speech delivered at *UIA Conference 'City Edge'*, Shanghai, 22 April.
—— (2008) Interview with Johannes Dell. Shanghai, 19 May.
Derrida, J. (1993) *Spectres de Marx*; trans. P. Kamuf (1994) *Spectres of Marx*, London: Routledge.
Dexter, E. and Weski, T. (eds) (2003) *Cruel and Tender: The Real in the Twentieth-Century Photograph*, London: Tate Modern.

Doel, M. (2000) "Un-glunking Geography: Spatial Science after Dr Seuss and Gilles Deleuze", in M. Crang and N. Thrift (eds) *Thinking Space*, London: Routledge
Doel, M. and Hubbard, P. (2003) "Taking World Cities Literally: Marketing the City in a Global Space of Flows", *City* 6(3): 351–368.
Doevendans, K. and Schram, A. (2005) "Creation/Accumulation City", *Theory, Culture and Society* 22(2): 29–43.
Drews, G. (2003) "Weimar und Anting New Town", *Weimar Kultur Journal* 6: 17–19.
Du Gay, P. (ed.) (1997) *Production of Culture/Cultures of Production*, London: Sage.
Elliott, A. (2009) *Contemporary Social Theory: An Introduction*, London: Routledge.
Entman, R. (1993) "Framing: Toward Classification of a Fractured Paradigm", *Journal of Communication* 43(4): 870–888.
Erling, J. (2005) "Chinas neue Vorstadt", *Die Welt*, 24 October: 10.
—— (2007) "Wir sind jetzt halbe Chinesen", *Die Welt*, 15 April: 12.
Engels, F. (1845, new edn 1976) *Die Lage der arbeitenden Klasse in England*, Berlin: Dietz.
Esomar (2007) *Global Market Research 2007: Esomar Industry Report*, Amsterdam: Esomar.
Featherstone, M. (1998) "The *Flâneur*, the City and Virtual Public Life", *Urban Studies*, 35 (5–6): 909–925.
—— (2004) "Automobilities: An Introduction", *Theory, Culture and Society*, 21(4/5): 2–24.
—— (2009) "Ubiquitous Media: An Introduction", *Theory, Culture and Society* 26(2/3): 1–22.
Featherstone, M. and Lash, S. (1999) *Spaces of Culture*, London: Sage.
Fiske, J. (1994) *Media Matters: Everyday Culture and Political Change*, Minneapolis: University of Minnesota Press.
Flew, T. (2002) *New Media: An Introduction*, Oxford: Oxford University Press.
Florida, R. (2002) *The Rise of the Creative Class: And How It's Transforming Work, Leisure, Social and Community Life*, New York: Basic Books.
Fornäs. J. (2008) "Bridging Gaps: Ten Crosscurrents in Media Studies", *Media, Culture & Society* 30(6): 895–905.
Franck, G. (2005) "Werben und Überwachen: Zur Transformation des städtischen Raums", in L. Hempel and J. Metelmann (eds) *Bild – Raum – Kontrolle: Videoüberwachung als Zeichen gesellschaftlichen Wandels*, Frankfurt/Main: Suhrkamp.
Franklin, S., Lury, C. and Stacey, J. (2000) *Global Nature, Global Culture*, London: Sage.
Frauenfeld, J. (2005) (ed.) *Deutsch-Chinesische Projekte*, Wiesbaden: H. Nelte.
Freud, S. (1930) *Das Unbehagen in der Kultur*, Vienna: Internationaler Psychoanalytischer Verlag.
Frisby, D. (1985) *Fragments of Modernity*, Oxford: Polity Press.
Gaines-Ross, L. (2002) *CEO Capital: A Guide to Building and Leveraging CEO Reputation*, New York: John Wiley & Sons.
Gdaniec, C. (2000) "Cultural Industries, Information Technology and the Regeneration of Post-Industrial Urban Landscapes: Poblenou in Barcelona – a Virtual City?", *GeoJournal* 50(4): 379–387.
Giesen, B. (1998) *Intellectuals and the German Nation: Collective Identity in an Axial Age*, Cambridge: Cambridge University Press.

Giles, S. (2001) "Cracking the Cultural Code: Methodological Reflections on Kracauer's 'The Mass Ornament'", *Radical Philosophy* 99 (Jan/Feb): 31–39.
Gilloch, G. (1996) *Myth and Metropolis: Walter Benjamin and the City*, Cambridge: Polity Press.
Gilroy, P. (2001) "Driving while Black" in D. Miller (ed.) *Car Cultures*, Oxford: Berg, 81–104.
—— (2003) *The Black Atlantic: Modernity and Double Consciousness*, London: Verso.
Goffrey, G. (2008) "Abstract Experience", *Theory, Culture and Society* 25(4): 15–30.
Goffman, E. (1974) *Frame Analysis*, New York: Free Press.
Goldman, R. (2006) "Capital's Brandscapes", *Journal of Consumer Culture*, 6(3): 327–353.
Gottdiener, M. (1997, 2nd edn 2001) *The Theming of America: Dreams, Media Fantasies, and Themed Environments*, Boulder, Colorado: Westview Press.
Grabner, G. (2001) "Ecologies of Creativity: The Village, the Group and the Heterarchic Organization of the British Advertising Industry", *Environment and Planning* 33: 351–374.
Graml, H. (1990) "Die verdrängte Auseinandersetzung mit dem Nationalsozialismus", in M. Broszat (ed.) *Zäsuren nach 1945: Essays zur Periodisierung der deutschen Nachkriegsgeschichte*, Munich: Oldenbourg Wissenschaftsverlag.
Gregory, R. (2006) "Destination Wolfsburg: Burg or a Berg . . . Stronghold or Floating Mass? . . . Phaeno is Open to Interpretation", *Architectural Review* 4: 42–55.
Grosz, E. (2001) *Architecture from the Outside: Essays on Virtual and Real Space*, Cambridge, Mass.: The MIT Press.
Günzel, S. (2007) *Topologie: Zur Raumbeschreibung in den Kultur- und Medienwissenschaften*, Bielefeld: Transcript.
—— (2008a) "Spatial Turn – Topographical Turn – Topological Turn: Über die Unterschiede zwischen Raumparadigmen", in J. Döhring and T. Thielmann (eds) *Spatial Turn: Das Raumparadigma in den Kultur- und Sozialwissenschaften*, Bielefeld: Transcript.
—— (2008b) "Topologie und städtischer Raum", *der architect* 3: 8–10.
Gutzmer, A. (2009) "Willkommen in China", *Welt am Sonntag* 31: 27–29.
Hajer, M. (1999) "The Generic City", *Theory, Culture and Society* 16(4): 137–144.
Hall, P. (1990, 3rd edn 2002) *Cities of Tomorrow: An Intellectual History of Urban Planning and Design in the Twentieth Century*, Oxford: Blackwell.
Hall, S. (1999) "Cultural Identity and Racism", in C. Burgmer (ed.) *Rassismus in der Diskussion*, Berlin: Elefanten Press.
Hall, S., Hobson, D., Lowe, L. and Willis, P. (eds) *Culture, Media, Language: Working Papers in Cultural Studies 1972–1979*, London: Routledge.
Halstead, N. (2002) "Branding 'Perfection': Foreign as Self; Self as 'Foreign-Foreign'", *Journal of Material Culture* 7(3): 273–293.
Hannigan, J. (1998) *Fantasy City: Pleasure and Profit in the Postmodern Metropolis*, London: Routledge.
Haraway, D.J. (1991) *Simians, Cyborgs and Women: The Reinvention of Nature*, London: Free Association Books.
Hardt, M. and Negri, A. (2000) *Empire*, Cambridge, Mass.: Harvard University Press.
Harries, K. (1996) *The Ethical Function of Architecture*, New Haven, Conn.: Yale University Press.

Harrison, M. (1999) *Bournville: Model Village to Garden Suburb*, Chichester: Philimore.
Harvey, D. (1985) *The Urbanization of Capital: Studies in the Theory and History of Capitalist Urbanization*, Baltimore: Johns Hopkins University Press.
—— (1990) *The Condition of Postmodernity*, Oxford: Blackwell.
—— (1996) *Justice, Nature and the Geography of Difference*, London: Blackwell.
—— (2001) *Spaces of Capital: Towards a Critical Geography*, Edinburgh: Edinburgh University Press.
Harvey, P. (1996) *Hybrids of Modernity: Anthropology, the Nation State and the Universal Exhibition*, London: Routledge.
Hassenpflug, D. (ed.) (2004) *Die aufgeschlossene Stadt: Öffentlicher Raum in China von Anting bis Zhuhai*, Weimar: VDG.
Heidegger, M. (1927, 16th edn 1986) *Sein und Zeit*, Tübingen: Max Niemeyer.
Heineberg, H. (2001) *Grundriß allgemeine Geographie: Stadtgeographie*, Stuttgart: UTB.
Henn, G. (ed.) (2000) *Corporate Architecture: Autostadt Wolfsburg. Gläserne Manufaktur Dresden*, Berlin: Aedes.
—— (2005) Interview with Gunter Henn. Munich, 10 August.
Hepp, A. (2004) *Cultural Studies und Medienanalyse*, Opladen: Westdeutscher Verlag.
Hetherington, K. (1997) "In Place of Geometry: The Materiality of Place", in K. Hetherington and R. Munro (eds) *Ideas of Difference*, Oxford: Blackwell.
—— (1998) *Expressions of Identity: Space, Performance, Politics*, London: Sage.
Hirsch, N. (2009) "Die Pavillonisierung der Architektur", in P. Cachola Schmal (ed.) *Der Pavillon: Lust und Polemik in der Architektur*, Ostfildern: Hatje Cantz.
Hobson, D. (1982) *Crossroads: The Drama of a Soap Opera*, London: Methuen.
Honour, H. and Fleming, J. (2005) *A World History of Art*, London: Laurence King Publishing.
Horkheimer, M. (1939) "Die Juden und Europa", *Zeitschrift für Sozialforschung* 8: 115–137.
Hosoya, H. and Schaefer, M. (2001) "Brand Zone", in C.J. Chung, J. Inaba, R. Koolhaas and S.T. Leong (eds) *Harvard Design School Guide to Shopping*, Cologne: Taschen.
Jacobs, J. (1961) *The Death and Life of Great American Cities*, New York: Random House.
Jameson, F. (1991) *Postmodernism, or, The Cultural Logic of Late Capitalism*, London: Verso.
Jongen, M., van Tuinen, S. and Hemelsoet, K. (eds) (2009) *Die Vermessung des Ungeheuren: Philosophie nach Peter Sloterdijk*, Munich: Wilhelm Fink.
Kaltwasser, M., Majewska, E. and Szreder, K. (eds) (2007) *Industriestadtfuturismus: 100 Jahre Wolfsburg/Nowa Huta*, Frankfurt/Main: Revolver.
Keith, M. (2000) "Walter Benjamin, Urban Studies, and the Narratives of City Life", in G. Bridge and S. Watson (eds) *A Companion to the City*, Oxford: Blackwell.
Keller, K.L. (1998) *Strategic Brand Management*, Saddle River, New York: Prentice Hall.
Kim, W.C. and Mauborgne, R. (2005) *Blue Ocean Strategy: How to Create Uncontested Market Space and Make the Competition Irrelevant*, Cambridge, Mass.: Harvard Business School Press.

King, A. (1991) *Urbanism, Colonialism and the World Economy*, London: Routledge.
—— (2006) "World Cities: Global? Postcolonial? Postimperial? Or Just the Result of Happenstance? Some Cultural Comments", in N. Brenner and R. Keil (eds) *The Global Cities Reader*, London: Routledge.
Kittler, F. (1986) *Grammophone, Film, Typewriter*, Berlin: Merve.
—— (1988) "Die Stadt ist ein Medium", in G. Fuchs, B. Moltmann and W. Prigge (eds) *Mythos Metropole*, Frankfurt/Main: Suhrkamp.
—— (1993) *Draculas Vermächtnis: Technische Schriften*, Leipzig: Reclam.
—— (1985, 3rd revised edn 1995) *Aufschreibsysteme 1800–1900*, Munich: Wilhelm Fink.
—— (1997) *Literature, Media, Information Systems*, Amsterdam: OPA.
Klein, N. (1997, 2nd revised edn 2008) *The History of Forgetting: Los Angeles and the Erasure of Memory*, New York: Verso.
—— (2003) *The Vatican to Vegas: The History of Special Effects*, New York: Norton.
Kleinman, M. (2005) "Dome could be an $O_2$ 'bubble'". Available from <http://www.timesonline.co.uk/tol/news/uk/article432609.ece> [Accessed 25 November, 2010].
Klewer, D. (1999) *Inferno: Die Welt des Dario Argento*, Hamburg: MPW.
Klingmann, A. (2007) *Brandscapes: Architecture in the Experience Economy*, Cambridge, Mass.: The MIT Press.
Kloock, D. and Spahr, A. (1997) *Medientheorien: Eine Einführung*, Munich: Wilhelm Fink.
Knorr Cetina, K. (1999) *Epistemic Culture: How the Sciences Make Knowledge*, Cambridge, Mass.: Harvard University Press.
—— (2000) "Post-Social Theory", in G. Ritzer and B. Smart (eds) *Handbook of Social Theory*, London: Sage.
Koolhaas, R. (2001) "Junkspace", in C.J. Chung, J. Inaba, R. Koolhaas and S.T. Leong (eds) *Harvard Design School Guide to Shopping*, Cologne: Taschen.
—— (ed.) (2002) *Mutations*, Barcelona: Actar.
—— (2003) *Phenomenon Automobility*, Rotterdam: AMO. [Internal study on behalf of Autostadt].
—— (ed.) (2004) *Content*, Cologne: Taschen.
Koolhaas, R. and Mau, B. (1995) *S, M, L, XL*, Rotterdam/New York: 010 Publishers/The Monacelli Press.
Kopytoff, I. (1986) "The Cultural Biography of Things: Commoditization as Process", in A. Appadurai (ed.) *The Social Life of Things: Commodities in Cultural Perspective*, Cambridge: Cambridge University Press.
Kracauer, S. (1963) *Das Ornament der Masse: Essays*, Frankfurt/Main: Suhrkamp.
—— (1925, new edn 1971) *Der Detektiv-Roman*, Frankfurt/Main: Suhrkamp.
Krier, L. (1989) *Albert Speer Architecture*, New York: Princeton Architectural Press.
Kwinter, S. (2001) *Architectures of Time: Toward a Theory of the Event in Modernist Culture*, Cambridge, Mass.: The MIT Press.
—— (2007) "Architecture and Combustion", in K. Feireiss (ed.) *Dynamic Forces: Coop Himmelb(l)au, BMW Welt Munich*, Munich: Prestel, 8–15.
Lagerkvist, A. (2010) "The Future Is Here: Media, Memory, and Futurity in Shanghai", *Space and Culture*, 13/3: 220–238.

Lash, S. (1999) *Another Modernity: A Different Rationality*, Oxford: Basil Blackwell.
—— (2002) *Critique of Information*, London: Sage.
Lash, S. and Lury, C. (2007) *Global Culture Industry: The Mediation of Things*, Cambridge: Polity Press.
Lash, S. and Urry, J. (1994) *Economies of Signs and Space*, London: Sage.
Latour, B. (2009) "Ein vorsichtiger Prometheus? Einige Schritte hin zu einer Philosophie des Designs, unter besonderer Berücksichtigung von Peter Sloterdijk", in M. Jongen, S. van Tuinen and K. Hemelsoet (eds) *Die Vermessung des Ungeheuren: Philosophie nach Peter Sloterdijk*, Munich: Wilhelm Fink.
Law, J. (1999) "After ANT: Complexity, Naming and Topology", in J. Law and J. Hassard (eds) *Actor Network Theory and After*, Oxford: Blackwell.
—— (2002) "Objects and Spaces", *Theory, Culture and Society* 19(5/6): 91–105.
Leong, S.T. (2001) "Captive" in C.J. Chung, J. Inaba, R. Koolhaas and S.T. Leong (eds) *Harvard Design School Guide to Shopping*, Cologne: Taschen: 175–185.
Lefebvre, H. (1974) *La production de l'espace*; trans. D. Nicholson-Smith (1991) *The Production of Space*, Oxford: Blackwell.
—— (1979) *La révolution urbaine*; trans. R. Bonnano (2003) *Urban Revolution*, Minneapolis: University of Minnesota Press.
Leydecker, K. (2009) "Zelt und Schmetterling: Pavillonarchitektur im Deutschen Architekturmuseum in Frankfurt am Main", *Neue Zürcher Zeitung*, 15 September: 23.
Liu, K. (2003) *Globalization and Cultural Trends in China*, Honolulu: University of Hawaii Press.
Liu, L. (2004) *The Clash of Empires: The Invention of China in Modern World Making*, Cambridge, Mass.: Harvard University Press.
Long, J. (2004) "Shanghai Exponential", in R. Koolhaas (ed.) *Content*, Cologne: Taschen.
Loos, A. (1908, new edn 2000) *Ornament und Verbrechen*, Vienna: Prachner.
Luedicke, M. (2006) "Brand Community under Fire: The Role of Social Environments for the HUMMER Brand Community", *Advances in Consumer Research* 33: 486–493.
Luhmann, N. (1984) *Soziale Systeme: Grundriss einer allgemeinen Theorie*, Frankfurt/Main: Suhrkamp.
Lury, C. (2000) "The United Colors of Diversity: Essential and Inessential Culture", in S. Franklin, C. Lury and S. Stacey (eds) *Global Nature, Global Culture*, London: Sage.
—— (2004) *Brands: The Logos of the Global Economy*, London: Routledge.
Lury, C. and Warde, A. (1997) "Investments in the Imaginary Consumer: Conjectures Regarding Power, Knowledge and Advertising", in M. Nava, A. Blake, I. MacRury and B. Richards (eds) *Buy this Book: Studies in Advertising and Consumption*, London: Routledge.
Lynch, D. (2001) *Mulholland Drive*, Paris: Les Films Alain Sarde. [DVD].
Lynch, K. (1960) *The Image of the City*, Cambridge, Mass.: Harvard University Press.
Lyotard, J.F. (1974) *Économie libidinale*; trans. I.H. Grant (1993) *Libidinal Economy*, London: The Athlone Press.
Maffesoli, M. (1996) *The Time of the Tribes: The Decline of Individualism in Mass Society*, trans. D. Smith, London: Sage.
Malz, E. and Kohli, A.J. (2000) "Reducing Marketing's Conflict with Other

Functions: The Differential Effects of Integrating Mechanisms", *Journal of the Academy of Marketing Science* 28(4): 479–492.
Manovich, L. (2001) *The Language of New Media*, Cambridge, Mass.: The MIT Press.
—— (2003) "New Media From Borges to HTML", in N. Wardrip-Fruin and N. Montfort (eds) *The New Media Reader*, Cambridge, Mass.: The MIT Press.
Marbach, R., Bruch, P. and Eicher, J. (1998) *Cities, Cultures, Conversations: Readings for Writers*, Boston: Allyn & Bacon.
Martino, E. (2007) *The History of the Venice Biennale*, Venice: Papiro Arte.
Marx, K. (1858, new edn 1983) *Grundrisse der Kritik der politischen Ökonomie*, Berlin: Dietz.
Massey, D. (1984) *Spatial Divisions of Labour*, London: Macmillan.
—— (1999) "Cities in the World", in D. Massey, J. Allen and S. Pile (eds) *City Worlds*, London: Routledge.
Massumi, B. (2002) *Parables for the Virtual: Movement, Affect, Senzation*, Durham, NY: Duke University Press.
Maturana, H. and Varela, F. (1980) *Autopoiesis and Cognition: The Realization of the Living*, Boston: Reidel.
Mauss, M. (1976) *The Gift;* trans. I. Cunningham, New York: Norton.
Mayer, M. (2003) "Yin, Yang und Rem", *AD Architectural Digest* (German edn) 11: 137–143.
McCarthy, A. (2001) *Ambient Television: Visual Culture and Public Space*, Durham, NY: Duke University Press.
McGetrick, B. (2004) "Editor's Letter: Content is a Product of the Moment", in R. Koolhaas (ed.) *Content*, Cologne: Taschen.
McLuhan, M. (1962) *The Gutenberg Galaxy: The Making of Typographic Man*, Toronto: University of Toronto Press.
McLuhan, M. (1964) *Understanding Media: The Extensions of Man*, New York: McGraw-Hill.
McQuire, S. (2008) *The Media City: Media, Architecture and Urban Space*, London: Sage.
Merrifield, A. (2002) *Metromarxism*, London: Routledge.
Merriman, P. (2004) "Driving Places: Marc Augé, Non-Places and the Geographies of England's M1 Motorway", *Theory, Culture and Society* 21(4/5): 145–167.
Metzinger, P. (2003) *Business Campaigning: Was Unternehmen von Greenpeace und amerikanischen Wahlkämpfern lernen können*, Berlin: Springer.
Meyhöfer, D. (2006) "BauWerk: Das Phaeno in Wolfsburg: Abschied von Wand, Boden und Decke", *Deutsche BauZeitung* 1: 24–26.
Miles, S. and Miles, M. (2004) *Consuming Cities*, Basingstoke: Palgrave Macmillan.
Milev, Y. (2009) "Am Anfang war der Unfall oder: Die Befreiung der Krise als Wohnmedium", in M. Jongen, S. van Tuinen and K. Hemelsoet (eds) *Die Vermessung des Ungeheuren: Philosophie nach Peter Sloterdijk*, Munich: Wilhelm Fink.
Miller, D. (1998) "Conclusion: A Theory of Virtualism", in J.G. Carrier and D. Miller (eds) *Virtualism: A New Political Economy*, Oxford: Berg.
—— (ed.) (2001) *Car Cultures*, Oxford: Berg.
Mitchell, W.J. (2005) *Placing Words: Symbols, Place, and the City*, Cambridge, Mass.: The MIT Press.
Mises, L. (1922, new edn 1981) *Socialism: An Economic and Sociological Analysis*, Indianapolis: Liberty Fund.

Moor, L. (2003) "Branded Spaces: The Scope of 'New Marketing'", *Journal of Consumer Culture* 3(1): 39–60.
—— (2004) "Branded Spaces: The Mediation of Commercial Forms", unpublished PhD thesis, University of London.
—— (2006) "'The Buzz of Dressing': Commodity Culture, Fraternity, and Football Fandom", *South Atlantic Quarterly* 105(2): 327–347.
—— (2007) *The Rise of Brands*, Oxford: Berg.
Moore, R.E. (2003) "From Genericide to Viral Marketing: On 'Brand'", *Language and Communication* 23(3/4): 331–357.
Morley, D. (2006) *Media, Modernity and Technology: The Geography of the New*, London: Routledge.
Morley, D. and Robbins, K. (1989) "Spaces of Identity: Communications, Technologies and the Reconfiguration of Europe", *Screen* 30(4): 10–34.
—— (1995) *The Space of Identity: Global Media, Electronic Landscapes and Cultural Boundaries*, London: Routledge.
Morse, M. (1990) "An Ontology of Everyday Distraction: The Freeway, the Mall, and Television", in P. Mellencamp (ed.) *Logics of Television: Essays in Cultural Criticism*, Bloomington and Indianapolis: University of Indiana Press.
Moussavi, F. (2006) "The Function of Ornament", in F. Moussavi and M. Kubo (eds) *The Function of Ornament*, Barcelona: Actar.
Moussavi, F. and Kubo, M. (eds) (2006) *The Function of Ornament*, Barcelona: Actar.
Murdoch, J. (1997) "Towards a Geography of Heterogeneous Associations", *Progress in Human Geography* 21: 321–337.
—— (2006) *Poststructuralist Geography*, London: Sage.
Nerdinger, W. (2006) *Ort und Erinnerung: Nationalsozialismus in München*, Munich: Architekturmuseum München.
Nickson, D., Warhurst, C., Witz, A. and Cullen, A.M. (2001) "The Importance of Being Aesthetic: Work, Employment and Service Organization", in A. Studry, I. Gruglis and H. Wilmott (eds) *Customer Service: Empowerment and Entrapment*, New York: Palgrave.
Olds, K. and Yeung, H. (2005) "Pathways to Global City Formation: A View from the Developmental City-State of Singapore", in N. Brenner and R. Keil (eds) *The Global Cities Reader*, London: Routledge.
Osterwold, T. (2003) *Pop Art*, Cologne: Taschen.
Packard, V. (1961) *The Hidden Persuaders*, Harmondsworth: Penguin.
Pang, L. (2008) "China Who Makes and Fakes: A Semiotics of the Counterfeit", *Theory, Culture and Society* 25(6): 117–140.
Paricca, J. (2007) *Digital Contagions: A Media Archaeology of Computer Viruses*, New York: Peter Lang.
Penrose, E.T. (1959) *The Theory of the Growth of the Firm*, New York: Wiley.
Pickton, D. and Broderick, A. (2001) *Integrated Marketing Communications*, Harlow: Pearson.
Pile, S. (2000) "Sleepwalking in the Modern City: Walter Benjamin and Sigmund Freud in the World of Dreams", in G. Bridge and S. Watson (eds) *A Companion to the City*, Oxford: Blackwell.
Porter, M. (1995) "The Competitive Advantage of the Inner City", *Harvard Business Review* (May/June): 52–71.
Poster, M. (1995) *The Second Media Age*, Cambridge: Polity Press.

Powers, S. (2005) "German Car Makers Race to Enshrine Their Histories as Competition Heats Up", *Wall Street Journal Europe*, 13 April, A12.
Prakash, G. and Kruse, K.M. (2008) *The Spaces of the Modern City: Imaginaries, Politics, and Everyday Life*, New Jersey: Princeton University Press.
Prix, W. (2007) "The Story of the Hurricane: Kirsten Feireiss talks to Wolf D. Prix", in K. Feireiss (ed.) *Dynamic Forces: Coop Himmelb(l)au. BMW Welt Munich*. Munich: Prestel.
Rajchman, J. (1997) *Constructions*, Cambridge, Mass.: The MIT Press.
Read, A. (ed.) (2000) *Architecturally Speaking: Practices of Art, Architecture and the Everyday*, London: Routledge.
Rebaschus, M. (2005) "Elbphilharmonie: Es geht voran", *Hamburger Abendblatt*, 8 June: 17.
Reichel, P. (2006) *Der schöne Schein des Dritten Reiches: Faszination und Gewalt des deutschen Faschismus*, Hamburg: Ellert und Richter.
Reichle, J. (2003) "Erleben und erleben lassen", *Süddeutsche Zeitung*, 29 November: V1/1.
Reichow, H.B. (1959) *Die autogerechte Stadt: Ein Weg aus dem Verkehrschaos*, Ravensburg: Otto Maier Verlag.
Reifenrath, J. (2004) "Die Wiedergeburt der Marke Maybach", *kommunikationsmanager* 1: 5–9.
Reimann, H. (2003) *Neue Erlebniswelten im Städtetourimus: Die BMW Welt in München*, Dresden: Dresden University.
Ries, A. and Ries, L. (2002) *The Fall of Advertising and the Rise of PR*, New York: HarperCollins.
Rifkin, J. (2001) *The Age of Access: How the Shift from Ownership to Access is Transforming Modern Life*, Harmondsworth: Penguin.
Ritzer, G. (1993) *The McDonaldization of Society*, Thousand Oaks, CA: Sage.
Roland Berger Strategy Consultants (2009) *Chinese Consumer Report 2009*, Munich: Roland Berger.
Roost, F. (2007) "Perspektiven der Industriestädte im Wandel: Wolfsburgs Umbau vom Waren- zum Imageproduktionsstandort", in M. Kaltwasser, E. Majewska and K. Szreder (eds) *Industriestadtfuturismus: 100 Jahre Wolfsburg/Nowa Huta*, Frankfurt/Main: Revolver.
Ross, A. (2000) *The Celebration Chronicles. Life, Liberty, and the Pursuit of Property Value in Disney's New Town*, London: Verso.
Ruhkamp, C. (2010) "Die größte Autofabrik der Welt", *Frankfurter Allgemeine Zeitung*, 17 June: 18.
Saiki, M. (2003) *The Toyota City Stadium: Kisho Kurokawa Architects and Associates*, London: Edizioni Press.
Sandywell, B. (2003) "Metacritique of Information: On Scott Lash's *Critique of Information*", *Theory, Culture and Society* 20 (1): 109–122.
Sassen, S. (1991) *The Global City*, Princeton: Princeton University Press.
—— (1998) *Globalization and its Discontents*, New York: New Press.
Schildt, A. (2007) "Wolfsburg: eine neue Stadt im Wiederaufbau der Bundesrepublik", in M. Kaltwasser, E. Majewska and K. Szreder (eds) *Industriestadtfuturismus – 100 Jahre Wolfsburg/Nowa Huta*, Frankfurt/Main: Revolver.
Schmitt, B. (1999) *Experiential Marketing*, New York: The Free Press.
Schneider, D. (1979) *Stadtgründung im Dritten Reich: Wolfsburg und Salzgitter. Ideologie. Ressortpolitik. Repräsentation*, Munich: Heinz Moos.

Schneider, M. (2005) Interview with Maria Schneider, Wolfsburg, 6 June.
—— (2007) Interview with Maria Schneider, Wolfsburg, 7 August.
Schnierer, T. (1999) *Soziologie der Werbung*, Opladen: Leske + Budrich.
Schug, A. (2003) *History Marketing: Ein Leitfaden zum Umgang mit Geschichte im Unternehmen*, Bielefeld: Transcript.
Scott, A.J. (2000) *The Cultural Economy of Cities*, London: Sage.
Searle, A. (2003) "A Life More Ordinary", *The Guardian*, 3 June: 10.
Sennett, R. (1974) *The Fall of Public Man*, New York: Norton.
—— (1994) *Flesh and Stone*, London: Faber & Faber.
Sheller, M. (2004) "Automotive Emotions: Feeling the Car", *Theory, Culture and Society*, 2 (4/5): 221–242.
Sheller, M. and Urry, J. (2004) "Mobile Transformations of 'Public' and 'Private' Life", *Theory, Culture and Society* 21(4/5): 107–125.
Shields, R. (2003) *The Virtual*, London: Routledge.
—— (2005) "The Virtuality of Urban Culture: Blanks, Dark Moments and Blind Fields", in H. Berking and M. Löw (eds) *Die Wirklichkeit der Städte*, Baden Baden: Nomos.
Shoard, M. (1999) "The Urban Fringe", *Landscape* 15: 1–23.
Siemons, M. (2006) "Surreales Flair von Ruhe und Ordnung", *Frankfurter Allgemeine Zeitung*, 10 October: 41.
Sloterdijk, P. (1998) *Sphären I: Blasen*, Frankfurt/Main: Suhrkamp.
—— (1999) *Sphären II: Globen*, Frankfurt/Main: Suhrkamp.
—— (2004) *Sphären III: Schäume*, Frankfurt/Main: Suhrkamp.
—— (2005) *Im Weltinnenraum des Kapitals: Für eine philosophische Theorie der Globalisierung*, Frankfurt/Main: Suhrkamp.
—— (2006) *Zorn und Zeit: Politisch-Psychologischer Versuch*, Frankfurt/Main: Suhrkamp.
Soja, E. (1996) *Thirdspace*, Oxford: Blackwell.
—— (2000) *Postmetropolis: Critical Studies of Cities and Regions*, Oxford: Blackwell.
Sorkin, M. (1991) *Exquisite Corpse: Writing in Buildings*, London: Verso.
—— (1992) *Variations on a Theme Park*, New York: Hill & Wang.
Stille, A. (2002) *The Future of the Past*, New York: Farrar, Straus & Giroux.
Stoffer, H. (2008) "Desperate Industry Begs Feds for Help", *Automotive News*, 27 October: 8.
Swyngedouw, E. (2006) "Circulations and Metabolisms: (Hybrid) Natures and (Cyborg) Cities", *Science as Culture* 15(2): 105–121.
Taylor, R. (1974) *Word in Stone: The Role of Architecture in the National Socialist Ideology*, Berkeley: University of California Press.
Thrift, N. (1998) "Virtual Capitalism: The Globalization of Reflexive Business Knowledge", in J.G. Carrier and D. Miller (eds) *Virtualism: A New Political Economy*, Oxford: Berg.
—— (1999) "The Place of Complexity", *Theory, Culture and Society* 16(3): 31–69.
—— (2000) "With Child to See Any Strange Thing: Everyday Life in the City", in G. Bridge and S. Watson (eds) *A Companion to the City*, Oxford: Blackwell.
—— (2004) "Driving in the City", *Theory, Culture and Society* 21(4/5): 41–59.
—— (2008) *Non-Representational Theory: Space / Politics / Affect*, London: Routledge.
—— (2009) "Different Atmospheres: of Sloterdijk, China, and Site", *Environment and Planning D: Society and Space* 27(1): 119–138.

Toscano, A. (2008a) "The Culture of Abstraction", *Theory, Culture and Society* 25(4): 57–75.
—— (2008b) "The Open Secret of Real Abstraction", *Rethinking Marxism* 2: 273–287.
Tschumi, B. (1994) *Architecture and Disjunction*, Boston, Mass.: The MIT Press.
—— (2000) "Six Concepts" in A. Read (ed.) *Architecturally Speaking: Practices of Art, Architecture and the Everyday*, London: Routledge.
Uhlig, G. (2000) "Die Autostadt in Wolfsburg", in G. Henn (ed.) *Corporate Architecture: Autostadt Wolfsburg. Gläserne Manufaktur Dresden*, Berlin: Aedes.
Urry, J. (2004) "The 'System' of Automobility", *Theory, Culture and Society* 21 (4/5), 25–39.
Vattimo, G. (1990) *La società transparente*; trans. (1992) D. Webb, *The Transparent Society*, Cambridge: Polity Press.
Venturi, R., Scott Brown, D. and Izenour, S. (1972) *Learning from Las Vegas*, Cambridge, Mass.: The MIT Press.
Vidler, A. (1992) *The Architectural Uncanny: Essays in the Modern Unhomely*, Cambridge, Mass.: The MIT Press.
—— (2002) "Bodies in Space/Subjects in the City", in G. Bridge and S. Watson (eds) *The Blackwell City Reader*, Oxford: Blackwell.
Virilio, P. (1984) *L'Espace Critique*; trans. D. Moshenberg (1991) *The Lost Dimension*, New York: Semiotext(e).
Van Berkel, B. (2009) "Pavillons: Ein Interview von Karen Murphy", in P. Cachola Schmal (ed.) *Der Pavillon: Lust und Polemik in der Architektur*, Ostfildern: Hatje Cantz.
Van Tuinen, S. (2007) *Peter Sloterdijk: ein Profil*, Stuttgart: UTB.
Von Boddien, W. and Engel, H. (eds) (2000) *Die Berliner Schlossdebatte: Pro und Contra*, Berlin, BWV.
Von Borries, F. (2002) *Wer hat Angst vor Niketown? Nike-Urbanismus, Branding und die Markenstadt von morgen*, Rotterdam: Episode Publishers.
Von Oettinger, B. (2004) *Ist die Erde geschrumpft? Die Renaissance des Raumes in der Strategie*, Munich: The Boston Consulting Group.
Von Schmettow, A. (2003) "PR-Konzept für die BMW-Welt in München", unpublished thesis, Bayerische Akademie für Werbung und Marketing.
Waldmann, A. (2008) *Anting New Town: Interkulturelle Herausforderungen innerhalb eines deutsch-chinesischen Architekturprojekts*, Saarbrücken: VDM Verlag Dr. Müller.
Wang, J. (2008) *Brand New China: Advertising, Media, and Commercial Culture*, Cambridge, Mass.: Harvard University Press.
Ward, J. (2004) "Berlin, the Virtual Global City", *Journal of Visual Culture* 3(2): 239–256.
Watson, J. (ed.) (1997) *Golden Arches East: McDonald's in East Asia*, Stanford: Stanford University Press.
Westwood, S. and Williams, J. (eds) (1996) *Imagining Cities*, London: Routledge.
Whatmore, S. (2002) *Hybrid Geographies: Natures, Cultures, Spaces*, London: Sage.
Wightman, W. (1961) "Whitehead's Empiricism" in I. Leclerc (ed.) *The Relevance of Whitehead*, New York: Humanities Press.
Williams, J. (2003) *Gilles Deleuze's Difference and Repetition: A Critical Introduction and Guide*, Edinburgh: Edinburgh University Press.

Willis, P. (1980) "Notes on Method", in S. Hall, D. Hobson, A. Lowe and P. Willis (eds) *Culture, Media, Language: Working Papers in Cultural Studies 1972–1979*, London: Routledge.

Wolfsburg Press Department (2008) "Neue Porschestraße: Neue Spiel- und Erlebnisgeräte – 'Masterplan Spielen' geht in politische Gremien", [Online]. Available from <http://wolfsburg.de/presseservice/index.html?detail=/data.cfm/static/691549.html> [Accessed 9 December 2008].

Wright, H. (2006) *London High: A Guide to the Past, Present and Future of London's Skyscrapers*, London: Frances Lincoln.

Zukin, S. (1982) *Loft Living: Culture and Capital in Urban Change*, Baltimore: Johns Hopkins University Press.

—— (1991) *Landscapes of Power: From Detroit to Disney World*, Berkeley: University of California Press.

—— (1995) *The Culture of Cities*, Cambridge, Mass.: Blackwell.

# Index

abstraction 93
actor-network theory (ANT) 32–3
actualization of brands 55–8
affect 49, 63–5, 115–16; as production 70
AMO 44–5
Argento, D. 97–8
art 47–8
attention 112–14

Berlin 52–5
biopolitics; and architecture 21
bodies; and knowledge 66–7
Bourneville 30
Berliner Stadtschloss 142
Brandenburg Gate 52–3
branding (as opposed to advertising) 2

car; as pure image 64–5
car industry 9, 23
CEOs 10
China 22–26
competition 103–5
consumer (and the concept of the customer) 27
consumption 148; and immersion 136
Coop Himmelb(l)au 62–3
copies (in architecture) 59–60
Crystal Palace 139–42

dark space 73
Deleuze, G. 33–4, 48–51
dirt 104–5

event 88–90
excess 70

flow 76–7
foam *see* Schaum

global mass ornament 129–37
Gursky, A. 48–9

Hadid, Z. 116–18
history 59; as productive element 72
Hollywood 107–9
Hollywood sign 108–9
Hummer; as car-becoming-medium 68–9
hybrid history 95–7
hybridity 25

identity 114–15
image 49–50
immaterial labour 151–2
immersion 79–80, 109–11
information 36
information society; and disinformation 58

junkspace 73–4

Kittler, F. 34–7
Klein, N. 109–12
Koolhaas, R. 44–5
Kracauer, S. 37–8

Las Vegas 79–80
lighting 78–9
linguistics 77–8
logo; and architecture 105–6
Los Angeles 68; and Wolfsburg 93–5
Lynch, D. 95

marketing; and branding 27–8
mass ornament 128–9
McDonald's 83
media theory 34–7

mirror; and architecture 116–18
mobility; and brands 60–1
model cities 30
Moussavi, F. 132–3

nature; and architecture 62
new media theory *see* media theory
nonplaces 75
normalization of the subject 112

object-event 107

past; as threat 72–3
pavilion 139–42
pop art; and logo 106–7
productivity 45–6
public space 46

rhizomatic space 46
rhizome; and mass ornament 132
Ruscha, E. 106–9

Schaum 38–40; 123–8
screen 111; and architecture 78, 116–18
semiotics 51–2
Sloterdijk, P. 38–40
Shanghai 22–6; as global city 119–21
subjectivity 152–3
surface 137–9

topology 103–5; 134

Unbehagen; of brand space 74
uncanny *see* Unbehagen
universalization of Chinese culture 84–5

virtual space 33–4, 48–51

Wolfsburg 17–18

Zukin, S. 59